CUNNINGHAM'S
ENCYCLOPEDIA OF

*wicca in the
kitchen*

Food has played a significant role in human celebrations of all kinds. In earlier times, the Earth and its bounty were connected with goddesses and gods. Fruit, seed, root, and flower were all manifestations of divinity.

As we've lost the knowledge of the old magics, so too have we forgotten the mystic lore of food. But timeless energies still vibrate within our meals. They wait for us to sense and use them.

About the Author

Scott Cunningham practiced elemental magic for more than twenty years. He was the author of more than thirty books, both fiction and nonfiction. Cunningham's books reflect a broad range of interests within the New Age sphere, where he was highly regarded. He passed from this life on March 28, 1993, after a long illness.

CUNNINGHAM'S
ENCYCLOPEDIA OF

WICCA IN THE KITCHEN

SCOTT CUNNINGHAM

Llewellyn Publications
Woodbury, Minnesota

THIRD EDITION
Twentieth Printing, 2024

SECOND EDITION 1996, one printing (titled *The Magic of Food*)
FIRST EDITION, 1990, two printings (titled *The Magic in Food*)

Book design and editing by Kimberly Nightingale
Cover design by Kevin R. Brown
Cover illustration © 2003 by Jennifer Hewitson   FR

ISBN 13: 978-0-7387-0226-1
ISBN 10: 0-7387-0226-9
CIP data for this title is on file with the Library of Congress.

Llewellyn Worldwide does not participate in, endorse, or have any authority or responsibility concerning private business transactions between our authors and the public.

All mail addressed to the author is forwarded but the publisher cannot, unless specifically instructed by the author, give out an address or phone number.

Any Internet references contained in this work are current at publication time, but the publisher cannot guarantee that a specific location will continue to be maintained. Please refer to the publisher's website for links to authors' websites and other sources.

The old-fashioned remedies in this book are historical references used for teaching purposes only. The recipes are not for commercial use or profit. The contents are not meant to diagnose, treat, prescribe, or substitute consultation with a licensed healthcare professional.

Llewellyn Publications
A Division of Llewellyn Worldwide Ltd.
2143 Woodlane Drive
Woodbury, MN 55125-2989
www.llewellyn.com
Llewellyn is a registered trademark of Llewellyn Worldwide Ltd.

Printed in the United States of America

Other Books by Scott Cunningham

The Complete Book of Incense, Oils & Brews

Cunningham's Book of Shadows

Cunningham's Encyclopedia of Crystal, Gem & Metal Magic

Cunningham's Encyclopedia of Magical Herbs

Cunningham's Guide to Hawaiian Magic & Spirituality

Dreaming the Divine

Divination for Beginners

Earth, Air, Fire & Water

Earth Power

Living Wicca

Magical Aromatherapy

Magical Herbalism

The Magical Household *(with David Harrington)*

Spell Crafts *(with David Harrington)*

The Truth About Herb Magic

The Truth About Witchcraft Today

Wicca

Biography

Whispers of the Moon
 (written by David Harrington and deTraci Regula)

Video

Herb Magic

Acknowledgments

Many people have been of assistance during the seventeen years that it has taken to complete this book. In no particular order, some of them are:

Jeanne Rose, herbalist extraordinaire, for her inspiration, friendship, and also for supplying mail-order sources.

Morgan of Hawaii, for allowing me to publish her Fruit Salad Spell.

Barda of Nevada, for her early encouragement and sharing of food lore and recipes.

Vinnie Gaglione, of Spellbound in Bloomfield, New Jersey, for supplying me with Italian food lore.

Laurie Cabot of Salem, for sharing her notes with me while we were working on similar projects.

Virginia Thompson of Arizona, for information about Central American food magic and ritual uses.

Robert and Virginia Thompson, for Japanese food lore.

Ray T. Malbrough of Houma, Louisiana, for many long phone calls and for providing a copy of his paper concerning Louisiana plant magic.

deTraci Regula, for Chinese food magic.

Morgan, my first teacher, who introduced me to the idea that food could be magical.

Lou and Myrna of Las Vegas, for finding all those out-of-the-way print books.

And finally, to my mother, who rarely minded my licking the spoon for all those long years.

TABLE OF CONTENTS

PART TWO: **the magic of food**

PART THREE: magical food diets

PART FOUR: scott's favorite recipes

PART FIVE: supplemental material

Food is essential to our lives. For many of us, the art of cooking and eating is a chore. For others, it is a great delight. And for some, the culinary arts and their products are indulgences. Food is substituted for love. Food is an excuse. Food is a god.

You're about to embark on a journey into a familiar yet exciting realm. This book is a guide to choosing, ritually preparing, and eating foods to manifest necessary changes in our lives. The only tools that are necessary to practice this ancient branch of magic are food, common kitchen implements, and yourself. Food magic is a natural art, in which we unite our own energies with those that exist in food.

Part one of this book consists of introductory material: the processes of magic and cooking; foods associated with ancient festivals; vegetarianism; and a step-by-step guide to the practice of food magic.

Part two is an encyclopedia of magical foods. Concise articles explore the spiritual backgrounds and magical uses of hundreds of foods, including bread, fruits, vegetables, ice cream, tofu, sugar, chocolate, seafood, spices and herbs, nuts, coffee, tea, and alcoholic beverages. Many common and exotic foods are discussed. Why is bird's-nest soup so prized by some Asians? What magical energies lie within apple pie, sprouts, oatmeal, and chocolate bars?

Part three could be called "The Magical Diet Book." Eleven chapters describe fifteen diets, each designed to create a different change within the diner's life: protection, love, money, psychic awareness, health, magical weight loss, and much more.

In part five I've collated some of the information contained within part two into tables for easy reference. A list of foods ruled by the signs of the zodiac and a table of the magical properties of fast food complete this section.

Finally, two appendices discuss magical symbols and mail-order sources of unusual foods, herbs, and spices.

This isn't a book of gourmet cooking; nor is it a cookbook. It is a guide to transforming our lives with the foods that we eat. It's a practical introduction to an ancient subject.

A Note on Notes

I've chosen to use this method rather than standard footnoting with good reason: it doesn't burden the pages of the text with lengthy footnotes, yet it allows the reader to easily check the sources of any information.

Some statements aren't followed by a number. I've lost the source for a few of them. Others are part of the knowledge that I've accumulated over years of study. Still others stem from oral sources or from the results of my own experience. In any case, a published work is unavailable for these few statements.

Numbers following a statement in this book refer to a specific entry in the bibliography. To find the source of the information contained within the statement, see the number list of books in the bibliography.

Food is magic. Its power over us is undeniable. From the sweet, rich lure of a freshly baked brownie to an exquisitely steamed artichoke, food continues to seduce us.

Food is life. We can't continue to live without its magic. Food, however, also harbors energies. When we eat, our bodies absorb those energies, just as they absorb vitamins, minerals, amino acids, carbohydrates, and other nutrients. Though we may not be aware of any effect other than a sated appetite, the food has subtly changed us.

In times of scarcity as well as plenty, peoples around the world have subjected food to religious reverence. Rice in Asia; fruit throughout Europe; grains in Africa; pomegranates and beer in the Near East; acorns and pine nuts in the American Southwest; bananas and coconuts in the Pacific; vegetables in tropical America—these foods have all played significant roles in religous and magical rituals.

Sacred meals are shared with the goddesses and gods (or their priestesses and priests). Today, eating with others is still an act of energy sharing, bonding, and trust.

The magic of the hunt and the sacredness of gathering rituals in fields and groves are still remembered by a few isolated peoples. Most of us now, however, buy presliced bread, gather our fruits and vegetables from gleaming counters, and hunt in refrigerated cases.

As we've lost the knowledge of the old magics, so too have we forgotten the mystic lore of food. But timeless energies still vibrate within our meals. They wait for us to sense and to use them.

Lengthy magical spells aren't required, though a simple ritual is necessary to boost the food's effectiveness. If you have little knowledge of magic, follow the instructions presented in this book. You'll soon discover its power.*

I've tried to speak to all tastes in writing this practical food magic manual. It isn't strictly vegetarian, nor is it concerned solely with healthy or organic food. You'll find the magic of wine, sugar, and hotcross buns here, along with that of seaweed, carrots, and tofu. This book has something for everyone.

Eating is a merging with the earth. It is a life-affirmimg act. Ritually preparing and eating specific foods is an effective method of enhancing and improving our lives.

It's also fun. Magic pretzels? Sacred chocolate? Passionate pickles? They're all part of the magic of food, and the spells to create them begin in your own kitchen.

*Magic is a positive, loving art. Magic isn't supernatural, evil, or dangerous. See chapter 2 for more information.

the magic in your kitchen

CHAPTER ONE

Food Power!

The woman bent over the stone hearth, adding twisted branches to the embers that glowed behind the andirons. Once they'd sprung into flickering life, she stepped outside to pump water into the old iron pot.

She returned to her house and placed the heavy cauldron directly over the fire, positioning its three long legs evenly around the blaze.

As the water warmed, she carved a small heart on to a beeswax candle, placed it in a pewter holder on the kitchen table, and lit its wick. She uncovered the baskets of strawberries that she had gathered that morning. Removing one, she placed it on the cutting board.

"Love . . . for . . . me," she murmured.

Working slowly and deliberately, she transferred the luscious fruits to the board, placing them in a pattern. She soon had created a small heart fashioned of strawberries.

The woman made another heart around the first, then another and another, until her supply of strawberries was exhausted. She smiled and chopped the strawberries, imagining what her life would be like once she'd met a man.

While waiting for the water to boil, she took an apple from a string hung from the ceiling. She carefully carved a heart into its peel with a white-handled knife, saying:

"Love for me!"

The woman stared at the apple, smiled, and bit into the fruit. The sweetness refreshed her. She slowly ate the apple, biting clockwise around the fruit from where she'd first penetrated it, slowly consuming the heart.

Later, the woman rose from her spinning and checked the pot. It was nearly boiling. She took the cutting board to the open-faced hearth and, using the white-handled knife, slid the chopped strawberries into the rustling water. As the fruit dropped into the cauldron, she said:

"Love for me!"

The cake of sugar had sat undisturbed in its ceramic pot for three months, but now was the time. The woman gently added it to the simmering, fruit-filled cauldron. It absorbed the water and melted.

She sat beside the fire and took up a spoon made of cherry wood. Slowly stirring, and moving the spoon in the direction of the sun, the woman cooked her strawberry jam. As it boiled, she said, over and over again in a voice barely audible above the crackling wood and the bubbling water:

"Love for me!"

The practice of folk magic* utilizes a variety of tools to empower simple rituals. These tools include visualization, candles, colors, words, affirmations, herbs, essential oils, stones, and metals. Other tools, fashioned by our hands, are also used, but these are merely power-directors. They contain little energy save that which is provided by the magician.

Another magical tool is at our disposal, a tool that contains specific energies which we can use to create great changes in our lives. This tool is all around us. We encounter it every day without realizing the potential for change that exists within it; without

---

*See glossary for unfamiliar terms.

knowing that, with a few simple actions and a visualization or two, this tool can be as powerful as the rarest stone or the costliest sword.

What is this untapped source of power?

Food.

That's right, food. The oatmeal you had for breakfast, your salad-and-seafood lunch, even the chocolate ice cream that topped off your evening meal, are all potent magical tools.

This isn't a new idea. From antiquity, humans have honored food as the sustainer of all life, a gift from the unseen deities who graciously provided it. Food played an important role in religious rituals for most cultures of the Earth as they entered the earliest stages of civilization. Its essence was offered up to the deities that watched overhead, while its physical portion, if not burned, was shared by the priestesses and priests. Food became connected with rites of passage such as birth, puberty, initiation into mystical and social groups, marriage, childbirth, maturity, and death.

Not only was food linked with all early religions; it was also understood to possess a nonphysical energy. Different types of food were known to contain different types of energy. Certain foods were eaten for physical strength, for success in battle, for easy childbirth, for health, sex, prosperity, and fertility.

Though food magic was born in an earlier age, it hasn't died out. Foods are used in magic in both the East and West, though the rationale for including them may have changed. Birthday cakes are an example. Most birthday cakes contain iced wishes of good luck. Why should we eat words? Originally, the words were thought to contain the energies associated with them. So the birthday celebrant was believed to enjoy both the cake and the energy of the words. Birthday cakes are a contemporary form of food magic, whether or not those who perpetuate this ritual are aware of it.

While food magic has suffered from neglect in most of the Western world (outside of religious connections), there are many places where food is still viewed as a tool of personal transformation. In Japan and China, specific foods are eaten to ensure long life, health, love, even a passing grade on an examination.

Such rituals have continued for 2,000 to 3,000 years because they are effective.

In my twenty-year excursion into the realm of magic, I've realized that no part of our lives is divorced from its power. I began researching the magical uses of food about seventeen years ago, when I was struck with the knowledge that it, too, was a tool of magic and could be used to create positive, needed change.

Many of my peers expressed disbelief when I first explained the premise of this book. Locked into one particular viewpoint concerning magic, they couldn't grasp the simple idea that food itself could be a force for magical change. Most of them agreed that herbs contain energies. All right, I said. If herbs are properly chosen and used, the magician can release their energies to manifest a specific change. Right? Correct, they said. Well, herbs are plants. Plants are food. And if food is properly chosen and used, couldn't the magician release its energies for magical purposes?

Of course they could, and they do. Doesn't it make sense that the rosemary a magician burns during a love ceremony could be used in other magical ways—in cooking, perhaps? Since lemons have been used for centuries in purifying rituals, can't we bake a lemon pie and internalize its cleansing energies?

This is the magic of food.

Both familiar and strange dishes can be found on these pages. Their magical energies are clearly stated. Where needed, directions for preparation are also given. I've included recipes where I felt they were appropriate, though you've probably prepared, or at least eaten, most of these dishes.

Every meal and every snack offers us a chance to change ourselves and our world. We can empower our lives with the energies of food. With knowledge and a few short rituals, we can spark the powers naturally inherent in food, transforming them into edible versions of the stones, woods, and metals used by magicians.

We must eat to live. Similarly, we must take control of our lives to be truly happy. The tools for doing just this are in your cupboards, in your refrigerator, and on your kitchen table.

Turn the page, and discover the magic that awaits!

CHAPTER TWO

Magic

Some words are necessary here regarding the practices described in this book. This information is vital to the correct practice of food magic.

"Magic is supernatural."
"Magic is evil."
"Magic is dangerous."
"Magic is illusion."

These statements, all false, have been passed down to us by earlier generations of nonpractitioners. Only those who haven't worked magic believe these ideas to be true. All of the statements have also been made about many other practices in earlier times: mathematics, chemistry, psychology, psychics, astronomy, and surgery. These and many other arts and sciences have been pushed from the darkness that lurks behind such statements into the light. They are no longer considered to be supernatural, evil, too dangerous, or illusionary.

At least two aspects of our lives haven't yet been ushered into this august group: *magic* and the *religious experience*. Hardline scientists and those sharing their worldview lump these two together because, to them, they're fantasies with no basis in fact. Magic, to them, can't possibly be successful, because there are no known laws governing the mechanism at work in magic, and no known force that could empower it. They often view the religious experience with a similar mixture of amusement and contempt.

Unfortunately (for these scoffers, that is), magic works, and the religious experience does exist. Telling an individual who has established a personal relationship with deity that deity doesn't exist will produce predictable results. The same is true of magicians: they don't *believe* that magic is effective; they *know* that it is.

The basis of magic is power. Though magicians have used it for thousands of years, we still don't know exactly what "power" is. But we do know how to work with it.

Magic is the movement of natural but subtle energies to manifest needed change. These energies exist within ourselves, within our world, and within all natural objects on it. These energies, whether in avocados or in our own bodies, share a common source, even if their specific manifestations are quite different. What is this common source? Each religion has given it a different name.

Three types of energy are used in magic. These are *personal power,* the energy that our bodies possess; *earth power,* that which resides within our planet and within plants, stones, water, fire, the atmosphere, and animals; and *divine power,* which has not yet been brought to Earth in specific forms.

Magic always utilizes personal power. In folk magic, Earth power is used as well: the magician arouses (or awakens) her or his own power through visualization or physical exertion. Then Earth power (the energy that resides within natural objects) is awakened through visualization. Visualization (the process of creating images in the mind) fine tunes these energies, altering them in order to make them useful for a specific purpose. Once this has been accomplished, and it is easily done, the magician blends the two types of energies. This is usually done through visualization, but there are other techniques available. Food magic is unique in offering a very natural method of uniting these two energies.

For example: Marjorie wants to increase her income. She's working hard at her job and brings home a regular paycheck, but she can't seem to get ahead of her bills. She has a need: more money.

Being familiar with food magic, she decides to add one money-energizing food to each of her meals. She checks part three of this book and comes up with three foods for the first day: oatmeal for breakfast, a peanut butter-and-grape jelly sandwich for lunch, and fresh tomatoes for dinner. This won't be all that she'll eat, of course; Marjorie will simply include these foods in her meals.

The next morning, Marjorie lights a green candle in the kitchen. As the wick catches the flame and burns, Marjorie sees her self free from financial strain. She visualizes herself paying her bills on time and enjoying the use of more money. Marjorie doesn't hope that this happens—she sees it as if it has already occurred.

She continues to visualize as she pours water into a glass pot and measures the oatmeal. Once the measuring cup is full, she sets it on the kitchen counter and places her hands on either side of it. Marjorie visualizes as strongly as she can. She then adds the oatmeal to the water and cooks it as usual.

As she's waiting, Marjorie sections a grapefruit and pours a glass of low-fat milk. These foods aren't related to her magical need; they simply provide nourishment.

When the oatmeal has cooked, she moves the green candle to the kitchen table, spoons the cooked cereal into a bowl, pours a dab of maple syrup over it (another money food, she thinks), and looks down into the oatmeal. She may say this before she eats:

> *"Oats of prosperity and gain,*
> *lift away my financial pain.*
> *I'm flooded with prosperity;*
> *This is my will, so mote it be!"*

Marjorie may also not say anything, but simply renew her visualization. Then she finally eats the oatmeal. With every hot bite she feels money energy pouring into her body. She also senses her body responding, welcoming both the nourishing food and its prosperous energy.

Marjorie pinches out the candle flame and returns the taper to a kitchen drawer until her next magical meal. She repeats the same ritual for at least one food per meal. Though she'll have the peanut butter and jelly sandwich at work, she'll prepare it with the same care and visualization, and will eat it in the same way during her lunch break.

As she wipes her lips, she decides to add money foods to her meals for at least a week to give the magic time to do its work.

So that's an example. What exactly did Marjorie do?

—She recognized that she had a problem.

—She found the tools (foods) that could help her solve it.

—She tuned her own personal power to a prosperous pitch through visualization.

—She also used visualization to attune the earth power contained within the oats.

—She used a short, rhymed chant to strengthen her resolve and her visualization.

—She moved the prosperous energy that resided within the oats into her body by eating them.

The green candle that she lit is a physical manifestation of the change that she wished to make: green is an ancient symbol of growth, prosperity, and abundance. In our modern world, it is also a color of money and of the things that money can bring us.

Folk magicians say that burning a candle releases energy into the surrounding area. The type of energy is determined by the color of the candle. By lighting the green candle, Marjorie added extra money-attracting energy to her ritual. The candle isn't necessary, but it can be used if desired.

Visualization is important in any type of magic. Most of us can visualize what we've already seen quite well. Close your eyes for a minute or two, and see in your mind's eye a picture of a favorite food, your pet, or your next-door neighbor. Don't just think about these things; try to see them as if you were actually looking at them.

In magic, we use visualization to create images of the change that we've decided to make. It wouldn't have helped Marjorie to visualize stacks of unpaid bills, to see herself scrounging in her purse for her last few pennies, or to picture being thrown out of her apartment. These are symptoms of her problem, *and problems are never visualized.*

Instead, the solution to the problem and the outcome of the magical ritual is visualized. This is why Marjorie saw herself paying her bills and enjoying extra money. This isn't positive thinking, though that does play a part. Magical visualization is actually positive *imagining.*

On a subtle (but real) level, images created and sustained in the human mind affect us as well as objects around us. In visualizing, our heroine was setting both Marjorie-energies and oat-energies into motion and giving them purpose. The final step was introducing those energies into herself, which she accomplished by eating the oatmeal at breakfast.

Visualization is the most advanced magical technique necessary for the successful practice of food magic. Many good books are available on the subject. Read them if you feel you need help in this matter*, or attend a class if one is held nearby.

This is food magic. It consists of choosing foods, cooking or preparing them with a purpose, and eating them. Since we all have to eat to survive, why shouldn't we make our meals more than nourishment rituals?

Consider again the four statements that opened this chapter. Judging from the example I've given, it's obvious that the energies involved in magic aren't supernatural. On the contrary, they're the energies of food and our own bodies—and of life itself.

Magic certainly isn't evil, except to a minority of folks who, for religious reasons, have decided that it is. These same folks often consider exercise, psychological analysis, self-improvement, and

---

*Among the finest is Melita Denning and Osborne Phillips' *Practical Guide to Creative Visualization.*

many other aspects of personal growth to be evil as well. Though their bias is clear, it's meaningless to those who don't accept their religious views.

Is magic dangerous? No more dangerous than any other part of life, from taking a shower to using a ladder. The idea that this ancient practice is dangerous stems from the concept that "magic is evil." Magicians don't contact demonic energies, perform sacrifices, or worship fallen angels (see chapter 22).

The fourth statement, that magic is illusion, is also false. This idea is accepted by most of those who haven't practiced it and who don't belong to a fundamentalist religious group. It is difficult or impossible to prove to these cynics that magic is effective precisely because magic utilizes energies that these cynics haven't yet fully investigated.

Still, the effects can be seen. Magic doesn't produce miracles; it produces needed changes. Disbelievers usually discount the fruits of magic as coincidence, as accidents, or as pure psychology. These three explanations are quite handy, but if magic produces the desired results time and time again, and if its practitioners find within its simple rituals ways of improving the quality of their lives, then it isn't illusion, no matter what others may say.

The only way you can discover this is by practicing it. Don't believe that magic works. Try it, so that you'll know that it does.

CHAPTER THREE

The Tools of Food Magic & Magical Cooking

F ood magic is a direct and simple form of self-transformation. Its most important tools are food and the magician's personal power. Other implements, however, are necessary to prepare and to cook empowered dishes. This chapter describes the magical qualities of these tools and some basic magical cooking tips. Since this isn't a gourmet cookbook, no unusual objects are required. Your own kitchen should provide virtually everything you'll need.*

Cups, Bowls, and Pots

The earliest form of food container must have been cupped hands. Later, leather was shaped in imitation of this form and used to contain liquids and solid foods. In some parts of the globe, basketry was tightly woven into bowls and storage units. Baskets made of fresh leaves are still quite common in tropical parts of the world.

Clay was also shaped into bowls, and these forms were subjected to heat to firm their shapes and to prolong their

*Information about the elements and the planets can be found in part four.

lives. Gourds have been used as containers around the world for hundreds of years. Carved wooden bowls were in common use until quite recently.

With the coming of the Bronze and Iron Ages, peoples that possessed the knowledge of metalworking used these materials to create their bowls. Silver and gold vessels were also common grave goods in royal tombs in the ancient world.

Cups, bowls, and pots are certainly receptive; they *contain*. As implements related to the element of water and to the earth's moon, they possess loving energies and recall the loving cups—trophies—still awarded to exceptional individuals and teams.

Earlier cultures identified the pot as a symbol of the Great Mother. This concept is almost universal.[78] Rounded pots and bowls, associated with goddess energy, were also used to prepare food. Thus, a goddess symbol physically nourished humans. The Zuni, for example, saw the bowl as the emblem of the earth, which they described as "our Mother." They drew food and drink from the bowl, as does a baby from its mother's breast. The bowl's rim was as round as the horizon of the earth.[21]

Pottery was invented by women, and pottery remained a feminine craft among virtually all culturally unadvanced early peoples. One of the hallmarks of "advanced" culture was the forced transference of this women's art to men.[78]

Throughout the world, pots have been used for magical purposes. In Panama, a pot shaped like a human being was placed on the roof of a house for protection. In West Africa, shamans trapped the winds and rains in huge jars,[60] and ancient Hawaiian deities are said to have done much the same thing with gourds.

Chinese New Year's festivities often included stuffing a clay pot with stones and bits of iron, which represented the ills of the past year. Gunpowder was added to the pot, along with a fuse. The pot was buried, the fuse was lit, and the resulting explosion wiped out the evils of the past year.[60] On their ceremonial pots, the Pueblo Indians of North America rendered animals that are found near springs. This was done to ensure a steady supply of water.[9]

Any cup or bowl can be used in magic, as long as it's not made of plastic or aluminum. Earth colors (browns, beiges, and whites) are most appropriate for a container. Choose cooking pots of the same colors, and made preferably of glazed ceramic, glass, enameled metal, or stainless steel.

Avoid using aluminum implements in magical cooking.

The Oven

The oven is another symbol of the divine.[29] It encloses, performs a transformative process (cooking), and is warm and bright. Humans have used many types of ovens, from the mud-brick ovens of the Middle East to the earthen ovens used in both North America and Polynesia. Some cultures honored an oven goddess, such as Fornacalia of ancient Rome.[29] Others, like the Chinese, see a male deity within its sun-like warmth. In Europe, the oven didn't come into common use until the eighteenth century; the cauldron, a kind of portable oven, was used in its place.[71]

The oven's purpose is to retain heat from the burning fuel and to provide the even temperature necessary for proper cooking. Gas or electrically heated ovens are fine for magical cooking. Modern microwave ovens work on a completely different principle to heat the food. As food magic is a traditional practice, it's best to avoid microwaves and utilize the time-honored, traditional tools of food preparation.

The Cauldron

Long linked with Witches in the popular imagination, cauldrons were once the common cooking pots used throughout Europe. Made of iron, marked with ribs used for measuring, and standing on three long legs, millions of cauldrons have swung or stood on hearths to cook the family meal[104]—the stockpot so loved by contemporary cooks has its origins in the lowly cauldron. The cauldron's association with Witches derives from the infamous "three Witches" scene in Shakespeare's *Macbeth*. To use an iron pot for brewing (such as in making teas) or cooking wasn't unusual in the sixteenth century. What *was* unusual, and what attracted the public's attention, was the *type* of cooking being done by these three women.

Among modern Wiccans, the cauldron is honored as a symbol of the Mother Goddess, just as bowls, jars, and pots have been. Cast-iron, three-legged pots are still produced for decorative and occult purposes, but I don't recommend trying to cook in a cauldron unless you have an open hearth and plenty of time. It takes hours to boil water in one of these big iron pots.

Plates and Platters

Plates were probably used before bowls. The first plates were flat pieces of wood or stiff leaves, which came in handy for holding and slightly cooling cooked food prior to eating.

Plates are ruled by the sun and the element of earth. Generally speaking, they represent the physical world, money, and abundance. Any plate made of natural materials can be used for magic.

Mortar and Pestle

The blender and food processor of earlier times, the mortar and pestle is still used by some cooks to crush or to grind herbs and nuts. Prehistoric mortars have been found among the archaeological remains of many peoples dating back to Neolithic times.[104] Mortars identical to those used by preconquest Mexican peoples are still used in contemporary Mexico.

Many Indian tribes of southern California fashioned mortars by grinding holes into huge rocks. A round stone was used as the pestle. As a child, I often threw acorns into such *mortars* in the Laguna Mountains near San Diego. I even tried to grind the acorns, as had the Digueno Indians.

Food processors are important tools for many of us, and they do save time. They, or the mortar and pestle, can be used if you wish. Grinding two cups of almonds with a mortar and pestle is a lengthy business; but while doing so we can pour our personal power into the food and concentrate on its eventual use.

Pantry

Pantries were once common to every home. Today, most of us fill cupboards with staples and canned foods. The pantry is ruled by the element of earth and the moon; because it is a container that houses food, it's intimately linked with the Mother Goddess. For our purposes, your kitchen cabinets constitute a pantry.

The magical cook should keep a stock of basic culinary ingredients: salt; sugar (if you use it); honey; maple syrup; herbs and spices; whole grains; flours of all types; corn meal; vinegar; and vegetable oils and other similar foods, stored in airtight containers.

As a place where food is stored, the pantry should be protected. A rope of braided garlic or chili peppers hung in or on the pantry will serve it well. While hanging the rope, visualize the vegetable's forceful energies driving away anything that would contaminate the food.

Spoons and Spatulas

The spoon is a bowl with a handle. As such, it is related to the moon and to the element of water.

Spoons have been used for thousands of years. Until quite recently in Japan, the *shamoji,* or rice-spatula, was considered a magical object. Small spatulas were nailed over the front door of a house to guard it, and in the hope that its inhabitants would never go hungry for lack of rice.[54]

Forks

Though they are commonly found on Western tables today, forks were once used solely for noneating purposes such as spearing fish, working with hay, and digging. The first fork was probably a forked stick. Until late in the seventeenth century, most Western peoples ate with their fingers. Though the fork was introduced into Europe in the eleventh century, it took five hundred years for it to gain widespread use.[69]

The fork is ruled by Mars and the element of fire. As a tool for eating, it has been regarded as sacred, and bent forks played a role in European protective rituals. They were buried in gardens or placed inside walls to ward off negativity.

Knives

Knives were first created by flaking flint, jasper, and other crypto-crystalline quartzes into finely edged tools. The knife is ruled by Mars and the element of fire. This tool has been used both for life-threatening (stabbing) as well as life-affirming (cooking) purposes. It was the first implement used for eating, for it could both cut food as well as transfer it to the mouth.

A Note on Magical Cooking

—When preparing foods for specific magical purposes, cook with purpose and care. Keep your goal in mind. Know that the food contains the energies that you require.

—Always stir clockwise. Clockwise motion is thought to be in harmony with the apparent movement of the sun in the sky, and has been linked with life, health, and success.

—Cut foods into shapes symbolic of your magical goal; i.e., hearts, stars, or circles (see chapters 21 through 31 for specific ideas).

—If you're cooking food that will be consumed by others as well as by yourself, don't load the whole dish with energy. Prepare it as you normally would. Then, just before you eat, charge your own portion with visualization. Failing to separate your empowered share is treading on the dangerous ground of manipulative magic.

—Cook with love.

CHAPTER FOUR

The Ritual of Eating

E ating is a simple practice. We put food into our mouths, then chew and swallow it. Nothing mystical about that, right?

Perhaps not. But because of food's importance, it has been linked with politics, social structures, legal systems, health maintenance, magic and, oh yes, religion.

Our lives still contain vestiges of these earlier practices. Prayer (or "saying grace") before meals is perhaps the most common. It is popular not only in Christianity but also in many other religions. The urge to give thanks for food prior to eating has its origins in the Pagan sacrifices common in ancient Egypt, Sumer, Greece, Rome, and many other cultures. Portions of the food were burned or placed in offering bowls. The food is now simply blessed.*

The idea today is the same: verbally or psychologically linking food with deity. Long ago, humans spent most of their time ensuring a steady supply of food, which could be wiped out by fires, droughts, insect infestations, torrential rains, storms, and unseasonal freezes. Unable to physically prevent such catastrophes, humans naturally turned to their deities for protection.

*People continue to offer food to deities in a variety of religions around the world, especially on feast days. This is even found in some Christian groups.

When the harvest had been spared, our ancestors thanked their deities with offerings of food. This may have been buried, flung into the air, or tossed into a fire. The portion earmarked for the deities wasn't consumed by humans.

Even today, with tremendous botanical knowledge and global weather reporting, farmers in most parts of the world are still at the mercy of natural forces. The increased knowledge and tools available to farmers and agribusinesses can't stop such events from destroying their crops.

In many parts of the world that suffer food shortages, food has become a tool of politics. People *are* starving on every continent and within our own borders. Emergency supplies shipped to the hungry are often held up by government intervention, or are funneled to those in power.

These two factors—the uncertainty of our food supply and its scarcity in many parts of the world—should deepen our appreciation of food.

Our ancestors* worshipped food, seeing it as a gift from the hands of their deities. Food magicians don't worship food, though we respect it as a life-sustaining substance containing the energies of the earth. Food is a manifestation of divine energies that's vital to our survival. Approaching food from this frame of mind makes it easier for us to utilize it as a tool of self-transformation.

About prayer: if you don't subscribe to any particular religion, and haven't been in the habit of praying before meals, there's no reason for you to begin to do so. Prior to eating, simply attune with the food (all of the food, not just that which you're eating for magical purposes). You can easily do this by placing your hands on either side of your portion of the food before beginning to eat. Sense their energies for a few seconds. You need say nothing. This simple act, which you can do in front of those who know nothing about your magical studies, prepares your body to accept the food. You absorb its essence (power) before absorbing its manifestation.

---

*Everyone's ancestors: African-Americans; Asians; American Indians; Arabs; Pacific Islanders; Caucasians—everyone's!

If it is your custom to pray before meals, continue to do so. Religion and magic have always been closely linked—religion worships the energy that created all things; magic utilizes the energies in those things that have been created.

You can also include a prayer to your deity while eating, or address your conception of deity during the magical preparation and consumption of the food. Though this may seem to be a new idea, it isn't. It's performed around the world by millions of non-Christian, nonWestern peoples.

Eating (and the resultant digestion) is an act of transformation. Our bodies change food into the fuel necessary for our continued physical existence. Be aware also of the higher aspects of food every time that you eat.

CHAPTER FIVE

Vegetarianism

Many magicians are strict vegetarians. They shun meat, poultry, and fish; some even avoid eggs and milk products. They often believe that spiritual advancement and magical ability can only be obtained with such a diet.

There are many kinds of vegetarians. Those who follow a macrobiotic diet eat little more than grains. The more common type, commonly called "vegans," add fruits, vegetables, and nuts to their diet. Some more broad-based vegetarians also consume milk (usually goat's milk), cheese, and even eggs. A few "vegetarians" will also occasionally eat fish and seafood, or even poultry, but never red meat.

Most vegetarians rigidly adhere to their diets in the face of overwhelming odds. Their degree of adherence is usually determined by their reasons for adopting a vegetarian diet. Many of them see living creatures as our sisters and brothers—of different forms, but from the same source. They make a commitment not to ingest them.

Another rationale for vegetarianism seems to be that meat is a poison. It's true that much of the meat eaten today in the United States is injected with growth hormones and is too fatty for sustaining good health. But meat isn't poison. If it was, the entire world's population would have died out thousands of years ago. As members of a largely affluent society, many of us eat too much meat; but this dietary imbalance can be quickly corrected and need not preclude the ingestion of all meat.

Spirituality is the other major reason for following a strictly vegetarian diet. Some believe that if they eat meat, they're no higher than the animals that do the same thing. Therefore, they feel, they'll never receive true enlightenment. Many vegetarians are also following spiritual teachings or a religion that forbids eating meat.

This is sacred ground to many people. Still, it's a topic that must be discussed in a magical food book. I'm not trying to offend anyone—vegan or not—so don't be offended by the words that follow.

We're all separate, distinct persons, connected with the rest of our fellow creatures and with the universe, and yet apart. No one diet is correct for everyone, just as no single type of haircut, food, or religion is suitable for all.

Opinions vary, but it seems that people of most earlier cultures ate meat. One food scholar[29] states that no exclusively vegetarian society has ever been discovered. Certain members of a society may have avoided eating meat, but theirs wasn't the usual diet. The reason for this may be that a strictly vegetarian people would have disappeared long before they could have left any traces.

Many Westerners point to modern-day India, with its taboos against eating beef, as an example of a vegetarian society. This teaching is said to date back thousands of years. It does, but the Indian avoidance of beef-eating has had a checkered past.

The Brahmins, the highest caste of India, ate beef in about 1000 B.C.E.* The religious veneration of the cow began in India around 2,000 years ago, but it wasn't until India's independence in 1949 that cows gained legal protection against slaughter.[29] Vegetarianism among Buddhists is also common worldwide.

---

*I use B.C.E. ("Before the Common Era") in place of B.C. and C.E. ("Common Era") instead of A.D. throughout this book. These terms are nonreligious in nature.

But most Buddhists in India do eat dairy products, and the low yields of milk from the scrawny Indian cows provide a major source of protein for the Indians. Even Buddhist priests in Sri Lanka, Thailand, and other Buddhist countries eat meat. Most people of the lower castes in India, many of whom are starving, won't turn down meat when it's offered to them. In some cases, an empty stomach can overrule religious convictions.[29]

Still, there have always been vegetarians, and there have also always been omnivores (though most earlier cultures ate far less meat than we do today). Neither way is more "correct" or "ancient" or, indeed, spiritual, although many are likely to disagree with this statement.

Those in the West who feel that vegetarianism is necessary for magical and spiritual work are correct—for themselves. If they've made this commitment, it's best that they keep it. No one can make a commitment for another, however, and no one way is satisfying for everyone.

Life feeds on life. Our bodies cannot survive unless something else gives up its existence to sustain us—whether it's plankton, soybeans, or a chicken. This may seem cruel, but it's not. It's the reality of physical existence.

What you decide to eat or not to eat isn't as important as why you make this decision. If you're vegetarian because you feel that it's the only way in which you can achieve any form of spiritual enlightenment, fine. If you're vegetarian because you've decided that you can't practice magic if you eat meat, again, fine. But others can make alternate decisions. They can decide to be omnivores, achieve spiritual enlightenment, and still successfully practice magic. Neither position, once again, is correct for all.

Personally, I seem to be somewhat eclectic regarding foods—I enjoy different types. Though many of my friends are vegetarians, I'm not. That doesn't mean that I'll periodically run to the kitchen and fry up a steak, or that I'm psychologically addicted to eating meat. It simply means that I haven't made a commitment not to eat it.

I did, indeed, once try a strict vegetarian diet, under the guidance of a long-time vegetarian and ceremonial magician. He taught me how to combine proteins so that I wouldn't undernourished myself. It was an interesting experience avoiding all animal proteins and fat (did you know that lard is an ingredient of Oreo cookies?), but I quickly realized that it wasn't right for me. By the second week of my diet, my head was constantly bumping into the ceiling. Walking became a mystical experience. Colors were brighter, I felt lighter, and my awakened psychic abilities were always present. This was pleasantly surprising, but I soon had an experience that changed my feelings.

I was in a friend's occult supplies shop one night as she was closing. It was just after dark. I stood staring at a painting in my by-now usual "wow, man!" attitude as she turned off the lights. Though plenty of light shone in through the windows from the street, the painting dissolved into blackness. There, where the picture used to be, I saw something that I can't describe. It scared the heck out of me.

My friend's store was under physical and psychic bombardment from an evangelical, fundamentalist Christian organization that occupied an adjoining suite. Someone had recently thrown a brick through her store's window. In the inky painting, I saw an image of all the hatred being sent her way. In my completely opened psychic state (which was a direct result of my strict vegetarian diet), this manifestation of negative energy shocked my entire being. I went outside as soon as I could, shook it off, calmed myself, and went about my business.

Soon, I went back to my normal diet. Even though I'd been receiving the proper amount of protein, even though I'd been taking vitamin and mineral supplements, even though my food intake was being closely monitored by a vegetarian who'd followed a similar regimen for over fifteen years, the diet left me so spiritually and psychically open that I couldn't handle it.

Many naturally psychic persons have the same problem. They have years to learn ways to protect themselves. Taken completely by surprise, I had about fifteen seconds.

Despite my harrowing journey into vegetarianism, this book's main focus is on grains, vegetables, and fruits. Vegetarians can use the information contained within it to good effect. If you don't eat fish, choose other foods with similar energies. The same is true if you avoid dairy products.

Meat is rarely mentioned in this book for three reasons. First, meat was and still is scarce in many parts of the world. Most earlier people's daily diets revolved around dairy products, grains, fruit, and vegetables. Meat was usually reserved for special occasions and was not part of the normal diet.

Secondly, there's less ritual and magical information available regarding meat. In researching this book, I've found hundreds of references to corn, rice, beer, apples, and many other foods, but few concerning meat.

Also, many of us involved in magic are vegetarians, and I wanted this book to be useful to all. Therefore, save for a few isolated references (in parts three and four), this is a wholly non-meat book.

To close this chapter, I'll tell you a story I heard from Carl Weschcke, president of Llewellyn Worldwide. When I was visiting his home in Minnesota several years ago, he told me of a frantic phone call he'd received. A woman called him at the office screaming that she was under "psychic attack." Someone had cast an evil spell on her. She couldn't sleep, she was losing weight, and she could feel evil energies surrounding her. The curse had disrupted her entire life. She was weak and could do nothing to stop it. Wouldn't he help her?

Carl Weschcke asked the woman if she was a vegetarian. Surprised, she answered that she was. He promptly suggested that she eat a hamburger. The woman, desperate to end this attack, went to a fast-food restaurant, bought a hamburger, and ate it. The meat made her sick to her stomach, but it also ended the "psychic attack." She was fine after that and returned to her normal vegetarian diet.

Her problem may have been a lack of protein, which could have diminished her body's natural defenses. It might also have been a complete lack of grounding (connection with the physical world), or simply the product of an overactive imagination. In any case, the meat acted not only as a purgative but also as a shock to her system. Her problem—whatever its cause—vanished.

CHAPTER SIX

The Practice of Food Magic

As with any art, food magic should be practiced according to a few basic principles. My system of food magic, however, isn't rigid; it can be altered to fit your own lifestyle and changed for various occasions (i.e., eating in restaurants; eating with others; eating while camping; and so on). Following the basic structure presented here will produce the maximum results.

Though some of this material may seem to repeat parts of chapter 2, it is of such importance that I felt it deserved its own section. Chapter 2 discussed magic in general, with food as an example. This chapter is a practical guide to practicing food magic in particular. Additionally, putting all this information into one chapter makes it easier to find if you should need to reread it.

Here is the step-by-step process of food magic.

—**Decide what you wish to change about yourself.** This can be a minor problem, such as temporary depression, whose magical treatment can vary from meal to meal. If you need, however, to make a more important change, you should probably put yourself on a magical diet (see the introduction to part three for more information).

This major change may be one of the following (but is certainly not limited to this list):

Clearer thinking	More satisfying sexual activities
Protection	More energy
Money	A loving relationship with another
Purification	A loving relationship with yourself
Greater health	Peace and happiness
Magical strength	Physical strength
Spirituality	Breaking addictions
Fertility	Psychic awareness
Beauty	Success in your endeavors
Weight loss	Celibacy
Wisdom	"Luck"

As you can see, most of these are changes of ourselves. They don't affect others; in fact, food magic should never be used to affect others *without their permission*. Don't serve lust foods to an unsuspecting date with the purpose of coercing him or her to have sex with you. This probably won't be effective, since your belusted one isn't prepared to receive these energies. Such practices are manipulative and contrary to the very nature of magic, and they're a waste of time and energy. Seduction has its own form of magic that doesn't rely on food.

You can do many things to create these changes, and your magical work *must* be backed up by conscious effort and physical or mental exertion on your part. Telling your food what to do, eating it, and then expecting it to change your life isn't enough. You must involve yourself in the process.

—Select foods that contain energies suitable to your desired change. This book mentions many such correspondences. For quick reference, glance through chapters 22–31. Read chapters 8–20 for other ideas, or check the index under the appropriate heading.

—**Choose foods that you enjoy.** Why eat foods that you dislike or even detest just for their magical value? Still, you should eat a balanced diet. We can't perform effective magic if we're fueling our bodies with nothing but junk food.

—**Prepare the food with visualization.** Preparation may mean simply peeling a carrot or picking fruit from a tree. It may also involve chopping, slicing, and cooking However the food is prepared, use your visualization to awaken the needed energies within yourself and those within the food. Charge food with your purpose through the powers of your mind.

—**Attune with all food prior to eating.** This prepares it and you for the transformative process. This can be accomplished through prayer or with a simple awareness of the food's energies.

—**Visualize as you eat.** Even if you're carrying on a conversation with someone else, keep in mind what you're trying to accomplish. If necessary, draw a small picture of your goal and glance at it while eating.

—**Accept the energy that the food offers to you.** Make it a part of yourself.

—**Give the food time to do its work.** We didn't create our problems overnight, so we can't expect them to disappear overnight. Eat foods linked with your magical change for at least a week until they've had time to take effect.*

That's about it. Every food at every meal doesn't have to be geared toward your magical goal. As long as you eat with purpose and visualization, magic will be at work.

---

*This is one of the questions I'm asked most often about all forms of magic: "How long should I do it?" There's no set answer. Continue until the change has manifested. That's it!

CHAPTER SEVEN

Festival Foods

Food has played a significant role in human celebrations of all kinds. In earlier times, the earth and its bounty were connected with goddesses and gods. Fruit, seed, root, and flower were all manifestations of divinity.

Throughout Western Europe, the times of planting, flowering, maturation, and harvest were observed by the common folk with festivals that celebrated the fertility of the land. Foods came to be associated with certain seasons and days. Some of this old food lore has survived to this day in a suitably whitewashed form.*

The human diet was once routine and unimaginative. Grain cooked in every conceivable manner made up the bulk of the food consumed by persons who sometimes worked sixteen hours a day just to survive. Save for the upper classes, meat was a luxury.

Specific days of the year, however, were set aside for riotous feasting. Every resource was called upon to provide a memorable meal or two that lingered in the mind until the next feast day.

*Most of the festivals mentioned in this chapter are of European origin, but many of them originated in the Middle East. Virtually every culture has celebrated similar occasions.

These days were largely determined by astronomical phenomena and agricultural cycles, which were and still are closely linked. Planting and harvesting prompted the people to feast, as did the coming of spring, summer, fall, and winter. Persons living in harmony with the earth used its seasons as a natural calendar that structured their otherwise routine lives.

These festivals were more than times of heavy eating after the work had been finished. Such feasting revels were religious as well as secular in nature. In the frenzied baking, cooking, and eating was a real thanksgiving to the mysterious powers that created and watched over the fertility of the earth.

Only on such spiritual days (and nights) did the people expand their diets to include all manner of festive foods. Only then could they truly enjoy the fruits of their intensive food-producing labors.

These festival days are still with us. Some of them are sacred in the old Pagan sense of the word (see glossary). Others are seemingly secular rites with religious roots. This chapter is a guide to food magic throughout the year, with suggestions of dishes we can eat on feast days that attune us with the energies at work within the earth.

If you decide to prepare and eat any of these foods, do so with the meaning of the holiday in mind. Remember that these dishes link us with the endless cycle of the earth's fertility. Eat with knowledge and peace.

Most of these celebrations actually began on the night before the festival date. This originated during the age of lunar calendars. Beltane rituals, for example, were performed on April thirtieth and continued into the actual day itself. This practice dates to the time when lunar calendars were observed.

We'll begin our journey at the festival of Yule.

Yule

(circa December 21)

Yule—the winter solstice—is an old solar ritual that has been preserved in the Christian observance of Christmas. Its origins lie deep in the past, in the Mediterranean lands of the sun. The birthday of Mithras, an ancient solar deity, was celebrated on the winter solstice. Later, this holiday was brought to Europe, and an astonishing collection of folk rituals became associated with it.

Yule occurs during the depths of winter. Though some of us live beyond the reach of snow flurries and zero-degree temperatures, this is still the season in which the earth pauses to regenerate herself for the coming spring.

This holiday (holy day; sacred day) astronomically marks the waning of winter. After the winter solstice, the hours of light increase each day. Therefore, Yule is associated with the returning warmth of the sun.

Before the intercontinental shipment of food, this precious substance was usually meager at Yule. Most of it was preserved, dried in the sun; salted; put up in crocks; submerged in honey; buried in the earth; kept covered in baskets; or laid in the snow for natural refrigeration. Because of its scarcity, food was given a high degree of sacralness.

Over the centuries and in various countries, a wide variety of foods have been associated with Yule. Here are a few of them.

Apples are sacred foods, associated with many ancient deities (see chapter 11). Earlier peoples hung apples on Yule trees (the forerunners of the modern Christmas tree) to symbolize the continuing fertility of the earth. Mulled apple cider is a fine drink to sip on Yule while watching the fire. Any dishes that contain apples are also appropriate, as is wassail.

Gingerbread is the modern version of ancient cakes made of grain and honey, which were offered as sacrifices to the goddesses and gods at Yule. These cakes were also buried with the dead to ensure the passage of their souls into the other world.

When ginger was introduced into Europe from Asia, it was soon incorporated into the ritual Yule cake. This was the origin of gingerbread. Though ginger was once more expensive than diamonds, this spice is now easily within reach of us all.

You may wish to create a gingerbread house at Yule. If so, make it in the image of your own home. If this isn't possible, visualize your home while mixing, baking, forming, and decorating the house. See your household filled with warmth, love, and happiness—all gifts of ginger and the sun. Eat the house on Yule, sharing it with others who live under your roof, and invite its loving energies into yourself.

Cookies are standard Yule fare. If you wish to make the ubiquitous sugar cookies, cut them into shapes associated with the season: circles (symbolic of the sun); bells (originally used to drive away evil in pre-Christian times); stars (for protection against negativity); and, of course, trees (representing the continuing fertility of the earth during winter). For more cookie lore, see chapter 9.

The idea of creating and eating specially shaped desserts on Yule isn't new. Prehistoric graves in northern Europe contain cakes modeled in the rough shapes of deities, animals, suns, stars, and moons, and these cakes may have been consumed at the winter solstice in those frigid regions.

The New Year

(January 1)

Many cultures celebrate the New Year, but not always on the same date. Japanese and Chinese New Year festivals, for example, fall on different days each year (according to our calendar). The pre-Christian cultures of Europe didn't always celebrate New Year's on January 1. It has been observed on the evening of November 1 and at Yule. The actual date matters little, for the rituals performed at the beginning of the New Year remain quite similar.

New Year's was once a time full of magic. Many of the old customs concerned food and its abundance. Past concerns and cares were ritualistically swept away, and good was invited into the home. It was once thought that whatever occurred on the first day of the year forecast the next 364 days, and people acted accordingly.

In the United States, many people eat cabbage on New Year's Day. It is often cooked with a small piece of silver. The green color of the vegetable, along with the silver, ensures plenty of food and money in the coming year.[46, 66]

Black-eyed peas are another traditional favorite for "luck" in the New Year, particularly in the southern United States. Carrots eaten on the first day ensure a sweet year.[46]

An old ritual: on New Year's Eve, place a loaf of bread and a penny on a table. Leave overnight. This will provide plenty to eat in the coming year.

Be sure to have a well-stocked pantry at this time.

Imbolc

(February 2)

Imbolc is an old festival connected with the coming of spring and the growing warmth of the sun. In some areas of Europe, this day marked the emergence of a few brave plants from beneath the snow. As such, Imbolc was an occasion for feasting.

Because the sun was usually seen as the source of the earth's fertility, Imbolc (known in Catholicism as Candlemas) was a solar festival. Practitioners of pre-Christian religions lit fires and carried torches in ceremonial processions to urge the sun's "return."

Appropriate foods for Imbolc are spicy and hot, in honor of the Sun. Those utilizing garlic and chili peppers are suitable, as are curried dishes.

Ostara

(circa March 21)

Ostara, the spring solstice, marks the astronomical start of spring. This was a time of joyous celebration, for the killing months of winter were over. Plants sprang from the ground in ways that seemed miraculous to our ancestors.

Because the burgeoning growth hasn't yet fruited, sprouts are very appropriate. Seeds of any kind (including pine nuts, sesame, poppy, sunflower, and pumpkin) and green, leafy vegetables also vibrate with the season's energies.

Flower dishes are also traditional. Rose, mustard, squash blossom, nasturtium, carnation—all can be added to more conventional dishes to bring the flavor and energies of the season into your diet. Never use flowers that have been sprayed with pesticides.

Eggs are a welcome addition to the diet. If you wish, color them red, yellow, and gold in honor of the sun. Flavor foods with sage for good health.

Beltane

(May 1)

We still observe May Day, a contemporary version of an ancient European Pagan religious celebration. In earlier times, Beltane was connected with the dairy, and so ice cream, yogurt, cheese, custard, quiche, and all other dairy foods are appropriate fare.

Oatmeal cookies and oatmeal bread also fit the symbolism of Beltane, the high point of spring. This customary food comes from Scotland. Many centuries ago, oatmeal cakes known as bannocks were used in Scottish rituals.

May wine is a tasty drink. It is made from white wine, fresh woodruff, and strawberries.

Midsummer

(circa June 21)

The summer solstice is an ancient time of magic. Great fires were lit on hilltops in honor of the zenith of the sun's strength.

Fresh fruits (which are increasingly available as autumn nears) are fine midsummer foods, as are any dishes that use fruit as a major ingredient.

In keeping with the heat of this holiday, flaming foods are also appropriate.

Lughnasadh

(August 1)

Lughnasadh is the first harvest—the promise of spring's planting realized. Sometimes known as the Feast of Bread, Lughnasadh is a time for kneading, baking, slicing, and eating this basic food. Lughnasadh originally marked the first-harvest festivals of earlier European peoples, for whom it didn't fall on a specific date.

Prepare a few whole-grain loaves on this day if you make your own bread. For something simpler, yet in keeping with the energies at work, make some corn bread.

Other traditional foods include all berries, crab apples, and grains. Barley soup, popcorn, and even beer (due to its ingredients) are also appropriate foods.

Mabon

(circa September 21)

Mabon marks the second harvest. The bounty of nature is dwindling. Earth begins to pull her fertility from the land. Humans and wild animals alike scramble to gather as much food as possible in preparation for the hard winter ahead.

Grains are appropriate for Mabon—particularly corn. Corn chowder, boiled ears of corn, and creamed corn fit Mabon symbolism well.

Beans, squash, and all other fall vegetables are also perfect for this festival.

Samhain

(November 1)

This ancient Celtic festival lives on in the United States and in other countries as Halloween, a degraded version of both the earlier Pagan holiday as well as the later Christian variant—All Hallow's Eve. The word "eve" in the Christian name reminds us that this festival begins the night before its calendar date.

Samhain marks the close of the year. Skies may still be blue, but the wind is chilly and crisp. Apples are ripening. Red, yellow, orange, gold, and brown leaves skip across the ground. Nuts fall. The earth prepares for winter.

On this night, the souls of the dead were thought to walk the earth. All manner of fantastic customs and rituals were carried out on Samhain. One of these has continued to the present day. Many people leave a plate of food outside the home to provide nourishment to the souls of the dead.

Samhain foods include root crops such as potatoes, beets, turnips, and carrots. Grain, nuts, mulled wines, and ciders are also appropriate to Samhain.

In the United States, the pumpkin is the one food most frequently associated with this holiday. This vegetable, a squash, is usually served in the form of pumpkin pie. Many cookbooks also have recipes for pumpkin custard, pumpkin soup, and other dishes. Roasted pumpkin seeds are perfect Samhain fare.

Pomegranate seeds are linked with Samhain due to their connection with the underworld in classical mythology. They can be eaten raw or used in a variety of recipes. Apple dishes of all kinds— cakes, pies, salads—are also consumed with relish on the night of Samhain.

PART TWO

the magic of food

Each chapter in this section discusses a specific type of food. I use this format rather than my usual alphabetical listing because foods naturally fall into tidy groups. Those few that refused to be pigeonholed have been thrown together into chapter 15. Aside from this, the format is much the same as that used in my other books. Generally speaking, each listing contains the following information:

Common name, usually in English.

Specific name, in Latin, the nomenclature used by scientists around the world.

Ruling planet, one of the seven "planets" known to the ancients. Briefly, each plant (and food) is thought to be governed by a heavenly body. This ancient system of magical correspondence is one method of grouping foods. Knowledge of a food's planetary ruler provides information concerning its magical uses. See part four for descriptions of the energies of the sun, moon, Mercury, Venus, Mars, Jupiter, and Saturn. By the way, I'm aware that the sun and the earth's moon aren't planets. But early skywatchers didn't know this. The sun and the moon were included in what they called the "wanderers"—the planets.

Ruling element, simply another method of classifying items used in magic. The powers of the elements—earth, air, fire, and water—are discussed in part four.

Energies, each food's dominant energies and, thus, its magical uses.

Lore, historical, mythological, cultural, ritual, and magical uses of the food. Uses listed in this section aren't necessarily recommended. I've included bits of historical information to remind us of the importance of these foods in earlier times.

Magical uses, or the specific changes that can be brought about with each food, and suggestions on usage.

I feel it necessary to mention that food magic is a personal art. If a food isn't mentioned here, look in the listings in part four, or use common sense and intuition to determine its magical properties. Here are some clues:

> —Is the food spicy? If so, it's probably protective.
> —Is the food citrusy? Purification is probably its best magical use.
> —Is the food sweet? Loving energies are probably locked inside it.

Once you begin to think of foods from a magician's view, the process of determining their magical uses becomes second nature.

Some magicians will quibble about my selections for planetary and elemental rulers of certain foods, and will even point out that in previous books I've made different selections. Isn't it cut-and-dried?

No. After twenty years of study and practice, I'm still learning. As I increase my knowledge of the uses of plants (particularly diets) and of the dishes in which they're used, I may reassign some foods based on this expanded knowledge.

It isn't wrong to say that carrots are ruled by Venus, or that bay leaves are better suited to Mars, but I choose to place them under the rulership of different planets. Don't be confused by such seeming inaccuracies. They are minor matters. Just read, visualize, eat, and enjoy the fruits of food magic.*

Some of the chapters, such as chapter 16, aren't quite arranged in the fashion described here. Please be flexible.

*I had to mention this once again due to the number of letters I receive about the subject.

CHAPTER EIGHT

Bread & Grains

Humans have eaten bread for at least 8,000 years.[104] We have made it round, oblong, square, and triangular; flat as a pancake or fat as a loaf. Bread has been twisted into a symbol of the winter solstice, spiced, sweetened, garlicked, and filled with fresh vegetables. Though it has been made of every grain, it was the raised wheaten form that first inspired human and divine palates.

Bread has long been worshipped as the "staff of life." But in the West today, bread is usually encountered in plastic bags, presliced and stripped of nutrients, bran, and wheat germ. It is "fortified" with just enough vitamins to satisfy government standards and may be artificially flavored and preserved. Perhaps the greatest indignity to which our bread is subjected is being pumped with air. This creates what is known in the grocery trade as "balloon bread."

Not long ago, bread was a divine substance, directly linked with the goddesses and gods of the earth, lovingly crafted with grain and water. Flat, unleavened breads sustained millions of humans. Due to our forerunner dependence upon bread, these loaves also played important roles in birth celebrations, spirituality, and death.

Before the advent of agriculture, humans gathered wild grains and hunted. This forced them to live nomadic lives in small family groups. Eventually women—who had always gathered grain—discovered agriculture. As fields were planted with grain, people began putting down roots. Life stabilized and civilization began. Grain, most often eaten in the form of bread or grain paste,[104] soon became far more important than meat.

Earlier European civilizations dedicated grain to state deities: Inanna in Sumer; Ishtar in Babylon; Osiris in Egypt; Indra in India; Demeter in Greece; Spes and Ceres (from whose name we take our word "cereal") in Rome; Xipe, Cinteotl, and Mayauel in ancient Mexico; and various forms of the corn mother throughout the Americas.

Bread, the basic product of grain, was offered to the deities. Ishtar, Shamash, and Marduk were each given thirty loaves a day in Sumer.[24,51] Ra, Amon, Ptah, and Nekhbet received their share in Egypt.[29] Demeter, the Greek goddess of bread, grain, and agriculture, was also similarly honored. The Phoenicians stamped Astarte's loaves with a horned symbol (linked with the moon) to deify the bread.[29]

The ancient Egyptians, whom Herodotus described as "the bread eaters," probably invented leavened bread. Along with onions and beer, it became a basic part of their diet.[29, 104] The Egyptians offered bread to the deities and to sacred animals (including cats), and stocked tombs with enormous amounts of the divine food for future use by the deceased. They are said to have baked fifty varieties of bread in numerous shapes. Some were heavily spiced and salted, though the priests and priestesses dedicated to certain deities avoided salted breads.[29]

Bread pigs formed from dough were sometimes sacrificed in place of live pigs by those too poor to afford the real thing. The bread pig was accepted as a suitable sacrifice in ancient Egypt.[23]

Eventually, wheat (or barley) bread became a symbol of life itself. "Breaking bread" was more than a process of nourishing the body; it became a meal that bound together all those who ate it. Eating a simple meal was a part of many Pagan religions, and such a ritual meal, transformed into the ritual of communion, later became an established part of Christian ritual.

Bread has also had its magical uses. In seventeenth-century England, a loaf of bread was floated on the surface of water to find the body of a person who had drowned. Midwives placed bread into a woman's bed while she was in labor to prevent the theft of both the woman and her baby.[82]

In contemporary Greece, men being inducted into the army are sometimes given pieces of bread, which are thought to confer protection and victory in battle. Field workers in Greece may pack a bit of bread with their lunch. It isn't eaten at midday, but only upon safe return to the home each evening. A small piece of bread secreted under children's pillows guards them while they sleep.[29]

In other parts of Europe, bread is formally presented to children as soon as they recognize it. This ritual blesses the infant with food for its entire lifetime.[68] Carpathian Gypsies carried small pieces of bread in their pockets to avoid danger and trouble during their continuing journeys.[14]

British and American folklore still acknowledge the potency of bread. When moving into a new home, many carry in a loaf of bread and salt, for continued food and luck, before moving any thing else.[46] Other superstitions related to the baking, slicing, and eating of bread still survive in our technological lives.[46]

The techniques and information contained within this chapter have been gathered from around the globe and from every period of recorded history. Both grains as well as some products made from them are examined here.

Food historians speculate that humans have eaten bread in one form or another since at least the late Stone Age.[71] Raised (yeast) breads were probably first made in Egypt in around 4000 B.C.E.[71] As we rediscover the value of grains and add them to our diets, it's enriching to know the wonders once ascribed to these simple food stuffs that have been worshipped as life-giving gifts from the forces that watch us from above.

Barley

(*Hordeum* spp.)

Planet: Venus

Element: Earth

Energies: Money, fertility, sex

Lore: Barley was an important grain to the ancient Egyptians, who used it as a medium of exchange and stocked it in tombs, most notably that of Tutankhamun. Thutmose III offered barley to Ra every day, as well as on the New Moon and on the sixth day of every month.[23] According to one Egyptian legend, barley grew out of men (as wheat grew out of women). This was apparently linked to the genders of the words in the ancient Egyptian language.[23]

The Sumerians made barley a staple of their diet. Eight different types of barley beer were made. This drink was manufactured under the auspices of the goddess Ninkasi.[104]

In ancient India, barley was sacred to Indra, known as "He who ripens barley." This grain was used for rituals relating to childbirth and marriage, and played a role in funerals as well.[120] The Vedas state that barley was also used with fresh water for healing ceremonies.[96]

The Babylonians were brewing beer with barley as early as 2800 B.C.E., and the Greeks planted it around temples to Demeter while asking for human fertility.[29] In China, barley is a symbol of male sexual potency.[120]

Magical uses: As a wholesome food, barley is currently experiencing new popularity. It is useful for prosperity diets—those designed to bring additional money when needed or to generally boost your financial state. Awaken this energy through visualization while preparing and eating barley dishes.

Add barley to diets if fertility or male sexual potency is a problem.

Buckwheat

(Fagopyrum esculentum)

Planet: Jupiter

Element: Earth

Energies: Money

Lore: Buckwheat pancakes are common enough in the United States, but few seem to know the magical history behind buckwheat itself. In Japan, this grain is used to make *soba*— buckwheat noodles. These are eaten on the Japanese New Year for "money luck," i.e., the ability to amass large amounts of money in the coming year.[120]

Buckwheat noodles are also served on other festive occasions. Upon moving into a new home, the owners may give soba to the neighbors on each side and to the three houses across the road. This is a gift of good fortune and friendship.[120]

Japanese goldsmiths have long used buckwheat dough to collect gold dust in their shops. This ageless practice has firmly connected soba with the promise of riches.[120]

Magical uses: Because all grains are connected with abundance in one form or another (fertility, money, life), eat buckwheat pancakes to attract this energy. For even more money power, pour on a bit of maple syrup.

Corn

(Zea mays)

Planet: Sun

Element: Fire

Energies: Protection, spirituality

Lore: Corn has played a central role in North and Central American religion for thousands of years. The Quiche Mayas of Guatemala and the Navajo believed that the first humans were created from corn.[111] The Mayas, Incans, Aztecs, and nearly every American Indian tribe ate corn and incorporated it into their religious beliefs and rituals. The corn mother was perhaps the most widely worshipped deity in the pre-Columbian Americas.[120] As a symbol of life, fertility, eternity, and resurrection, corn was a sacred gift of the Mother Goddess.

To the Zuni, various colors of corn were related to the four directions:

Yellow corn—north
White corn—east
Red corn—south
Blue corn—west

Blue corn was often considered to be the most sacred form, and so was the most useful for spiritual rituals.[90]

The Hopi offered corn meal during religious rituals of all types in thanks to the corn mother.[111] Divination with corn was common throughout the Americas and Mexico, and a corn-divination ritual from early Mexico has survived. Originally used to diagnose illness or the extent of a sickness, this ritual can also be called upon to answer other types of questions.

Fill a small bowl with exactly thirty dried kernels of corn of any color. Concentrating on a specific question, take a random number of kernels from the bowl. Place them on the floor (or the table) and divide them into groups of four. If you create an even number of piles with an even number of leftover kernels, the answer is favorable. However, if you form an odd number of piles with an odd number of kernels, the answer is negative. Finally, if you come up with an even number of piles, but an odd number of leftovers, no answer can be given. [109]

Another form of corn divination was apparently practiced by the ancient Aztecs. During a preliminary curing session for a severe illness, a priestess would lay a piece of white bark cloth before an image of the god Quetzalcoatl. A bowl of corn was then placed before the cloth. Inspired by the god, the priestess would take a handful of the corn kernels and scatter them on the cloth. If the corn was evenly scattered, the patient would eventually attain good health. If the corn was separated into two portions, death would eventually result from the illness.[10]

Corn was one of America's priceless gifts to the world. As it was introduced into other countries, its sacredness was forgotten; but it still feeds millions of persons, especially vegetarians who combine beans with corn to form a complete protein.

It is still used in magic. A curious Ozark ritual for curing hiccups consists of naming three kernels of corn for three friends, placing these into a vessel of water, and holding it above the head.[87]

Many still feel that corn is sacred, and that wasting it will cause poverty. This belief is similar to the Asian taboo against wasting rice.

Magical uses: Place ears of blue corn on the altar or hang them in the home to induce spirituality. Scatter corn meal around outdoor ritual sites for blessings and heightened spiritual rituals.

Now that blue corn is being offered for retail sale, utilize it in spirituality producing diets. Blue popcorn and blue cornbread are two possibilities (see appendix 2 for possible sources).

Place ears of red corn in baskets on the floor to protect the home. Corn is also added to protection diets. To make cornbread for this purpose, run a knife through the top of the unbaked dough in the shape of a pentagram.* Bake and eat with visualization.

Maize (from the Haitian or Cuban name for corn) is known as corn only in the United States. In other English-speaking countries, "corn" refers to any grain except maize. Maize is not an Indian term.

---

*The pentagram is a five-pointed star, with one point up and two points down. It is an ancient symbol of protection and has no connection with the modern, spurious practice of Satanism.

Lentil

(Lens culinaris)

Planet: Moon

Element: Water

Energies: Peace

Lore: In 1085 B.C.E., Egyptians traded lentils for the prized cedars of Lebanon. During Graeco-Roman times, the Egyptians offered lentils to Harpocrates.[23] This wonderful food was also eaten by the Sumerians.[104] The Roman naturalist Pliny prescribed lentil soup for creating an even temper.[86]

Magical uses: Lentil soup is a warm, nourishing staple of many diets around the world. Eat it for peace. The Romans believed that lentils hindered sleep, so it might be better to eat them at midday.

Millet *(Pucium miliacaeum)*

Planet: Jupiter

Element: Earth

Energies: Money

Lore: In ancient China, grains of millet were used as a unit of measure: ten millet grains placed end to end constituted one inch, one hundred grains was the measurement of one foot, and so on.[76]

Magical uses: If you find it difficult to enjoy this grain, visualize millet as compact, concentrated money energy before eating.

An old German custom: eat millet on the first day of the year to bring riches into your life.[22]

Oat

(Avena sativa)

Planet: Venus

Element: Earth

Energies: Money

Lore: In Scotland, cakes known as *bannocks* were baked and eaten at Beltane, the old Pagan observance of May Day. Oat cakes are still eaten during some contemporary Wiccan rituals.

Magical uses: Use only whole-grain oats.

Remember Marjorie from chapter 2? We can prepare and eat oatmeal first thing in the morning to bring money and prosperity into our lives. Other magical possibilities include oat cookies and oat bread.

Pretzel

Planet: Sun

Element: Fire

Energies: Protection

Lore: You may be surprised to see this food listed here, but pretzels have a long magical history.

According to legend, the winter solstice was observed with a special bread in Europe during the Middle Ages. This bread was circular, in honor of the sun, but twisted at the center to form an equal-armed cross symbolic of the four seasons. This was called a "bret-zel" or "pretzel," and was a familiar festival food denoting the rebirth of the sun in European folk religion.

Our pretzel is the direct descendant of these early breads. Its shape reveals Pagan origins, although it has been slightly altered. The salt seems to be a later addition.[29]

Magical uses: Though pretzels can be enjoyed at any time, eat them on the winter solstice in honor of the sun. Also, pretzels are appropriate to protective diets due to their planetary ruler, the salt, and the bread's twisted shape.

Rice

(Oryza sativa)

Planet: Sun

Element: Air

Energies: Money, Sex, Fertility, Protection

Lore: Rice is to Asia what corn is to the Americas. It has been laboriously cultivated and eaten in the East for thousands of years. Linked with deity and served at every meal, rice was and still is a vital staple food for many peoples.

More than half of the world's population regularly eats rice. It's of central importance in China, Japan, and throughout the Pacific area. Because of this, numerous rituals and customs have been attached to rice.

Among some peoples, if a man and a woman eat rice out of a common bowl, it is a binding declaration of marriage.[31] In China, rice is thrown at newlywed couples to confer luck and many children. This is the origin of our similar custom.[3]

The Japanese, who still revere rice, eat it with red beans (*azuki*) to bring good fortune. Interestingly enough, these are the same beans added to shaved ice (a flavored ice treat) enjoyed in Hawaii; and red beans and rice is an old Cajun luck food in Louisiana. In Japan, red rice, produced by cooking a special type of rice with azuki beans, was once eaten on the first and fifteenth days of each month for good luck, as well as on birthdays and festivals. Red is a color of joy.[54]

Wasting rice, to a Japanese, is an inexcusable action. In feudal times, rice was used as money to pay salaries, allowances, and retainers.[120]

The Japanese used rice to startle and scatter "evil spirits." In the past, one spirit in particular was believed to disturb babies who cried in the night without apparent cause. A bowl of rice was always placed near the infant. When trouble began, the mother or father threw a handful of rice from the bowl onto the floor. This frightened away the spirit and allowed the child to peacefully sleep all night.

Ancient magic clings to rice. In cooking rice, if a ring forms around the edge of the pot, the owner will become rich.[22] Cooked rice, mixed with sugar and cinnamon (a common treat), is believed to "make a man skillfull in his relation with the ladies."[59]

Magical uses: Though white rice has outstripped brown rice in popularity, choose the brown variety for the best nutritional and magical effects.

Rice cakes, those cute circles of pressed, puffed rice, are a deliciously simple way to bring rice energy into your life. Hold a plain rice cake in your hand and visualize money, enhanced sexuality, fertility, or protection. Eat the cake while retaining the visualization.

Before cooking brown rice (never use the quick-cooking type), pour some of the rice to be used onto a clean, flat surface one grain thick. While visualizing, use a finger to trace an image of your needed change in the rice (a heart for luck, a dollar sign for money, and so on).* Cook and eat this charged rice.

Rye

(*Secale* spp.)

Planet: Venus

Element: Earth

Energies: Love

---

*See Symbols, pages 341–344, for magical symbols and runes.

Magical uses: The familiar taste and smell of rye bread comes from the caraway seeds used in its creation, not from the rye. Rye, however, is a powerful addition to diets designed to increase your ability to give and to receive love. Caraway fits in here as well.

Tamales

Lore: Tamales (corn meal wrapped around a filling and cooked in a husk) were used in Zuni healing ceremonies. These tamales were presented as gifts to the shaman about to perform the ritual. Prayers accompanied the offering of the tamales. Those receiving them returned the gesture with further prayers.[111] Tamales are still offered to the deities by contemporary Huichols in Mexico.

Tortilla

Planet: Sun

Element: Fire

Energies: Spirituality, protection

Lore: Tortillas are a standard Mexican food. They are still made in the same way as they were during Aztec times. Round, containing sacred corn, tortillas are an indispensible part of the Latino diet.

The Huichols of Mexico also offer tortillas to their deities. Tortillas made of yellow corn are believed to be more satisfying and to give more energy to the body than those of other colors.[109]

Magical uses: Corn tortillas are best. Wheat tortillas, which were first made in northern Mexico, simply don't have the same symbolism or energies as corn tortillas

If you buy tortillas prepackaged, check the label. Choose only those that contain no artificial preservatives. They can be made at home (any good Mexican cookbook has directions) or, in many U.S. towns, can be purchased at tortillerias.

Warm tortillas, with butter or cheese, are wonderful foods at any time, but are particularly satisfying after intense magical workings. They instantly nourish the body and refuel it.

Round tortillas can also be added to spirituality diets. Warmed and spread with garlic butter, corn tortillas are a delicious part of a protective diet.

Wheat

(Triticum spp.)

Planet: Venus

Element: Earth

Energies: various (see below)

Lore: Wheat has long played a part in the human diet. After rice, it's the second-most commonly used grain for human food, and was first cultivated during the Neolithic age.[120]

The Egyptians, Sumerians, Babylonians, Hittites, Greeks, and Romans all worshipped harvest deities associated with wheat. Wheat is particularly a symbol of the Mother Goddess. She taught the secrets of agriculture to women, the grain's first farmers and cultivators.

In ancient Greece, newly married couples were pelted with sweetmeats and grains of wheat.[31] The Romans crowned brides and grooms with wreaths of wheat and with lilies to symbolize purity and fertility.[75]

Magical uses: Whole wheat is best for magical (and nutritional) purposes. Bleached wheat has had more than its vitamins, minerals, and bran removed: it also lacks magical energy. Though white bread was eaten by the Roman upper classes, it's a spiritually dead food.

Eat wheat-based foods (breads and all dough products) to bring prosperity and money into your life.

Before baking a loaf of bread, use a sharp knife to ritually incise a symbol of a specific energy that you wish to bring into your life. Do this with visualization. Various types of wheat bread have diverse energies and magical uses. Here are some of them:

Twisted breads (any bread-recipe book contains directions) are fine additions to protective diets. The more twists, the more protection. Visualize as you braid the dough.

Egg breads are baked and eaten, with visualization, to promote physical fertility.

Saffron bread enhances spirituality. To a lesser extent, so too do all round loaves.

Sprouted bread is excellent for increasing psychic awareness.

Pita bread (also known as "pocket bread") is a fine spirituality food.

Seven-grain bread (or its eight-grain cousin) is a fine money attractant.

Dill bread promotes love.

Garlic bread, created by slathering slices of bread with garlic-flavored butter, is a delicious and powerful addition to protection diets.

Most European countries produce **sweetened breads** for use during spring festivals (which are now connected with later Christian holidays such as Easter). Sweetened breads are discussed in chapter 9.

CHAPTER NINE

Cakes, Sweetened Breads, Cookies, & Pies

Humans have always eaten sweetened foods. Honey has been in use since at least 8000 B.C.E. Cave paintings of humans gathering honey attest to this.[71] Date syrup and grape syrup were also commonly used throughout Mesopotamia and the Mediterranean region for sweetening purposes.[29] Until fairly recently, only India and Hawaii used sugar as their major sweetener (see chapter 13 for further information about sweeteners).

Sweetened breads and cakes have always been linked with religion and folk magic. The history of these foods is a journey through dozens of cultures and peoples around the globe.

Babylonians baked cakes for the goddess Ishtar in the shape of male and female human genitalia, and served them during fertility festivals.[12] Selene was honored with crescent-shaped cakes; Hermes with those in the form of a herald's rod.[93] Cakes marked with the images of the horns of the moon were offered to Astarte.[29] The Greek goddess Artemis was honored each month with round cakes, upon which burning candles were placed.[124]

In China, moon cakes are baked in honor of the autumn moon festival. A small table is placed on a patio and piled with the round cakes and fruit. Family and relatives eat them in sight of the lunar orb.[3]

In Teutonic Europe, sweetened breads were formed into the images of humans and animals and were offered in place of living sacrificial victims. The twisted breads now made in Germany have a religious and magical origin. They were made and given to the goddess Holle by her worshippers to avoid her punishment: rumpling of the hair.[93]

Serbian Gypsies transferred the power of edible cakes to their symbolic form. To cure headaches cakes, roosters, suns, knives, snakes, and acorns were embroidered upon the affected person's clothing. These symbols dispelled the evil eye, once believed to be the true cause of headaches.[14]

All cakes and sweetened breads are ruled by the planet Venus and the element of water, and so are imbued with loving energies. Today, cakes and sweetened breads are still important symbolic foods at birthdays, weddings, and religious festivals throughout the world. Here is some of this magic.

Birthday Cakes

Offering a special cake to a person enjoying a birthday is a custom of obscure origin, but almost certainly is meant to magically ensure that the recipient won't suffer poverty or hunger during the coming year. Birthday cakes may also be related, in some way, to astrology, for the sun is (obviously) in the same position in the zodiac on the day of birth every year. Small candles might have originally been placed upon the cake in the shape of the person's zodiac sign. Created from sacred foods (grain, butter, sugar, and eggs), cakes are uniquely linked with the divine and are perfect gifts on birthdays.

Why do we write on special-occasion foods, such as birthday cakes? This involves the idea that the act of eating words (even those created out of icing) magically transfers the energies represented by those words to their eaters. "Happy Birthday" and "Good Luck" carefully written on cakes were originally more than kind gestures—they were ritual assurances of just these things.

Some scholars claim that our modern birthday cakes, topped with candles, are related to those once created for Artemis.[124] The lit candles are reminders of the sacred fires of this goddess. Additionally, when a child woke on its birthday, German peasants lit cake-borne candles.

Blowing out the candles and "making a wish" are obviously remnants of forgotten magical rituals—perhaps those performed to gain the favor of Artemis. The next time you're presented with a candlelit cake, visualize your wish as you blow.

The color of the candles is important. Use white candles for protection and purification; pink for spiritual love; red for sexuality; blue for peace and healing; purple for healing and spirituality; green for growth, abundance, and money; yellow for clear thinking, and orange for energy.

Round cakes represent spirituality, while square and rectangular cakes symbolize prosperity. If you make a cake for a friend's birthday, put much love and positive energy into it. Ice it with appropriate symbols, and words, visualizing all the time. If you wish, place the candles on the table around the table, instead of on top of the cake.

All-natural cakes, sweetened with honey, frosted with honey icing, and containing whole grains, can be served to those who forgo conventional "junk foods." Fresh, chopped fruits can also be added while keeping their magical energies in mind (see chapter 11).

Wedding Cakes

The history of wedding cakes is quite long. These nuptial goodies have their origins in the ancient custom of couples ritually eating sacred foods during the marriage rite. At some times and in some places, a couple needed only to eat or drink food together to be married.

It seems that the wedding cake is descended from the Roman *confarreatio*. This special cake was crumbled over the bride's head during marriage feasts to ensure fertility and plenty during the couple's life together.[31] The cake was, of course, sweetened with honey. Guests kept pieces of the cake, much as wedding guests of our own time take home slices for "good luck."[46] In the Victorian era, unmarried English women placed pieces of wedding cake under their pillows for dreams of their future husbands.[82]

Some American Indian tribes made cakes for marriage celebrations. An Iroquois bride, for example, baked a cornmeal cake and gave it to the groom. This was an important part of the ceremony.[31]

The roses so often found decorating wedding cakes today are symbolic wishes for love. They are probably the modern form of the crystallized rose petals and violets that were once placed on the completed cake.

Such an important part of an important ceremony is still fraught with superstitions: the bride should never make her own wedding cake; neither bride nor groom should taste it until the appropriate time;[46] the bride should keep a piece of the cake (as long as she has it, she'll have the love of her husband); spice wedding cakes denote a spicy relationship.

In 1861, the wife of Horace Mann wrote *Christianity in the Kitchen*, a curious conglomeration of information based on the theory that an unhealthy diet hindered morals. Among her astounding conclusions: since wedding cake is difficult to digest, it is immoral and un-Christian.[104]

Is it just a coincidence that the two substances most often used to flavor wedding cakes, chocolate and vanilla, are both powerful love stimulants?

Sweetened Breads

The major difference between cakes and sweetened breads is that the latter usually contain yeast, whereas cakes do not. As soon as the art of leavened bread-making became popular, honey or date syrup was certainly added, along with spices and other ingredients, in order to produce a pleasing variety.

Sweetened breads are still baked during religious festivals in Europe (especially for Easter) and Mexico (for All Soul's Day). Certain cakes baked for Halloween and Christmas are quite popular in Scotland, and German *stollens* are well-known. Pre-Christian

Brits baked cakes for spring festivals. One of these breads is still with us today, in a conveniently sanitized form.

Hot-Cross Buns

Long before the advent of Christianity, Europeans celebrated the coming of spring with rituals dedicated to the sun and to the earth, which were viewed as symbols of the God and the Goddess. The spring solstice, which falls on a day between March 21 and March 24 each year, was a welcome breath of life after the chilling months of winter.[29, 44, 114]

In these rituals, some of which were dedicated to Eostra (from which our word "Easter" is derived), small, sweetened buns were baked and eaten to encourage the returning fertility of the earth. These ritual breads, created with carefully stored grain and honey, were marked with phallic symbols as visual representations of the sun's fertilizing influence upon the earth and humans.[29, 44, 114]

As Christianity spread across Europe, the uses of these Pagan breads was altered by the new faith. The phallic symbols, regarded with unnatural horror, were transformed into more "seemly" crosses.*[125] Hot-cross buns became a part of Easter celebrations and were dedicated, if a bit tardily, to the Christian story of resurrection. The conversion was so complete that hot-cross buns were even given to religious pilgrims traveling through English villages.[119]

Perhaps not curiously, hot-cross buns retained their mystic energies in the popular mind. They were eaten on Good Friday to bring a year of good luck. They were used to cure certain illnesses. Hung in the house, they guarded it from fire and evil of all kinds and were said to last indefinitely without getting moldy. (In Cornwall they were hung from the bacon-rack.)[114] Sailors believed that having one on board prevented shipwrecks, and hot-cross buns were even placed in granaries to keep out rats. A modern American superstition states that placing a hot-cross bun in a

*Which are themselves phallic symbols.

cupboard on the spring equinox ensures that "you'll know no hunger for ages."[46]

The magical properties ascribed to the simple hot-cross bun are memories of a time when they were much more interesting symbols firmly linked with the old Pagan religions of Europe.

Pan de Muerto

On November 2, All Soul's Day, many Mexicans visit family graves to perform a ritual rooted in pre-Christian times. Along with orange marigolds, they bring a special sweetened bread baked only for this occasion.

This joyous time includes a feast in which the dead are invited to participate. The feast affirms the inevitability of death in the minds of the living and reaffirms the value of the departed. This is quite a healthy ritual.[83]

In the United States, All Soul's Day (a Catholic holy day) is exoterically celebrated as Halloween, with its attendant masquerades, parties, and occult themes. Some of the European-based motifs have been transferred to Mexico, but the honoring of the dead is of ancient, pre-conquest origin.

In late October, bakeries throughout Mexico and the southwestern United States offer *pan de muerto,* "bread of the dead." I've long relished the unique flavor of this specialty food. If you have Mexican bakeries (*panaderia*) in your part of the world, check them during this month for pan de muerto. If they don't have it, ask for it. If you still can't find any, make some yourself next Halloween—and revere.

Pan de Muerto

> 1 teaspoon anise seeds
>
> 3 tablespoons water
>
> 1 package dry yeast
>
> ½ cup warm milk
>
> 3½ cups sifted, all-purpose flour

1 teaspoon salt

1 cup melted butter

6 eggs lightly beaten

1 tablespoon orange flower water

Grated rind of 1 orange

1 egg, beaten

Coarse or red sugar (for topping)

The night before, place anise seeds in 3 tablespooons of water in a pan. Bring to a boil, turn off heat, and let stand overnight. On the following day, strain out seeds and discard. Sprinkle yeast over warm milk to soften. Add anise water to the yeast. Add enough flour to make a light dough. Knead and shape into a ball. Let stand in a warm place until doubled in bulk (about 1 hour). Sift together the remaining flour with salt and sugar. Beat in melted (and cooled) butter, eggs, orange flower water, and grated rind. Knead on a lightly floured board until smooth. Add the dough ball. Knead together until smooth and elastic. Cover with cloth and let the dough rest for 1½ hours, or until doubled in bulk.

Pinch off 2 walnut-sized chunks of dough (for decoration). Divide remaining dough and shape into round loaves. Place on greased baking sheets. Roll out some of the reserved dough with a rolling pin into 4 thin ropes about 5 inches long. Stretch out ropes, flattening ends until they resemble bones. Allow to rise. Cross two bones on each loaf, attaching with beaten egg (to resemble crossed bones). Roll remaining dough into another thin rope. Cut off small pieces, shape into teardrops, and attach to loaf with beaten egg between bones.

Remember, as you do this, to recall the symbolism of the season—the deepening of winter and the lessening of the earth's fertile energies. Recall passed loved ones and friends with happiness, not sadness.

Cover lightly with a cloth and let stand until just doubled in bulk. Lightly brush loaves with beaten egg. Sprinkle with coarse sugar (or red-dyed sugar). Or, leave plain. Bake in preheated 375°F (190°C). oven for about 30 minutes. Yield: 2 loaves.

Cookies

Cookies are sweetened, distant relatives of the flat breads served by our Neolithic predecessors. Cookies have always been baked into specific shapes for ritual and magical purposes.

Sugar Cookies

Many of us have eaten cut-out sugar cookies at Yule. As mentioned in chapter 7, bell-shaped cookies were once eaten for protection and to drive away evil. Cookies in the shapes of animals represent the sacrifices that were once offered to the goddesses and gods.

If you make simple sugar cookies, cut them into specific shapes representing your magical goals. Such cookies make strong magical tools. Remember to visualize as you mix, cut, and slide them into the oven (see Symbols, p. 341, for more ideas).

A wide variety of cookie cutters is available. Specialty cutters available at Yule and Halloween offer a wealth of possibilities. Crescents, stars, brooms, "Witches," suns, and many other styles are available. Use your imagination (and, if all else fails, a sharp knife) to carve your magical symbols.

Fortune Cookies

Ah yes, those ancient Chinese divinatory devices! Actually, fortune cookies were probably invented to advertise a Chinese restaurant in California during the 1920s. Still, they bear a resemblance to an ancient Roman practice. This method, known as aleuromancy, consisted of writing messages on slips of paper that were enclosed in balls of flour paste. These were mixed together and randomly distributed in order to reveal their receiver's fortunes.

The modern version is more pleasing to the palate. Making your own gives you the opportunity to truly personalize the fortunes, and it's a good way to spend a rainy afternoon. Try it—your fortune cookies will be the hit of your next party, dinner, or ritual gathering.

Take a large piece of clean white paper. Cut into 48 strips of paper, each about ½ inch wide and 3 inches long.

Sitting before them with a pencil, close your eyes and clear your mind. Contact your psychic awareness. Allow it to send messages to your conscious mind.

Then start writing the fortunes. Write whatever pops into your head. Write neatly. If nothing comes to you, here are some samples that you can use to spark your imagination:

> —*Those who wait, do not*
> —*Luck lies around the corner*
> —*Speak not to strangers*
> —*Wait until the wind rises*
> —*Happiness is found within*
> —*You will not want*
> —*Love is on the breeze*
> —*Rippling water answers you*
> —*The stars shine upon you*
> —*You are blessed*
> —*Wealth lies before you*
> —*Do it!*

Or, if you're as bad at writing fortunes as I seem to be, draw one magical symbol on to each slip of paper.

Now, to making the cookies. The "secret" here is to use soft, clean cotton gloves. These are indispensable (unless you're really into pain) for the process of folding the cookies. Cardboard (*not plastic*) egg cartons are also essential. Here's how to do it:

Fortune Cookies

½ cup melted butter

3 egg whites

¾ cup sugar

⅛ teaspoon salt

¼ teaspoon vanilla extract

1 cup flour

1 teaspoon instant tea

2 tablespoons water

The fortunes

Burn a light blue candle in the kitchen as you work. Mix together the egg whites, sugar, and salt in a bowl. Stir in vanilla, flour, tea, water, and melted butter individually. When well mixed, chill for at least thirty minutes. Heat oven to 350°F (177°C).

Drop a rounded teaspoon of the chilled dough onto a greased baking sheet. Using the back of the spoon, spread the batter until it makes a thin, 3-inch circle. Repeat to form a second circle—but form no more than two at a time. Bake 3 to 5 minutes or until the edges turn brown. Just before they're done, put on the cotton gloves. Remove the pan from the oven. Using a spatula, lift one cookie from the sheet. Place on a clean, unfloured surface. Working quickly, lay one fortune across the center of the cookie. Lift one edge and fold over to form a half circle. Holding the cookie at the ends, place the middle of the fold over the rim of the cardboard egg carton. Bend down the ends. Carefully place the cookie into an egg hole in the carton to cool. Quickly repeat this entire process with the second cookie.

Continue until you've used up the dough. Bake no more than two cookies at a time; otherwise they'll stiffen and you'll be unable to bend them.

Pies

Pastry probably originated in ancient Greece.[105] It was learned by the conquering Romans, who spread the art throughout their empire. Pastry isn't used only to hold sweet foods, of course; English pasties and dough-wrapped fish come to mind. The lore of sweet pies, however, is so compelling that I'm limiting my remarks to them.

Pies were once illegal. Oliver Cromwell, that humorless gent who ruined countless English parties in the 1600s, banned all pies in the Commonwealth. Why? Because they gave people pleasure, which was the last thing this tyrannical, fanatical Puritan wanted. Fortunately, Charles II ascended to the throne in 1660 and restored the enjoyment of pies throughout the land. A new royal was rarely so well-received.[105]

Why are American pies round and not square? This custom began during colonial times in the United States (I guess our Puritans were open to some forms of pleasure). The deep square or oblong pans used in Europe required far too much precious fruit, so the corners were cut off and the pan was made shallow. Hence, our round pies.[105]

Magically speaking, round pies induce spirituality, and square pies promote prosperity. Pies topped with intricate lattice-work crusts are useful in protective diets. The choice of fruits is important when making (or even buying) a pie. Choose them for their magical energies. Here's a quick list of some of the more common pies and their magical qualities (fruit is more thoroughly discussed in chapter 11):

Apple: Love, healing, peace
Apricot: Peace
Banana cream: Money
Blackberry: Money, sex
Blueberry: Protection
Chess (custard): Spirituality
Chocolate cream: Money, love
Coconut cream: Spirituality
Cherry: Love
Key lime: Love, purification
Lemon: purification, love
Mince: "Luck," money
Peach: Love, health, happiness, wisdom
Pecan: Money

Pineapple: Love, healing, money, protection
Pumpkin: Money, healing
Raspberry: Happiness, love, protection
Rhubarb: Protection, love
Strawberry: Love

This magical information also relates to tarts, cobblers, and turnovers. Visualize as you mix, bake, and eat!

Mince pie is a special case. Throughout England and Europe, mince pies are baked and served on New Year's Eve. Just after midnight, a piece is eaten, with a wish (and attendant visualization). This also bestows money on the eater.

While baking pies, lightly mark a pentagram on the upper crust (if it has one; if not, mark on the lower crust before baking. This guards the pie during the baking process. Or, cut slits. Alternately, lightly trace symbols related to your magical goal into the pie's crusts (see "Symbols," page 341).

At one time, pastry left over from forming the crusts was baked and left as an offering to the spirits who were thought to inhabit the kitchen. I remember my mother baking these remnants, sprinkled with sugar and cinnamon, and serving them to us. They often seemed to taste better than the pies themselves.

Pancakes

To close this chapter, a short look at pancakes—those bubbly, light-brown things that fly off the griddle and often hit the bottom of our stomachs like a pound of granite.

Pancakes are "luck" foods around the world. In England, Shrove Tuesday is known as Pancake Day. To eat a pancake on this day ensures a year with plenty of money, food, and luck. This custom stems from pre-Christian roots.

Before the destruction of their folk practices, Russians used to celebrate the coming of spring with a special ritual. They drove an image of Masslianitsa, the goddess of butter, on a sledge around the villages, singing and enjoying themselves. The decorated figure was then burned (ouch!) and the celebrants feasted on *blinni*, a traditional Russian pancake, to end this Pagan festival.[79]

Today, many groups still call upon the power of this basic dish. They do this by having fund-raising pancake breakfasts that dimly echo the wild feasts of earlier times.

Pancakes are linked with the two most important gifts of the earth—grain and milk. No wonder they've been honored. Here's some of my pancake magic:

For Money

Short on cash? Make up some buckwheat pancakes. Pour them onto the griddle in the shape of a dollar sign. Visualize. Cook, flip, and serve with maple syrup (another money-attractant).

An All-Purpose Pancake Ritual

While visualizing, quickly pour any pancake batter onto the griddle in the reversed shape of some magical symbol (such as a pentagram). Flip, cook, and eat.

A Pancake Divination Ritual

Several years ago, I ran across a simple and delicious pancake divination that I've shared with many friends.

Make the batter from scratch, stirring clockwise and visualizing your question. If you have no specific question, simply blank your mind.

Pour the batter onto the griddle. Push the rounded tip of a wooden spoon into the center of the uncooked pancake against the griddle. Randomly move it, asking your question.

When it's time, remove the spoon and flip the pancake. Symbols will appear on the browned side. Use your psychic awareness. Interpret them to give you a glimpse of possible tomorrows.

CHAPTER TEN

Vegetables

"Wait a minute!" you might be thinking. "Vegetables aren't as interesting as other foods!" Perhaps. These green (red, purple, brown, white, yellow, and orange) foods, however, are just as important as desserts in magic. We've been trained by our society to desire sweet foods and to ignore veggies. Despite our transient desires, we can't limit ourselves to eating only sweets.

That said, read on and enjoy yourself.

Artichoke

(Cynara scolymus)

Planet: Mars

Element: Fire

Energies: Protection

Lore: Greek legend states that the first artichoke was originally a beautiful woman. Some angry god (frankly, I don't know which) was so jealous of her beauty that he transformed her into an artichoke.[92]

The artichoke seems to have originated in the Mediterranean region and in the Canary Islands. This vegetable was enjoyed in ancient Rome as a luxury food.

The Romans preserved it in brine or vinegar (much as we pack artichoke "hearts" in oil).[53, 92]

Magical uses: The artichoke is certainly delicious. Because it is a member of the thistle family, and due to its flower's sharp points, the artichoke is eaten as part of protective diets.

Flavor with garlic or bay leaves for additional protective energy.

Asparagus

(*Asparagus officianlis*)

Planet: Mars

Element: Fire

Energies: Sex

Magical uses: As you prepare the asparagus to be cooked or steamed, visualize yourself enjoying sex. Eat with power.

Bamboo

(*Bambusa* spp.)

Planet: Sun

Element: Air

Energies: Protection, psychic awareness

Lore: Bamboo is an ancient symbol of longevity in China and Japan.[3] It is also planted around homes to guard them. Hawaiian religion is rife with bamboo lore.[7]

Fresh bamboo shoots are poisonous. They must be cooked before they can be safely eaten.[71]

Magical uses: Bamboo shoots are added to protective diets. To further empower them with protective energy, mark a small pentagram on each shoot with a knife before adding it to food.

Bamboo shoots are also eaten to enhance psychic awareness. Use in salads with fresh sprouts to open your deep mind.

Bean

(*Phaseolus* spp.)

Planet: Mercury

Element: Air

Energies: Money, sex

Lore: Beans were a major part of the diets of many Mesoamerican cultures, including the Maya and the Aztecs. They're still an important food throughout Latin America.

Plutarch states that beans were given in sacrifice to Harpocrates (the Graeco-Roman deity) in the month of Mesore. Apollo was also offered beans in sacrifice. The Egyptian king Ramses III offered 11,998 jars of shelled beans to the deities on one occasion.[23] Several ancient religions forbade priests and priestesses to eat beans.

The Romans offered beans to the dead at certain festivals. The Greeks and Romans also used beans for ballots: white beans for yes, black beans for no. Apollo was offered beans in sacrifice.

Beans were long thought to promote sexual desire if eaten. The famous English herbalist Culpeper recommended them for this purpose, while a father of the Church, Saint Jerome, forbade nuns to eat beans because they "tickled the genitals."[71]

In England, insanity was thought to be the result of sleeping overnight in a bean field.[99] The white flowered beans, however, have long been sacred to the Goddess and were revered by many peoples.

Colonists learned the art of cooking Boston baked beans from American Indians.[29]

Magical uses: Add beans to diets designed to increase wealth. If you make your own baked beans, add a touch of ginger, maple syrup, and other money-attracting foods during their preparation, and visualize as you mix and cook. Or, eat beans with the appropriate visualization to increase your interest in sexual activity.

Hot chili with beans is a protective dish.

Beet

(Beta vulgaris)

Planet: Saturn

Element: Earth

Energies: Love, beauty

Lore: Beets have been eaten for centuries by persons wishing to lengthen their life spans. Aphrodite, the ancient Greek goddess of love, was said to have used beets to maintain and increase her beauty.[56]

The redness of this food dictates its use during harvest and for winter religious festivals such as Lughnasadh (August 1) and Samhain (November 1).

Magical uses: Folk magic states that if a man and a woman eat from the same beet, they'll fall in love with each other. While this may not be the case (love is far more complex), beets should be added to love-attracting diets.

Cook and eat beets while visualizing yourself enjoying increased beauty. Remember: beauty is internal as well as external.

Broccoli

(Brassica spp.)

Planet: Moon

Element: Water

Energies: Protection

Magical uses: Broccoli is a fine addition to protective diets. Season with basil, garlic, and mustard seed for increased power.

Brussels Sprouts

(Brassica spp.)

Planet: Moon

Element: Water

Energies: Protection

Lore: Legend has it that brussel sprouts were created from wild forms of cabbage growing in Babylon. Nebuchadnezzar relied on cabbage to prevent or to cure the hangovers that usually resulted from his fabulous, excessive feasts. He was naturally disturbed that no fresh cabbage was available during the winter.

According to this myth, he ordered his head gardener, Brussel, to devise a method of growing cabbage year-round. By hybridizing, Brussel eventually succeeded in creating today's brussel sprouts, which, indeed, are small cabbages and belong to the cabbage family.[56]

Magical uses: Eat Brussels sprouts as a part of protective diets. Adding a bit of salt to them is fine, since salt is also a protective substance, but too much of anything (especially salt) results in ill health. Ill health leads to a lack of our body's normal psychic protections. As an alternative to salt, try basil, dill weed, and mustard, all of which are protective flavorings.

Cabbage

(Brassica spp.)

Planet: Moon

Element: Water

Energies: Protection, money

Lore: Superstitious persons once placed cabbage leaves on their foreheads on the dreaded Friday the 13th to keep evil far from them—and, most probably, to keep them far from everyone else.[56]

Around 621 B.C.E., officials in Greece passed a law calling for the death penalty for anyone caught stealing cabbages, a favored food.[56] Also, in Greece, the sad idea arose that eating several heads of cabbage everyday would cure insanity and nervous conditions.[56]

Magical uses: Cabbage is a fine lunar food. Serve it by the light of the Full Moon after magical and spiritual rituals.

Like brussel sprouts and broccoli, cabbage is eaten to internalize protection. Flavor it with basil and mustard for this purpose. Or, eat salty sauerkraut for protection.

Green cabbage is added to money-drawing diets. For this purpose it is cooked with a solid silver coin. Or, flavor with dill seeds to attract prosperity. Cabbage soup is a tasty way to bring money energy into your life. The Roman naturalist Pliny recommended cabbage before sleep to prevent nightmares.

Carrot

(Daucus carota)

Planet: Mars

Element: Fire

Energies: Sex

Magical uses: Carrots have been consumed since the days of ancient Greece to induce the desire for sexual contact. Prepared and eaten with the correct visualization, carrots may play a part in overcoming psychological impotency.

Cook them with parsley and caraway for the best results.

Cauliflower

(Brassica spp.)

Planet: Moon

Element: Water

Energies: Protection

Magical uses: Eat fresh or cooked cauliflower as part of a protection diet. To increase its effectiveness, cook cauliflower with dill, mustard seeds, or rosemary.

Celery

(Apium graveolens)

Planet: Mercury

Element: Fire

Energies: Sex, peace, psychic awareness, weight loss

Lore: Roman women ate celery to increase their sexual appetites.

Magical uses: This plant's aphrodisiac powers have long been celebrated. Celery soup was one of Madame de Pompadour's favorite dishes for this purpose. Curiously, heated celery seems to emit a type of pheromone, the chemical sex-attractant naturally secreted by humans and animals. This could be why celery has been favored for this use for 2,000 years.[52]

If you make celery soup, cook it with visualization. Such sex-stimulating foods are, of course, only effective if *you* eat them. They will have little or no effect when served to others.

With a different visualization, eating fresh or cooked celery is soothing and brings peace.

Add celery seed (as a seasoning) to foods to strengthen psychic awareness. Celery is also a part of weight-loss plans.

Chervil

(Anthriscus cerefolium)

Planet: Mercury

Element: Air

Energies: Weight Loss

Lore: Folk magicians once boiled chervil with pennyroyal. The resulting brew was thought to cause its drinker to see double.[56] The plant was named *cerefolium* to honor its ancient use in festivities directed to Ceres, the goddess of grain and vegetation.[94]

In earlier, rougher times, many died from combat wounds due to infection. In the 1500s, wounded men were given chervil juice to drink. If they kept it down the chervil predicted that they would live. If they "cast it up," the wound was mortal.[56]

Magical uses: Chervil can be hard to find, but is well worth seeking, especially as it can be of help when trying to lose weight. Juice a bit of this plant every day, visualize, and drink to maintain or to regain your desired figure. For added power, eat in a salad with chickweed.

Chili

(Capsicum spp.)

Planet: Mars

Element: Fire

Energies: Protection

Lore: From archaeological evidence found in Mexican caves, chili peppers seem to have first been cultivated 9,000 years ago.[29, 90] The Aztecs are said to have used chili peppers in rituals designed to exorcise spirits from possessed persons.[100]

Chili peppers were recently banned from one state's prison system because the burning vegetables could be used as weapons. Curiously enough, during the seventeenth century, Spanish invaders were repelled in some parts of South America by the smoke from burning chilis.[29] In contemporary New Mexico, the core of a red bell pepper is still burned on a Friday night to prevent evil from harming humans.[80]

Magical uses: Though there are dozens of varieties, the most commonly seen in U.S. markets are jalapeno, cayenne, and "bell" peppers. Add any of these to diets designed to guard against negative energies. Chile rellenos, stuffed (vegetarian or otherwise) peppers, and jalapeno jelly are three examples of protective foods.

By the way, all peppers (except black pepper) are members of the same family. If you don't like extremely hot peppers, try the milder pepperoni (the ones served in Italian restaurants), a dash of cayenne, pimento, or the sweet, firmly fleshed bell peppers in your magical protective diet.

Chives

(Allium spp.)

Planet: Mars

Element: Fire

Energies: Weight loss, protection

Lore: Chives may have been first grown in what is now Siberia, near the shores of Lake Baikal, one of the deepest lakes in the world.[56] Chives were considered to be powerful aphrodisiacs.[56]

Magical uses: The great herbalist Gerarde stated that eating chives would surely "attenuate or make thinne," and these mildly flavored onions are worth trying if you're adopting a weight-loss way of life. Though they are difficult to find fresh in grocery stores, they are easily grown at home. Chives even grow well in containers.

For protection, tie a chive into a knot, add to food, and eat. Do this with visualization!

To be rid of a nasty habit or some personal problem that has been vexing you, tie the problem into a chive with a knot and bury. Do not uncover it.

Cucumber

(Cucumus sativus)

Planet: Moon

Element: Water

Energies: Peace, healing

Lore: Fresh cucumbers were once placed under swooning women's noses (remember swooning?). The odor was supposed to rouse them from their faint.

In Africa, the Nuer sometimes consecrate a small wild cucumber and sacrifice it in place of a treasured ox during important ceremonies.[29]

Magical uses: Add cucumbers to peace-inducing diets. Peel and munch on one of these raw, whole fruits for quick relief from stress. Or, eat cucumbers while recovering from illness to speed the healing process. Visualize as you eat.

Eggplant

(Solanum melogena var. *esculentum)*

Planet: Jupiter

Element: Earth

Energies: Spirituality, money

Magical uses: These natives of China were originally small, egg-shaped and white, unlike our massive purple specimens. Eat cooked eggplants to increase spirituality. If you're fine in this department, visualize increased money while dining on the vegetable.

Many people dislike the strong taste of eggplant. If you happen to be one of them, you'll be happy to hear that you don't even have to eat this purplish food to benefit from its energies. To manifest additional money in your life, split an eggplant into two equal pieces. Place a one-dollar bill between the pieces, tie them together, bury them in the earth, and never dig them up. Money will come to you (but you'll be out a buck).

Endive

(Cichorium endivia)

Planet: Jupiter

Element: Air

Energies: Physical strength, sex

Magical uses: Endive is overlooked today as a salad green. This is a shame, because it can be eaten to promote physical strength (and is certainly safer than steroids).

Endive is another of the many foods that are thought to create sexual desire. Who am I to argue with long-standing tradition?

Greens

In general: Greens are linked with fairies in Scotland and Ireland. This may be one reason why green has long been thought to be an unlucky color. Additionally, greens were once rarely found at wedding feasts and receptions for the same reason—the celebrants didn't wish to offend the little people.[35]

In folk magic, greens of all kinds are eaten for money.

Leek

(Alliurn spp.)

Planet: Mars

Element: Fire

Energies: Protection, physical strength

Lore: Leeks are steeped in myth and folklore. In twelfth-century Persia they were worn over the left ear to prevent intoxication. Gerarde, who lived in sixteenth-century England, thought they produced nightmares. In his time, a leek was hidden inside a black cloth and placed under the pillow of an ill person to effect a cure.[56] Leeks were also regarded as solemn protection against fire and lightning.

Magical uses: Leeks are good protectants, as you might expect from a member of the onion family. Make leek soup or add leeks to a stew for this purpose.

Additionally, they can be eaten for increased physical strength. According to tradition, Welsh soldiers rubbed fresh leeks on their bodies for success and vigor in battle. They also believed that the magic juice would protect them from wounds. The leek is still a national symbol of Wales.[114]

Lettuce

(Lactuca sativa)

Planet: Moon

Element: Water

Energies: Peace, money, celibacy

Lore: Lettuce was sacred to the god Min in ancient Egypt. Min, whose graphic depictions as a phallic god were deemed obscene a hundred years ago, also ruled over vegetation of all kinds.[23]

Lettuce seems to have been his favorite due to its greenness and the fact that the core, when squeezed, exudes a milky sap that was probably associated with semen. Lettuce was naturally related to the act of procreation and to fertility. It was commonly stocked in tombs and offered to Min.[23]

At least one Roman emperor was so enamored with this vegetable's restorative properties that he had an altar, complete with a statue, built to the plant.[15]

Magical uses: A Mexican woman once told me that when her young children were "crybabyish" or hyperactive, she'd simply put them in a bathtub with lettuce leaves. This calmed them.

Wild lettuce contains opiates and the juice was once drunk to bring on natural sleep. Today, lettuce is eaten with visualization for peace and tranquillity, even though the common head lettuce found in grocery stores contains virtually no opiates.

Like other salad greens, lettuce is added to money-attracting diets. Use in a salad with fresh dill weed for increased money.

Lettuce is also eaten (in direct contrast to most other foods) to cool sexual desire and, curiously enough, to prevent seasickness.

Mushroom

Planet: Moon

Element: Earth

Energies: Psychic awareness

Lore: Pharaohs in ancient Egypt ate mushrooms, but the common people did not. Romans believed that mushrooms provided strength to the body.[53]

Mushrooms, like all fungi, have long been regarded with suspicion. Their seemingly miraculous appearance overnight after a good rain, their mysterious ways of propagation, and their eerie appearance have put them into a thousand magical spellbooks and fairy tales.

Some mushrooms are delicious and quite safe to eat. Others are delicious and quite deadly. Accidental deaths still occur each year when amateur mushroom hunters pick the wrong kind of wild mushrooms to enjoy in natural meals.

Mushrooms containing hallucinogenic substances have been used for ritual purposes in Mexico, South America, Siberia, and in many other parts of the world.[123] They remain a popular (and illegal) street drug in parts of the United States.

Magical uses: Add normal culinary mushrooms to meals to heighten psychic awareness.

Olive

(Olea europaea)

Planet: Sun

Element: Air

Energies: Spirituality, health, peace, sex

Lore: The olive was sacred to Aten in ancient Egypt.[69] Olive oil, which was in great demand in the ancient world, actually led to the downfall of Greece. Farmers began growing olives almost exclusively while ignoring food crops. This began Greece's dependence on imported foods. When import lines were cut, Greece and its populace suffered.[104]

Oil was used in hundreds of ways in the ancient world, but it was always linked with religion. It was necessary for the creation of the scented oils used in both religious and magical rituals. In Greece, olive oil was the most popular ingredient for these purposes.

The Romans disdained the use of butter in cooking. They moistened bread with olive oil (as we use butter) and also cooked food in oil.[104]

Magical uses: Add olives or olive oil to spirituality inducing diets. Olives are perfect for post-ritual feasts.

Small amounts of olive oil can be added to health diets. Visualize!

Olives are also eaten for peace and for the release of stress. If this isn't a problem, olives (and the oil) are suitable for arousing sexual desire.

Onion

(Allium cepa)

Planet: Mars

Element: Fire

Energies: Protection, weight loss

Lore: The great city of Chicago was named for the local Indians' word for the wild onions growing in the area—*chicago*.[56]

According to ancient Egyptian incantations, onions were included in charms designed to keep potentially harmful ghosts from children.[23] Celebrants at winter solstice festivals in Egypt wore onions around their necks.[23] Onions also played a role in the mummification process.[69] Though it has often been written that the pyramids were built by onion- and garlic-fed slaves, all Egyptians ate onions in those days. Onions, bread, and beer made up the basic ancient Egyptian diet.[104]

In old Rome, the naturalist Pliny wrote that runners should eat onions daily for speed and endurance.[86] About 1394, an Arab writer recommended onions boiled together with green peas and spiced with cardamom, cinnamon, and ginger to create sexual desire.[56]

Three hundred years later, the English herbalist Gerarde prescribed the use of onions in weight-loss diets; their low caloric content makes them ideal for this. Even if they are well boiled, he states, onions will not lose their "attenuating" quality.[36]

In contemporary Guatemala, men eat onions to retain virility and to procreate children, even into advanced age.

Magical uses: This sharply scented plant has long been revered and utilized in magical ritual. In general, onions are eaten to boost our protective armor, which is created by a flow of energy from the body. They can be used in any form whatsoever for this purpose; the sharper the taste, the more effective the onion will be. Onions have long been kept in the kitchen, halved, to absorb evil.

Or, as Gerarde recommended, eat onions daily as part of a weight-loss plan.

Pea

(Psium sativum)

Planet: Venus

Element: Water

Energies: Love

Lore: During the Inquisition, peas were thought to be standard food for "Witches." They have always been sacred to the Mother Goddess.

Magical uses: Cook peas with basil, coriander, dill, or marjoram. Cook while visualizing this simple food as a powerful love attractant. Then eat.

Poke

(Phytolacca americana)

Planet: Mars

Element: Fire

Energies: Protection

Magical uses: All parts of this Native American plant are poisonous, save for the young shoots. These are cooked and eaten for protection.

Potato

(Solanum tuberosum)

Planet: Moon

Element: Earth

Energies: Protection, compassion

Lore: The potato is a native of Peru, where it was first cultivated by about 34000 B.C.E.[104] It was introduced to Spain (and subsequently throughout Europe) in 1534.[120] It was immediately claimed that the potato was a sure-fire cure for impotency. At times, it was sold for the equivalent of 1,000 dollars a pound.[104]

Potatoes lost favor in 1728 in Scotland, where cultivation of the potato was prohibited because it was an *unholy* nightshade that wasn't mentioned in the Bible.[120]

Practitioners of American folk medicine carried potatoes in their pockets to cure rheumatism.[44] In England, toothache sufferers carried a piece of potato to vanquish the pain (this was probably most effective while going to see a dentist).[35] Those who dine on new potatoes are granted a wish.[68]

Magical uses: As with many root crops, potatoes are added to protective diets. They should be seasoned with onions, chives, dill weed, rosemary, or parsley for the strongest effect.

Additionally, owing to this vegetable's lunar rulership, potatoes can be eaten to instill compassion.

Pumpkin

(Curcurbita spp.)

Planet: Moon

Element: Earth

Energies: Healing, money

Lore: According to early American lore, if half a pumpkin is left exposed in the kitchen, negative energies will arrive to spoil the cooking.[22]

The pumpkins carved with faces and lit with candles on the last night of October in the United States are related to the similarly prepared turnips carried by children in the U.K. They are created to scare away evil.

Pumpkins are sometimes featured in Samhain celebrations by Wiccans as symbols of the fruitfulness of the earth and of the God's death beneath the sickle of time. These round, orange vegetables are also symbols of the Mother Goddess.

Magical uses: Add pumpkin dishes to health diets. Dry, roast, and eat the seeds, or enjoy such delicious treats as pumpkin pie and pumpkin bread.

Pumpkin is also a nutritious money-attractant. Make a pumpkin pie and add cinnamon, ginger, and nutmeg to flavor it with money-drawing energies.

Radish

(Raphanus sativus)

Planet: Mars

Element: Fire

Energies: Protection

Lore: Wild radishes, eaten before breakfast, were once thought to protect the diner from being flogged and to enable one to overcome all obstacles and enemies.

Magical uses: Slice thinly and eat for protection, especially in salads with onions, bell peppers, and other protective foods.

Rhubarb

(Rheum spp.)

Planet: Venus

Element: Earth

Energies: Love, protection

Magical uses: Rhubarb is native to China, where it is still used in medicinal herbalism.[104] All parts of the plant are poisonous save for the red stalks.

Rhubarb is a love food. The zingy taste ensures zingy, exciting relationships, if rhubarb is prepared with visualization. Rhubarb or rhubarb/strawberry pie is one of the ultimate love foods. The addition of sugar (necessary if rhubarb is to be enjoyed) seals the loving qualities of this Venusian vegetable.

A wedge of rhubarb pie makes an excellent protective dessert.

Seaweed

Planet: Moon

Element: Water

Energies: Weight loss

Lore: Seaweed (more correctly, sea vegetables) are surprisingly nutritious foods that are rarely found in Western diets, except as processed food additives (such as carageenan).

In Cornwall, pieces of a seaweed known as Lady's Tresses were placed on small stands near the chimney to guard seaside cottages from fire.[35]

Seaweed is eaten throughout the year by the Japanese, who also serve it on their lunar New Year for happiness.[46]

Magical uses: Add seaweed to your diet if you wish to lose weight. Seaweed has been prescribed for this purpose since ancient times. Dried kelp (a generic term for seaweed) is available in all health-food stores.

Soy

(Glycine max)

Planet: Moon

Element: Earth

Energies: Protections, psychic awareness, spirituality

Lore: We know soy in two forms: soy sauce and tofu. While soy sauce has always enjoyed popularity in the West as a flavoring for Chinese food, tofu is only now gaining ground as a nutritious alternative to meat. It is especially popular with vegetarians.

The Chinese have eaten soybeans for at least 2,000 years and the Japanese for 1,000.[98] People in both cultures usually eat them in the form of tofu. In Japan, two deities, Ebisu and Daikotu, are involved in the old-style preparation of tofu. Symbols of these deities are burned into the side of the wooden boxes used to measure the soybeans to be processed into tofu. This blesses them with the energies of Ebisu and Daikotu.[98]

Throughout Japan, fried tofu is an acceptable offering at the *inami,* agricultural shrines that dot the countryside. These shrines are dedicated to agricultural deities.[54] On the Japanese New Year, handfuls of roasted soybeans are scattered onto the floor in homes and temples. These "beans of good fortune" are then thrown through an open window to the chant of "Out with evil; in with good fortune!"[54, 60]

In the 1600s, the Emperor Nintoku established the Women's Mass for Needles. In this ceremony, a cake of tofu is situated on the household altar. Women push all the needles which have been bent or broken in the past year into the cake of tofu. This is done to give the needles—thought to be the spirits of people whose bodies have been sacrificed in service—a gentle resting place.[54]

Magical uses: Add soy sauce or tofu to protective diets. Soy sauce is ideal for this due to its extreme saltiness (though too much is, of course, hazardous to good health). For protection, stirfry tofu with onions and other vegetables of similar energies.

Tofu is also eaten for psychic awareness (particularly if one is searching for alternatives to meat), and to induce spirituality.

Spinach

(Spinacea oleracea)

Planet: Jupiter

Element: Earth

Energies: Money

Lore: In the United States, spinach is remembered as the favorite food of a popular cartoon character, upon whom it magically bestowed great physical strength. This green, leafy vegetable seems to have been introduced from Persia (present-day Iran) to Europe in the fifteenth century; it was soon used on fasting days.[45]

Magical uses: Steam spinach and eat as a part of prosperity diets. Flavor with sesame seeds or nutmeg for added power.

Spirulina

Planet: Venus

Element: Water

Energies: Physical energy

Lore: After they'd arrived in what is now known as Mexico, the Spaniards observed the Aztecs eating what was described as "green foam" or "green mud." The custom disappeared as the lakes surrounding what is now Mexico City were drained, and the food remained a mystery for hundreds of years.

It seems that the Aztecs ate large quantities of spirulina, the "modern" wonder algae that thrived in the lakes. Spirulina, which is nearly 70 percent protein, contains all the amino acids necessary for human life, as well as seven vitamins.[29]

Magical uses: Spirulina is available in tablet and powder form. It can be added to food or eaten alone, with visualization, to boost physical energy. All health-food stores stock it.

Sprouts

Planet: Various

Element: Various

Energies: Various

Magical uses: Though sprouted seeds have long been a part of Asian cooking,[71] we've only recently introduced them to our salads and breads.

Generally, all sprouts are fine for promoting psychic awareness. Here's a list of some specific sprouts and their energies:

Alfalfa (Venus, earth): Money, psychic awareness
Bean (Mercury, air): Protection
Mung (Mercury, air): Spirituality
Soy (Moon, earth): Spirituality, psychic awareness, protection
Sunflower (Sun, fire): Protection

Squash

(Curcurbita spp.)

Planet: Sun

Element: Fire

Energies: Spirituality

Lore: Squash was cultivated in the Americas as early as 4000 B.C.E.[104] Several American Indian tribes honored this plant. One striking Hopi kachina is depicted with a squash head, and squash-blossom necklaces are modern reminders of the original sacredness of this simple plant.

Magical uses: Eat this vegetable in dishes designed to increase awareness of the nonphysical reality around us. It is a fine spirituality-inducing food. At least for magical purposes, a squash is a squash, baked or fresh, acorn, hubbard, or zucchini.

Many people, of course, dislike squash. If you're one of them, avoid this food or eat sweetened zucchini bread.

Sunflower

(Helianthus annuus)

Planet: Sun

Element: Fire

Energies: Protection, success

Lore: Sunflowers were viewed as symbols of the sun by the ancient Incas of Peru. Gold crowns inspired by this flower were reportedly worn by solar priestesses during rituals.[90]

Many Mexican gardens contain sunflowers, since their presence is thought to confer "luck." Women still eat sunflower seeds for help in conceiving a child. In the United States, the seeds are gathered at sunset and eaten to gain a wish.

Magical uses: Hold your hands over a small bowl of roasted sunflower seeds. Visualize them bursting with the energies of the sun—protection, success, triumph. Then eat them to bring these powers inside yourself. Or, add to protective salads and other dishes.

Sweet Potato

(Ipomoea batatas)

Planet: Venus

Element: Water

Energies: Love, sex

Lore: An English cookbook of 1596 includes the preparation of a sweet potato tart intended to excite sexual desires. [29]

Those sweetened, orange tubers often served at Thanksgiving are actually sweet potatoes, not yams. Yams certainly do exist and are eaten in large quantities in Africa, Central and South America, and the West Indies, but not in the U.S. True yams are massive tubers, growing to as long as seven feet and tipping the scales at more than one hundred pounds. Compare these to our "yams" of November and you'll readily see the difference.

Magical uses: Cook and eat sweet potatoes to expand your ability to receive as well as to give love. Flavor with cinnamon, ginger, and a dash of honey or sugar to further empower them with loving energies.

Or, prepare them with visualization and share with a mate for enhanced sexuality. Inform your partner of the food's power.

Tomato

(*Lycopersicon* spp.)

Planet: Venus

Element: Water

Energies: Health, money, love, protection

Lore: Known as *zictomatl* by the Aztecs,[83] the tomato is an ancient food. When it was introduced into Europe in the sixteenth century, the tomato was regarded with suspicion. It is botanically related to nightshade, which is obvious from studying the plant's leaves, flowers, and even fruit. Everyone assumed that its fruits were also poisonous, despite the tales of the inhabitants of New Spain (Mexico) eating it and surviving.[104]

The fruits became known as "love apples" and were finally accepted into the dietary regime. At some point in the past, the tomato was considered to be a lucky food, and the red tomato pincushions that are still made today are a survival of this idea.

Lonely women once dried tomato seeds and enclosed them in a piece of cloth. They wore this charm around their necks in the hope of attracting men.[25]

Magical uses: Tomatoes can be used in a number of ways. Tomato sauce, tomato juice, and the popular Italian combination of sun-dried tomatoes, mozzarella cheese, and basil are just some of them.

For health, eat fresh tomatoes, or cook them with sage and rosemary.

Mixing basil, cinnamon, or dill weed with tomatoes creates an especially potent, money-attracting food.

For love, season tomatoes with rosemary, or eat them while they're fresh and bursting with juice.

To bring protective energy inside yourself, flavor tomatoes with black pepper, bay, dill, or rosemary.

Truffle

(Tuber melanospermum)

Planet: Venus

Element: Water

Energies: Love, sex

Magical uses: The Romans believed that truffles were created by thunder.[27] Add truffles to foods designed to increase your ability to give and to receive love. If that's not the important issue, eat truffles to increase sexual desire.

Watercress

Planet: Mars

Element: Fire

Energies: Protection, fertility

Lore: In the ancient world, watercress was thought to strengthen the conscious mind. The Greeks (who knew the plant as *kardamon*) ate watercress to gain wit.[55] Classical Romans munched the spicy green leaves to stimulate their brains.[86]

Magical uses: Add watercress to protective diets. The sharp taste and the plant's habit of growing near flowing water makes it ideal for this purpose. Eat with visualization, as always.

Watercress is also eaten to promote physical fertility.

CHAPTER ELEVEN

Fruit

Naturally sweet, refreshing and fragrant, fruits of all kinds have given humans millions of hours of culinary enjoyment.

It once surprised me that the Buddhist altars I'd seen in San Diego, Los Angeles, San Francisco, and throughout Hawaii usually contained offerings of fruit, not vegetables. Oranges are perhaps the most favored of these.

Why is fruit favored over vegetables? Perhaps because vegetables (and grains) have been the mainstays of the human diet. They grow in or on the ground. Fruit, however, generally grows on trees. Perhaps it seemed "higher," more exalted than other foodstuffs. Fruit's unique sweetness probably has something to do with this reverence as well.

The pomegranate of Mesopotamia; the strawberries of the Teutons; the coconut and banana of the Pacific Islanders; the apples of Avalon; the pear and peach of China—these are some of the fruits that have been revered as direct links with deity.

I've tried to list the most popular fruits in this section, as well as a few that are only now appearing in our grocery carts and at farmer's markets. But even the most familiar fruit assumes a new importance in the realm of food magic: its potential as a tool of self-transformation.

Apple

(Pyrus malus)

Planet: Venus

Element: Water

Energies: Love, health, peace

Lore: The peoples who inhabited the prehistoric lake dwellings of Switzerland enjoyed apples, as shown by apple remains found there.[105] Apples may have been eaten as long ago as the Paleolithic era.

They were a valued food in ancient Egypt. Ramses III offered 848 baskets of apples to Hapy, the Egyptian god of the Nile.[23] Among the Norse, Iduna safeguarded a store of apples. When eaten, the apples gave the gift of perpetual youth to the goddesses and gods.[90] It is said that certain Norse priests were forbidden to eat apples, due to the fruit's legendary lustful properties.[62] Apples are still offered to Chango among the Yoruba.

Apple trees once grew around the sacred island of Avalon in England, and apples were intimately linked with spirituality in the British Isles.

At one time, apples were always rubbed before they were eaten to remove all the demons or evil spirits that were thought to reside within them. Even the smell of fresh apples was thought to bestow longevity and restore flagging physical strength.

Magical uses: *Love.* Simply eat a fresh apple. Carve a heart into the skin before devouring it. Drink apple cider. Bake an apple pie (flavored with cinnamon, ginger, and sugar). Share an apple with a lover.

Health. Place a glass of apple cider between your palms. Visualize health and healing energies flowing into it between your hands. Visualize your body's natural healing ability gaining in strength. See yourself as being healed. Then drink the cider. Or, cut an apple into three parts with a sharp knife while visualizing. Eat all three parts.

Peace. Add applesauce, apple cake, apple dumplings, or some other cooked form of apples to your diet.

Apricot

(Prunus armeniaca)

Planet: Venus

Element: Water

Energies: Love, peace

Lore: Apricots probably originated in China, where they were cultivated as early as 2000 B.C.E.[71] They arrived in England by 1562 C.E.[53]

Magical uses: These fleshy fruits are ideal additions to love-expanding diets. They can be used fresh or cooked. Apricot nectar, a combination of fruit pulp, sugar, and water, can be drunk for love.

Love sauce. Stew ripe apricots with warm water until soft and mushy. Taste and add a bit of honey or sugar if desired. Run through a blender or food processor until smooth. Pour on to vanilla ice cream for a love-inducing treat.

Also, eat apricots in any form for peace.

Avocado

(Persea americana)

Planet: Venus

Element: Earth

Energies: Beauty, love

Lore: Avocados have been enjoyed in Central America for at least 7,000 years.[71] The Aztecs made a type of guacamole with avocado, tomato, and chili peppers that is similar to the dish we enjoy today. The Aztecs also considered avocados to be aphrodisiacs.

Magical uses: To promote beauty, hold a ripe avocado in your hands. Visualize your new appearance as strongly as you can. Maintain your visualization as you peel and eat the avocado. Eat at least one a day (plain) for blossoming beauty.

Avocados are also a useful love food.

Banana

(Musa spp.)

Planet: Mars

Element: Air

Energies: Spirituality, love, money

Lore: The banana is mentioned throughout the sacred books of India, and is still considered to be a holy food. A valued offering to Hindu deities, the banana's leaves are used to decorate marriage altars.[2]

Stalks of the banana plant (it is not a tree) were sometimes offered in place of humans during sacrificial rites in the Pacific.[7] Polynesian legends tell of the creation of the original banana plant from the bodies of slain heroes.[7]

In old New Orleans, the plants were grown for luck near the home. In Hawaii, food wrapped in large banana leaves was thought to be safe from intruding negativity.[7]

Though we know little of the banana's orgins, it's certain that people in India were enjoying the slippery fruits in about 2000 B.C.E.; that bananas arrived in Africa in 500 C.E., in Polynesia around 1000 C.E., and in tropical America during the fifteenth and sixteenth centuries.[71] Bananas were introduced to consumers in North America at the 1876 Philadelphia Exposition. Not long afterward, thousands of tons were being imported and purchased by an appreciative populace.[2] Most of the bananas we eat today are grown in Ecuador.

During the 1960s, banana peels were sometimes smoked as a replacement for marijuana. Though this had little or no effect beyond suggestion, it is curious that banana peels actually do contain minute amounts of the psychoactive substances serotonin, norepinephrine, and dopamine.[52, 71] Fortunately, smoking the peels had little effect and the fad quickly died out.

Don't eat bright yellow bananas. Those who dislike the taste of bananas may have never eaten a ripe one. Bananas are ripe only when the peel has begun to turn brown. The more brown spots, the more sugar that has been formed within the fruit.

Magical uses: The fruits form upward on the stalk, reaching toward the sky. Eating bananas stimulates spirituality. Choose fresh bananas, baked bananas, or that exquisite Chinese treat, candied (toffied) bananas.

Also add the fruit to love and prosperity diets.

Blackberry

(Rubus villosus)

Planet: Venus

Element: Water

Energies: Money, sex

Magical uses: Blackberries are traditionally eaten during the harvest festivals.

Bake a blackberry pie, eat blackberry jam, or consume fresh blackberries to draw money. A bowl of oat cereal topped with fresh blackberries is a delicious money-charged breakfast. Or, eat the delicious, seedy berries to increase your interest in sex. Visualize!

Blueberry

(Vaccinum frondosum)

Planet: Moon

Element: Water

Energies: Protection

Magical uses: This delicious Native American food is a welcome addition to the arsenal of protective foods. Eaten with visualization, it increases our magical defense systems.

Here are some suggestions: eat blueberry pie. Add the fruits to coffee cake with protective spices (see chapter 12). Have a dish of blueberry ice cream. Sprinkle fresh blueberries onto a bowl of cooked rice or corn flakes for a doubly protective breakfast.

To make a protective kitchen charm, crush fresh blueberries. With a finger dipped into the juice, mark the sign of the pentagram (see appendix 2) on to a piece of white paper. Keep this in the kitchen (it doesn't have to be in plain sight) to guard the room itself as well as the food that is stored and prepared there. Wash your finger after making the sign. It'll need it.

Carambola

(Averrhoa carambola)

Planet: Sun

Element: Fire

Energies: Protection

Lore: Carambola (starfruit) is one of the "new" fruits that have only recently begun appearing in our markets. A native to Indonesia,[89] carambola ripens and is available during the winter months. It's commercially grown in Florida, Texas, and California. I've also seen it in stores from Denver to Hawaii.

The fruit itself is an unusual ribbed oblong of yellow flesh. When sliced, it produces star-shaped sections. The flesh is usually sweet, firm, and crisp. Seeds, peel, and all can be eaten.

Magical uses: The first time that I saw a starfruit, I was amazed at its resemblance to the pentagram. This tasty fruit should be sliced with visualization, then simply eaten or added to protective dishes. A protective fruit salad can be made with carambola slices, whole blueberries, mango chunks, pineapple slices, whole raspberries, and tangerine sections. Carambola slices can also be used to garnish other protective foods.

Cherry

(Prunus spp.)

Planet: Venus

Element: Water

Energies: Love

Magical uses: The sight of cherry blossoms portends further delights once the round red fruits have matured.

Make a killer cherry pie using as much love-visualization as you possibly can. Lightly trace a heart on the bottom crust before baking. Eat one piece of the pie each day until it is gone, while creating a mental image of yourself involved in a loving relationship.

Citron

(Citrus medica)

Planet: Sun

Element: Fire

Energies: Strength

Lore: Citron was first used in Egypt in the second century C.E.[23] Though we may not encounter this fruit except in Yuletide fruitcakes, citron was once accorded a lofty place in the world. Pliny wrote that it was grown around temples dedicated to Amon in ancient Egypt. Citron was thought to have been created by Ge (the Egyptian god of the earth) to celebrate the wedding of Zeus and Hera. This myth was obviously formed during the influx of Greek thought into Egypt.[23]

In Mediterranean countries, citron is still used to drive away the "evil eye."

Magical uses: Fresh citron is rarely available, but the candied fruit can be added to foods designed to strengthen your physical body.

Cranberry

(Vaccinium oxycoccus)

Planet: Mars

Element: Water

Energies: Protection

Lore: Cranberries, native to North America and Europe,[53] were eaten by Indians long before being introduced to the Pilgrims.[53]

A close relative of the cranberry lives in Hawaii. The *ohelo (Vaccinium reticulatum)* grows on short plants found at higher elevations.[58] The juicy red fruits, which taste like cranberries but are sweeter, are made into jam and are the central ingredient in the famous ohelo berry pie served at Volcano House, on the rim of Kilauea crater on the Big Island.

Magical uses: The sourness of cranberries makes them an ideal protective food. Eat sweetened cranberry sauce during protective meals.

Date

(Phoenix dactylifera)

Planet: Sun

Element: Air

Energies: Spirituality, strength

Lore: The date palm may have grown in some areas as early as 48,000 years ago. Humans have always eaten the fruit.[104]

Dates were once thought to be eaten by the spirits of the dead.[35] Babylonians dried dates and ate them as we eat candies.[104] They also offered them to their deities. Dates from both Babylon and Dilmun, presented on a slice of bread soaked in oil, were given to Anu. Ea, Shamash, and Marduk were similarly offered this food.[24, 51] Date syrup was a popular sweetener in Mesopotamia, and date wine was another sacred food.[104] The date tree was an ancient symbol of fertility.

Magical uses: If you enjoy the taste and texture of dates, add them to a spirituality enhancing diet. Switch to date sugar for sweetening purposes. Or, simply eat the delicious fruits one at a time.

Also, consume dates to increase your physical strength.

Dates are an important part of fertility diets.

Fig

(Ficus carica)

Planet: Jupiter

Element: Fire

Energies: Strength, money, sex

Lore: Figs are often depicted on Egyptian tomb paintings and reliefs. At ancient Thebes, Pharaoh Ramses III offered 15,500 measures of figs to Amon-Ra.[23] They were also apparently eaten during certain rituals, such as those in honor of Thoth.[23]

The fig was sacred in ancient Greece and was associated with many deities, including Dionysius and Juno.

A fig isn't actually a fruit; it is a hollow, bud-like object filled with immature flowers and mature seeds.[90]

Magical uses: Eat figs as the Greeks did, to gain both physical strength and energy. Or, add them to money-attracting diets.

Figs can also be eaten to boost sexual desire and fertility. Figs regained their reputation as an erotic food during a scene in the Ken Russell film *Women In Love.*

Fig Newtons, the popular, prepackaged food, can be used for any of these purposes.

Grape, Raisin

(Vitis vinifera)

Planet: Moon

Element: Water

Energies: Dreams, fertility, money

Lore: Most ancient Egyptian tombs were stocked with grapes.[23]

On one occasion, Ramses III offered 11,872 jars of raisins, which the Egyptians created by drying grapes in the sun.[23] In Greece and Rome, grapes were sacred to Dionysius and Bacchus, respectively.

Magical uses: Eat grapes to produce dreams.[22] Grapes are also eaten to encourage physical fertility. When planted in temperate gardens, they strengthen the other plants situated nearby.

Surround a bunch of green grapes with solid silver coins. Hold your hands over the grapes and visualize money coming into your life. Then eat the grapes. Or simply add grape juice or grape jelly to your diet.

Raisins. Due to the sun-drying process used to create them, raisins are ruled by the sun and by the element of fire. They're eaten to develop the conscious mind.

Grapefruit

(Citrus paradisi)

Planet: Sun

Element: Water

Energies: Purification

Magical uses: The grapefruit has been cultivated in India and Malaysia for 4,000 years.[53]

Drink the juice or enjoy a half grapefruit for purification.

Guava

(Psidium guajava)

Planet: Venus

Element: Water

Energies: Love, purification

Lore: The guava is native to Mexico, Central America, Brazil, and Peru. Though we often associate guavas with Hawaii, they were introduced there just over a hundred years ago. Still, they have already made their way into Hawaiian folk magic. To purify themselves, Filipino families returning home from funerals in Hawaii often wash their feet with water that has been boiled with guava leaves.[18]

Magical uses: Fresh guavas are rare in most mainland U.S. markets. Other closely related fruits are now appearing here, such as feijoas (but these aren't true guavas). Guavas are, however, occasionally found at farmer's stands, especially near the Mexican border. If you have no luck, guava jelly and guava nectars are readily available. (See appendix 2 for mail-order sources.)

In Hawaii, many bakeries offer such delicacies as guava chiffon cake—an unforgettable taste sensation. Mexican cooks use guava paste in their culinary efforts.

This is another love food. Drink guava juice or nectar with visualization. The sweetness of the fruit foretells the sweetness of the coming relationship.

Guava nectar is also drunk for internal purification.

Kumquat

(Fortunella spp.)

Planet: Sun

Element: Air

Energies: Money, "luck"

Lore: These small, golden-orange fruits are native to China. The Chinese exchange small sprays of kumquat leaves and fruits at their New Year's festivities to ensure good fortune and money during the coming year.

Magical uses: Add these fruits to diets designed to bring "gold" into your life. Alternately, eat kumquats to stimulate good fortune.

Lemon

(Citrus limon)

Planet: Moon

Element: Water

Energies: Love, happiness, purification

Lore: Probably native to China, lemons first gained notice in the West when British sailors were given rations of the vitamin C–rich lemon juice to prevent scurvy on long voyages. Later, lime juice (just as effective, but less expensive) replaced the lemon, subjecting these British seamen to the derogatory term "Limeys."[104]

Lemon-flavored foods are used in Wiccan lunar feasts.

Magical uses: Lemon is a love fruit, but should be mixed with sugar for maximum results. Lemon pies, the British lemon curd, and lemon puddings are all love-inducing. Women once served lemon pies to their husbands to keep them home at night. As the cads ate the dessert, they'd feel their wives' love for them.

Lemon dishes (such as lemon chicken) spread warmth among friends when shared at intimate dinners. They also promote happiness.

For an internal purification, squeeze half a lemon into a glass of water. Sip or drink this straight down. The acidic juice is not only good for you, it will also give you a boost of physical energy as well.

Also, drink this mixture during all rituals designed to banish negative habits and thought patterns.

Lime

(Citrus limetta)

Planet: Sun

Element: Fire

Energies: Love, purification

Lore: In present-day Peru, shamans use sweetened lime juice in purification rituals.[97]

Magical uses: Lime is used in precisely the same way as lemon—to promote love and purification.

Key lime pie, a traditional Florida dessert, is an evocative love enhancer and one of my personal favorites. If you make this pie, visualize as you mix. You might cut out small hearts from the green portion of lime peel and place these onto the pie before serving.

Mango

(Mangifera indica)

Planet: Mars

Element: Fire

Energies: Protection, sex, love

Lore: The mango is native to India and Malaysia and has been cultivated in those countries for 4,000 years.[58] Around 600 B.C.E., in India, a special mango grove was presented to Buddha as a quiet place for meditation. Vedic magicians used mangos in preparing love philtres.[106] Today, Hindus use mango leaves as symbols of prosperity and happiness in various religious festivals.[58]

The mango is extremely popular in Central America and Mexico. In Guatemala, women eat the juicy, fleshy fruits to promote sexual excitement. In Hawaii, dreams filled with the fruit indicate prosperous times ahead.[102]

Eating this gooey fruit involves all the senses: the texture of the peel and the meat; the golden-reddish color of the flesh; the scent of the juice; the sound of the fruit squishing between your teeth; and the delicious taste. I've often ended up completely drenched with mango juice after a particularly satisfying encounter with this sacred fruit of India.

Magical uses: Mangos are useful in protection diets. It is a, however, member of the poison ivy and poison sumac family; some people develop rashes when touching the sap in the fruit's skin. Never eat the skin! Simply peel and enjoy.

Eat fresh mangos to stimulate the desire for sex, or to promote love. Recall the importance of visualization in food magic. Simply eating mangos with no visualization won't create sexual desire within the diner. The visualization is what causes the magical change. Yes, it's safe to serve mangos to young children!

May Apple

(Podophyllum petaltum)

Planet: Mercury

Element: Fire

Energies: Love, money

Lore: The may apple is also known as the American mandrake. It grows wild throughout the eastern and midwestern states.

In my files I have recipes for may apple pie and may apple jam. Although the fruits are safe, the root is poisonous and should never be taken internally. May apple roots were used in suicide teas among the Huron and Iroquois Indian tribes.

Magical uses: Eat the "apples" for love and money.

Melon

Planet: Moon

Element: Water

Energies: Healing, purification

Lore: The honeydew and cantaloupe were being eaten as early as 2000 B.C.E. Melons are native to Africa and India.[53] Egyptians are believed to have been eating honeydew melons in 2400 B.C.E.[53] Among continental Gypsies, melons were used as love-inducing foods.[14]

Magical uses: In general, melons are added to health-bestowing diets. Eat fresh melons once a day with the proper visualization. Any kind can be used—crenshaw, musk (also known as cantaloupe), honeydew, cassava, and so on. Melons are also eaten for purification, especially when trying to break a negative habit or way of thinking. See also the entry for *Watermelon* in this chapter.

Mulberry

(Morus rubra)

Planet: Mercury

Element: Air

Energies: Wisdom, fertility, psychic awareness

Lore: These curious, tree-borne berries were once thought to be sacred to Minerva.[90] Ray T. Malbrough, in an unpublished paper on Cajun herbal medicine and magic, states that mulberries are eaten before acts of divination for better glimpses of the future. They're also used for fertility.[67]

Magical uses: Eat ripe mulberries to gain wisdom, or as a part of fertility diets. Also, add mulberries to diets designed to increase psychic awareness.

Nectarine

(Prunus spp.)

Planet: Venus

Element: Water

Energies: Love

Magical uses: The name of this fruit has its origins in the Greek word *nekter,* the drink of the gods.[53] The nectarine is actually a smooth-skinned peach.

Add fresh nectarines to diets that promote love.

Orange

(Citrus sinensis)

Planet: Sun

Element: Fire

Energies: Love, purification

Lore: Probably native to China, the orange was used in imperial sacrifices to the deities. Oranges are exchanged at the

Chinese New Year to spread happiness and prosperity[3]

Oranges were once eaten to prevent drunkenness. It is curious that a slice of fresh orange is still added to many mixed drinks.

Magical uses: Those who have seen orange blossoms used at weddings won't be surprised to learn that this fruit is an age-old love stimulator. It can be added to love diets; however, the juice, when taken internally, is thought to "hinder lust." Orange juice and the fruit itself produce spiritual love, like that shared by friends and family.

For a quick internal purification, drink orange juice every morning while visualizing the refreshing juice cleaning your system from the inside out. Fresh-squeezed juice is best.

Orange flower water can be used in desserts for love. Flavor whipped cream with orange flower water; stir a bit into vanilla ice cream; or add to all types of food. Use only genuine orange flower water (check gourmet stores).

Papaya

(Papya carica)

Planet: Moon

Element: Water

Energies: Love

Lore: Papaya seems to be native to the tropical Americas. The Incas and Mayas ate it, and it is still a popular fruit in Mexico. [85] It was introduced to Hawaii about one hundred years ago and quickly became a standard food there as well.

Papayas taste like flowers. Many dislike the aroma of the fruit, but this has never been a problem to me. Papaya contains the digestive enzyme papain. Skindivers and bathers in Hawaii use it (or meat tenderizers consisting largely of papain) to remove the pain of Portuguese man-of-war stings. In Guatemala, men eat papaya as an aphrodisiac. Women use the mango.

Magical uses: Eat the fruit or drink the juice (usually in the form of sugared "nectars") for love. Use papaya-seed dressing on salads to further stimulate love.

Passion Fruit

(Passiflora edulis)

Planet: Moon

Element: Water

Energies: Love, peace

Lore: This vine is a native of Brazil.[89] Christian folklore associates the unusual flowers of this tropical vine with the crucifixion. This is curious, since the plant doesn't grow in biblical lands.

The Cajuns, among others, use passion fruit to calm anger and to promote friendships.[67]

The fruit is about the size of an egg, and is usually purple and wrinkled when ripe. Each fruit produces less than a tablespoon of juice. Fresh passion fruits are sold in many markets in the United States.

Magical uses: Known as *liliko'i* in Hawaii, passion fruit produces an exquisitely tart juice. When diluted and sweetened, its taste becomes rich and mysterious.

Add passion fruit to love diets. Fortunately, passion fruit juice is currently a popular flavoring ingredient in mixed "tropical punches," and so some form of passion fruit is readily available.

The sweetened juice is also drunk for peace.

Peach

(Prunus persica)

Planet: Venus

Element: Water

Energies: Love, health, happiness, wisdom

Lore: The famous Chinese heroine Ho Hsien-Ku, who lived in
the seventh century C.E., was transformed into a fairy by eating a supernatural peach. Thereafter she lived on a diet of
powdered mother-of-pearl and moonbeams, which caused
her to be immortal.[3]

The peach has always been a sacred tree to the Chinese,
whose longevity deity is sometimes depicted emerging from a
peach tree. The "pits" are carved into lock shapes and given to
children as amulets against death. Sprays of peach blossoms
are placed over the front door to guard it against negativity
during the Chinese New Year. [3, 114]

Magical uses: Eat fresh peaches, peach jam, or peach pie to
expand your ability to give and to receive love. Peaches are also
eaten (with appropriate visualization) to induce health, happiness, and wisdom, as they have been in China for centuries.

Pear

(Pyrus communis)

Planet: Venus

Element: Water

Energies: Longevity, money

Lore: Pear trees can continue to bear fruit for as long as 300
years, according to ancient Chinese lore. Due to their extraordinary longevity, pears are eaten to impart magical life exten-
sion to humans.

Athena was worshipped as the mother of pear trees in ancient Greece; in Russia, cows were protected with pear charms.[112] In the U.S., pears are eaten for good "luck" on Thanksgiving.[46]

Magical uses: These fruits are eaten for longer life and for money. They can be used fresh or in the form of pear bread, pear tarts, and other desserts.

Persimmon

(Diospyros virginiana)

Planet: Venus

Element: Water

Energies: Happiness

Magical uses: This native of North America produces large orange fruits. Add persimmons to your diet for happiness and joy. Eating persimmon jam is a pleasant way of adding this fruit's energy to your life.

Pineapple

(Ananas comusus)

Planet: Sun

Element: Fire

Energies: Healing, money, protection, love

Lore: In early America, the pineapple was a symbol of hospitality. Its image was often carved into furniture and into household items such as newel posts. The fruit is used in Mexican healing rituals.[109]

Magical uses: Add fresh or cooked pineapple to healing diets. Eat the fruit to garner money.

Pineapple is useful for two seemingly contradictory but inked magical changes: protection and love.

Plum

(Prunus spp.)

Planet: Venus

Element: Water

Energies: Protection, sex

Lore: Plum tree branches were placed above doors and windows to keep negativity from European homes.[35] In China, the fruit was eaten to guard against evil. It was also consumed for long life. Prunes, the dried form of plums, are thought to be sexually arousing. They were served free to customers in Elizabethan brothels (probably the only thing in these establishments that was free).[29]

Magical uses: Eat these tartly sweet fruits for internal protection and to stimulate the desire for sex. Visualize!

Pomegranate

(Punica granatum)

Planet: Mercury

Element: Fire

Energies: Fertility, creativity, money

Lore: Throughout Mesopotamia and the Mediterranean, this many-seeded fruit was linked with deity. The Hittites attributed the pomegranate to Ibritz, their god of agriculture. The Greeks depicted Zeus holding a pomegranate;[23] the redness of the seeds also suggested that the fruit sprung from the blood of Dionysius. The pomegranate also played a symbolic role in early Judaic symbolism.[23]

Representations of pomegranates abound in the art of antiquity, such as the famous pomegranate-shaped silver jar found in Tutankhaman's tomb. The fruits were used as money—barter and cash—in ancient Egypt.[23]

Pomegranates were served at Babylonian marriage banquets. Pomegranate seeds were also offered to guests during Asian weddings, much as we put out bowls of nuts.

In contemporary American folklore, these are "lucky" fruits. A wish is always made before eating the fruit's first seeds.

Magical uses: A fine food for autumn seasonal festivals, particularly Samhain (Halloween); the redness of the juicy flesh surrounding the seeds symbolizes the blood of life that will continue during the coming winter months.

The pomegranate was used in fertility magic due to its numerous seeds. While this was perhaps "superstitious," pomegranate seeds can be added to diets geared toward physical fertility. Simply eat with visualization. Alternately, eat pomegranate (or drink the sieved juice) to stimulate creativity (there are many forms of fertility).

Eat pomegranates with visualization to promote increased income. Or, rub fresh pomegranate seeds on to money before spending it to ensure its return. Don't try this at the checkout counter, however.

Prickly Pear

(*Opuntia* spp.)

Planet: Mars

Element: Fire

Energies: Protection

Magical uses: Prickly pears, known as *tunas* in Spanish, produce deliciously juicy fruits. They are sometimes available in Southwestern markets, or can be picked straight off the plants—but take care not to prick your fingers on the spines. (Those for sale in stores have been despined.)

The fruit is surprisingly sweet and quite delicious. Eat it as a part of protection diets. Prickly pear jelly and jam are sometimes available in grocery stores, and can also be eaten for protection.

Quince

(*Cydonia* spp.)

Planet: Saturn

Element: Earth

Energies: Love, Protection

Lore: The Roman naturalist Pliny wrote that the fruit of the quince wards off the influence of evil.[86] The quince was also a symbol of love and happiness in ancient Greece. Newly married couples often ate the fruit.[64] Some groups of European Gypsies used the quince for love magic.[14]

Magical uses: Many people today have never eaten a quince, but that's no cause for fear. It must be cooked to be enjoyed. Simply eat foods containing quince to stimulate love. Alternately, add quinces to protective diets.

Raspberry

(*Rubus idaeus*)

Planet: Venus

Element: Water

Energies: Happiness, protection, love

Magical uses: There's something magical about a rambling tangle of raspberry brambles. The white flowers, scarlet fruit, and painful spines add to the mystery of this common fruit, which has been introduced throughout the world. It even grows untended on the lonely trails that lace through the Hawaiian islands.

The scent of the ripe berries, even if they're packed in a carton, can be cheering. Smell and eat for happiness. Raspberries are also useful in promoting both protection and love.

Strawberry

(Fragaria vesca)

Planet: Venus

Element: Water

Energies: Love

Lore: The strawberry is native to both the Americas and Europe.[71] Romans planted it in their gardens,[71] and the fruit was sacred to Freya in old Europe.

Magical uses: This delicious fruit is useful in love diets. Some examples? Strawberry ice cream. Chocolate-dipped strawberries. Sliced strawberries and whole raspberries mixed with a few fresh, shredded mint leaves. I'm sure you can think of other love-inducing strawberry delights.

Tamarind

(Tamarindus indicus)

Planet: Saturn

Element: Water

Energies: Love

Magical uses: The tamarind is native to India. It is a long, bean-shaped fruit that is rather distressing in appearance, but it produces a refreshing, sweet drink known in Mexico as *tamarindo*. I'm not sure if it is drunk there to stimulate love, but it should be.

Tangerine

(Citrus spp.)

Planet: Sun

Element: Air

Energies: Protection

Lore: I was once walking through a heavily Asian neighborhood to the grocery store. As usual, I was being nosy, looking into the cars that were parked along the road. One of the cars stood out. The usual red-and-gold ornament, placed there for protection, hung from the rearview mirror. Beside it, the car's owner had suspended a small branch with dried tangerines still attached to it. I did a double take and smiled, knowing that the tangerine is a fruit of protection throughout Asia. It is also a common offering on contemporary Buddhist altars.

Magical uses: Tangerines, solar fruits, are drenched with the energies of the sun. Eat for internal personal protection. Alternately, place a fresh tangerine on your kitchen table (or household altar, if you have one) to guard your home, particularly during short vacations and trips. Replace with a fresh tangerine as needed. Bury the used tangerines in the ground.

Watermelon

(Citrullus vulgaris)

Planet: Moon

Element: Water

Energies: Healing

Lore: What could be a more all-American food than watermelon? Many plants, in fact, including wild rice, corn, and potatoes. The watermelon is native to Africa and was brought to our continent during the saddest and most savage time in our history—the time of trafficking of human beings.[29]

The watermelon was introduced to Egypt in about 2000 B.C.E.[71] Ancient Egyptians mixed watermelon juice with wine and gave this drink to ill persons who were believed to be possessed by illness-causing demons.[69] Watermelon was mythological related to the god Set, and Egyptian women may have eaten watermelon in prescriptions designed to cause weight gain.[69]

In Hawaii, a watermelon is sometimes rolled out of the house through the front door to ease the spirit of a deceased person into the next world.[18]

Watermelon is sacred to the goddess Yemaya in the various manifestations of the Yoruba religion.

Magical uses: Nothing is more refreshing on a hot summer day than ice-cold watermelon. This is a healing fruit. Simply eat with visualization. Like all melons, the scent alone is also healing.

CHAPTER TWELVE

Spices & Herbs

Spices were once more costly than gold. They were imported at great expense from distant lands. China produced cinnamon. Ceylon (now Sri Lanka) grew black pepper. The Molucca Islands were home to cloves. India and Zanzibar produced ginger. Banda exported nutmeg.

In their homelands, spices were liberally used to spark up otherwise drab meals. But the cost of spices in Europe forbade their use in cooking. Instead, these treasured substances were used solely for medicine and for ritual. In Egypt, Greece, and Rome, spices were burned in sacrifice to the deities and were added to remedies. It took hundreds of years and sharp drops in cost before Europeans began flavoring food with spices.

Those bottles of cloves that we find so expensive today (approximately three dollars per ounce, retail) would have at one time started wars. Men* killed and were killed for them.

The bloody history of spices is fraught with political struggles and with slavery. Only in the last fifty or so years have spice plantations been successfully founded in lands

---

*My use of the sexist term here is deliberate.

near the equator. Crops have increased in volume and prices have fallen.

Though Western nations no longer use these fragrant treasures in religious ceremonies, spices continue to spellbind us.

Herbs

What's an herb? Few experts can agree. Originally "herb" referred to perennial, woody-stemmed plants. Today it is usually applied to all plants possessing strong fragrances, flavors, and/or medicinal properties.

The first medicines were composed of plants. So, too, were the first offerings to the goddesses and gods that watched over early peoples. Throughout the centuries, the cupboards of village wise women and magicians were crammed with aromatic flowers, leaves, seeds, and barks—the materials of a thousand-and-one mystic rites.

In our times, herbs have largely been limited to the status of luxury items. At one time, every household had a kitchen garden. Today, chefs rush to markets to purchase fresh herbs. The scented products, such as air fresheners, used in our homes usually derive their fragrance from laboratory compositions, not plants. The medicinal properties of plants are synthesized and combined in unnatural formulations.

But the continuing awareness of the value of herbs for healing, ritual, and cooking has brought many of these fragrant plants into the light once again.

Spices and herbs are more than simple flavoring materials. Chosen with care and added with visualization, they can be used to fortify a number of dishes with specific energies related to magical goals.

This chapter examines some versatile herbs, with tips on how they can manifest necessary changes. Here's a quick guide to incorporating them into magical cooking:

—Use the appropriate herbs and spices for each dish: love herbs and spices in love foods, protective flavorings in protective dishes, etc. Adding, say, horseradish (a protective flavoring) to a love food cancels out the food's desired effect.

—Herbs and spices should subtly enhance the flavors of foods, not drown or disguise them. Add sparingly to taste.

—If using fresh herbs while making recipes that call for dried herbs, use two and a half times the amount of the fresh herb.

—Before using any dried herb or spice, measure it and pour onto a clean, flat plate or countertop. Visualize strongly. Place the index finger of your projective hand (the hand that you write with) into the middle of the spice. Draw a symbol that represents your goal in the spice while continuing to visualize (see Symbols, p. 341). Add to the dish as usual.

Allspice

(Pimenta officinalis)

Planet: Jupiter

Element: Earth

Energies: Money, healing

Magical uses: Allspice is native to the West Indies and to tropical America. Its small, round berries are said to combine the flavors of cinnamon, nutmeg, and cloves.

Add allspice to money and healing foods.

Anise

(Pimpinella anisum)

Planet: Jupiter

Element: Air

Energies: Love

Magical uses: Use anise to flavor wedding cakes. This helps to ensure continuing love for the couple. Anise cookies (recipes can be found in any cookie cookbook) are also useful for promoting love and establishing relationships.

Basil

(Ocimum basilicum)

Planet: Mars

Element: Fire

Energies: Love, protection, money

Lore: The magical history of this Indian herb is long and fascinating. As soon as it was introduced into Europe, it was used for magical as well as culinary pursuits.

    The famous herbalist Culpeper states that "women in early pregnancy should never smell its [basil's] scent which could quickly expelleth birth [the fetus]."[56] Another famous belief concerning basil was that smelling it too long might breed a scorpion in the sniffer's head—perhaps meaning a headache.[56]

    Some Latina women in the United States and in parts of Mexico sprinkle their bodies with powdered basil in an attempt to halt their wandering husbands' infidelity.[101]

Magical uses: Basil-flavored foods create loving feelings. Pesto sauce (containing basil and pine nuts, among other ingredients) over noodles (made with wheat, ruled by Venus) is an excellent love food.

For protection, eat basil-flavored foods prepared with the proper visualization. Also add to money foods.

Use fresh basil for the strongest effects. (Most supermarkets contain a section of fresh herbs. Ask in the produce department.) The dried herb can be used in a pinch, but will be less effective.

Bay

(Laurus nobilis)

Planet: Sun

Element: Fire

Energies: Protection, psychic awareness, healing, purification.

Lore: Long associated with Greek and Roman deities, bay (laurel) leaves were used to crown Olympic victors. Bay was dedicated to many deities in the classical world.

In the United States, any diner who received a bay leaf in her or his bowl of food made a wish. The bay leaf made the wish come true.[46]

Magical uses: Bay leaves are just as powerful today as they were in the past. Sparingly add the dried leaves to protection, psychic awareness, healing, and purification foods.

Black Pepper

(Piper nigrum)

Planet: Mars

Element: Fire

Energies: Protection, purification

Lore: Though you may casually ask the waiter to add a few grinds of black pepper to your salad, or sprinkle some of the spice onto your food without a second thought, black pepper is an ancient plant with a long history.

Used medicinally in Greece as early as 500 B.C.E.,[104] the most common food flavoring of our times was used there for gynecological problems.[104] Pepper has been in use for cooking and medicine in Asia for over 4,000 years. It just took us awhile to catch up with the rest of the world.

As soon as I learned something of black pepper's history, I became fascinated by it. I finally had the pleasure of seeing a living black pepper vine in 1984 at Foster's Botanical Gardens in Honolulu, Hawaii.

Black pepper isn't related to chili peppers.

Magical uses: Add black pepper to protective foods, such as chili, tomato juice, and nachos. Sprinkle with visualization. Naturally, freshly ground pepper is best.

Black pepper is also used in purification diets. It's powerful. Don't overuse this or any other spice.

Caraway

(Carum carvi)

Planet: Mercury

Element: Air

Energies: Sex, love

Lore: The remains of caraway seeds were found in the prehistoric lake dwellings of Switzerland, proving that this commonplace herb has been in use for thousands of years. In about 500 C.E., Persians sometimes paid taxes with bags of the most sought after currency: caraway.[56]

Magical uses: Caraway fruits (commonly misnamed "seeds") have long been celebrated as promoting the desire for sex. Chew them or add to food to create the effect. Naturally, expectation of the caraway producing the result you desire comes into play. But if used with visualization, caraway might bring you what you need. Also add to love foods.

Remember that giving someone a food laced with caraway seeds won't make them jump into bed with you—unless the person already wanted to do so.

Cardamom

(Elletaria cardamom)

Planet: Venus

Element: Water

Energies: Love, sex

Lore: Greece imported cardamom seeds from the East as early as 400 B.C.E. Later, in spite of its high cost, cardamom became the most popular spice in Rome.[71] Today, cardamom seeds are still expensive. They're the third costliest spice, after saffron and vanilla.[71]

Magical uses: When crushed, cardamom seeds emit an exquisite scent. Long linked with love and sex, the spice is useful in promoting both. Flavor coffee or herbal tea with a few cardamom seeds. Or, bake cardamom cookies for a tasty love and lust treat.

Chickweed

(Stellaria media)

Planet: Moon

Element: Water

Energies: Weight loss

Magical uses: This simple, common herb is said to "discourage obesity."[90] Add small amounts to foods if you wish to slim your body. An ideal way to do this is to place a few leaves into a salad and enjoy.

Though the plant isn't available in markets, it spreads itself over disturbed ground all across the country. Get an herb or plant identification handbook and go hunting!

Chicory

(Chicoriurn intybus)

Planet: Sun

Element: Air

Energies: Love

Magical uses: Many who have tasted chicory coffee have developed a fondness for it. The brew—a mixture of coffee beans and ground, roasted chicory root—is useful for love.

Cinnamon

(Cinnamomum zeylanicum)

Planet: Sun

Element: Fire

Energies: Love, psychic awareness, money

Lore: The ancient Egyptians used cinnamon in medicine and religion as early as 1450 B.C.E.[104] Ramses III presented many offerings of this fragrant spice to the deities in 1200 B.C.E. In Greece, it played a part in processions to Dionysius.[24]

Most cinnamon sold in the United States, no matter how it's labeled, is actually cassia. Cassia is a dark spice, usually reddish brown, while true cinnamon is actually tan-colored.[71] However, there's virtually no difference between the taste and magical effects of cinnamon and cassia.

Cinnamon is a love spice. When added to apples, it is doubly powerful. Applesauce flavored with cinnamon is a good love food. So, too, is cinnamon-rich apple pie.

For a morning love-enhancer, fill a teaspoon with ground cinnamon. Carefully pour a bit of the spice in the shape of a heart on a toasted piece of bread. While visualizing, spread it out with a knife and eat.

Or, add cinnamon to money or psychic foods.

Cloves

(Syzygium aromaticum; Caryophyllus aromaticus)

Planet: Jupiter

Element: Fire

Energies: Love, money, protection

Magical uses: Cloves lend a wonderfully spicy flavor if added sparingly to protective foods. They're also useful in love and money foods. Eat small amounts.

Coriander

(Coriandrum sativum)

Planet: Mars

Element: Fire

Energies: Love, sex

Lore: A sprig of fresh cilantro (coriander leaves) is placed in many Central American kitchens to guard against "evil."

Magical uses: Coriander is a love herb. The fruits (misnamed seeds) are added to appropriate foods with appropriate visualization. The powdered fruits are placed in warm wine and drunk to stimulate the desire for sexual activity.

Cumin

(Cuminum cyminum)

Planet: Mars

Element: Fire

Energies: Peace, happiness

Lore: Cumin was a favorite of Egyptian deities; at least that's what many pharaohs thought while they sacrificed tons of the herb.[237] In Greece, it was worn around the neck as a protection against negative magic. Cumin is one of the most popular Mexican culinary spices.

Magical uses: Add cumin to foods of peace and happiness.

Dandelion

(Taraxum officinale)

Planet: Jupiter

Element: Air

Energies: Psychic awareness

Lore: The ground, dried, and roasted roots of dandelions were once brewed and drunk as a substitute for Chinese tea. Many still favor this drink as an alternative to coffee.

   Drink dandelion tea with visualization to promote psychic awareness.

Dill

(Anethum graveolens)

Planet: Mercury

Element: Fire

Energies: Conscious mind, money, weight loss, love

Lore: To those of us familiar with dill only in the form of pickles, its history may come as a surprise. The Egyptians knew of it and considered dill sacred to Amsety, one of Horus' four sons who guarded the canopic jars in which a mummified person's internal organs were kept.[23] The ancient Greeks used dill fruits (seeds) as money.[56] To fortify themselves prior to battle, Roman gladiators rubbed their bodies with dill-scented oil,[94] while emperors placed crowns of dill on their heads to ensure lengthy and successful reigns.[56]

   Europeans have long used dill in spells and rites. In France, dill was a strong protectant against "evil." Spaniards wore snippets of dill on their clothing to drive away demons, and brides in Germany carried wedding bouquets that contained dill for "good luck."[56]

Though a Mediterranean plant, dill has travelled around the world. Fresh stalks of dill are still sold in India for both culinary and protective use.[56]

A few generations ago, cranky children were fed dill water to cause them to fall asleep. In herbal medicine of the Renaissance, dill was prescribed for exactly the same purposes. It was chewed, eaten, or worn to bed for this purpose.[56, 94]

Magical uses: Dill's strong, fresh scent was probably responsible for its constant use in folk magic and religion throughout the ages. Its powers have not yet faded from the mind: eating pickles before sleep is said to create strange dreams, and pregnant women sometimes crave dill-flavored pickles.

Fish cooked with dill leaves is said to "exhilarate" the brain, leading to increased mental faculties.[56] This may be true for two reasons: the effects of the herb itself and the fact that such a meal would be less of a digestive burden than others.

Ruled by Mercury, the planet of intelligence, dill "seed" (actually fruits) or "weed" (leaves) may be added to diets designed to increase the ability to use the conscious mind.

Or, eat dill-flavored foods to bring money into your life, to help your business prosper, and to ensure that the money you do receive is spent wisely. Dill pickles are perfect for this use.

What other miracles have been attributed to dill? For centuries, dill has been used to lose weight. Dill tea or pickles are both said to be helpful in achieving this common goal. Just don't sprinkle dill onto a hot-fudge sundae and expect it to work weight-loss magic.

Dill is also added to love foods.

Fennel

(Foeniculum vulgare)

Planet: Mercury

Element: Fire

Energies: Physical strength, weight loss, protection

Magical uses: Add these fragrant seeds to dishes designed to promote physical strength. Fennel has been used for this purpose for hundreds of years.

Additionally, use fennel as part of a weight-reducing diet. The seeds are also added to protective dishes.

Garlic

(Allium sativum)

Planet: Mars

Element: Fire

Energies: Protection, health

Lore: In antiquity, garlic was given to insane persons in the belief that it would cure them.[23] The conquering Romans spread garlic throughout their newly acquired lands, and Roman soldiers ate garlic for courage in battle.

Around the Mediterranean, and particularly in Italy, garlic is considered an excellent protection against "evil." The power of the smelly bulb against vampires is another example of this belief from Eastern Europe.

In 1597, an Englishman wrote: "If a woman cannot smell the savor of Garlike being set by her bedside in the night, she is undoubtedly with childe."[56]

Garlic was once also thought to keep rats and mice from fruit-bearing trees.

Magical uses: The intensity of the smell and taste of fresh garlic make it useful in protective diets. If you enjoy garlic, by all means add it to a diet designed to guard yourself.

Some experts say that we should eat a clove of fresh garlic every day for good health. This presents no problem to garlic lovers (who even enjoy garlic ice cream). If you're not ready for a daily clove, simply add some garlic to your food every day for continuing good health. Visualize as you cook and eat. Use only fresh garlic. No freeze-dried, dehydrated, or bottled garlic!

Ginger

(Zingiber officinalis)

Planet: Mars

Element: Fire

Energies: Love, money

Lore: Ginger is native to Asia and seems to have been introduced to the West by Alexander the Great in about 340 B.C.E.[56] The Chinese placed ginger in tombs to feed the dead, and hung portions of the root over doorways to guard mother and baby during childbirth. They also saw in the spicy plant a tool for communicating with their deities. Ginger was and still is an important part of religious offerings throughout China and in Hong Kong.[19]

Pacific Islanders chewed fresh ginger rhizome* during healing rituals and, while at sea, spat the masticated spice at oncoming storms to stop their progress.

Since this is a book about food, I feel compelled to write that a dime-sized piece of crystallized ginger is one of the best remedies for an upset stomach. So, too, is ginger tea, made by pouring hot water over sliced fresh ginger.

Magical uses: Ginger is rarely used in Western cooking, which is a shame because it's so versatile. If used, it must be sparingly added, however, due to its intense flavor.

---

*A rhizome is an underground stem that looks like a root.

Gingerbread and ginger ale—when they're made with real ginger—are both love-inducing foods. Ginger can be added to other dishes of this nature. The easiest way to add ginger to your diet is to simply chew a very small piece of crystallized (candied) ginger while visualizing. Though you may fear the ginger will burn you tongue, it won't. It is hot, yes, but not as hot as chili pepper. Eat no more than a dime-sized piece.

Ginger-flavored dishes are also excellent for increasing income. Visualize as you cook and eat, of course.

Horseradish

(Cochleria armoracia)

Planet: Mars

Element: Fire

Energies: Purification, protection

Magical uses: American folklore states that the best horseradish is made from roots that are dug at the Full Moon (this is when they're at their tangiest).[46] Add prepared horseradish sauce to purification and protection diets. Eat it only if you enjoy its curiously strong taste.

Licorice

(Glycyrrhiza glabra)

Planet: Venus

Element: Water

Energies: Love, sex

Lore: The Roman Pliny wrote that keeping a piece of licorice root in the mouth staved off hunger and thirst.[59]

In American folk magic, a cross made by tying together two pieces of licorice root with red yarn is carried for protection against injury and negativity.[101]

Magical uses: Licorice, and the candy after which it is named, has long been linked with love and sexuality. Licorice created from artificial flavors possesses no special energies, but black licorice made from true licorice extract can still occasionally be found, and can be chewed for love. Check for it in health-food stores. Failing this, chew on a piece of licorice root while visualizing love or enhanced sexual activities.

Mace

(Myristica fragrans)

Planet: Jupiter

Element: Earth

Energies: Psychic awareness

Magical uses: Mace is the bright red aril (covering) removed from nutmegs. It is added in small amounts to foods in order to strengthen psychic awareness.

Marigold

(Calendula officinalis)

Planet: Sun

Element: Fire

Energies: Happiness, protection

Lore: Several centuries ago, the marigold was as common as dill or sage. Its bright orange petals were used in making custards and were added to soups and stews. The color and vibrancy of the flowers make them perfect for garnishing autumn and winter foods.

 The flowers of this true marigold (not to be confused with the Mexican variety, *Tagetes* spp.) were dried and made into a tea which was drunk for happiness.

Magical uses: Add fresh marigold petals to foods to promote happiness. Or, add to protective foods to boost their energies.

Marjoram

(Origanum marjorana)

Planet: Mercury

Element: Air

Energies: Love, peace

Lore: According to Pliny, a species of this plant (gold marjoram) was grown in Roman and Greek gardens. If it flourished, the gardener was guaranteed plentiful money. If it died, however, the owner faced ruin. This belief survived until the 1400s in Venice.[56]

Magical uses: Use marjoram in love foods. Drink tea made of one teaspoon mixed marjoram and thyme steeped in a cup of water. Sweeten with honey, visualize. Marjoram is also used in peaceful foods.

Mustard

(Brassica spp.)

Planet: Mars

Element: Fire

Energies: Protection, courage

Lore: The Greeks believed that Aesculepius discovered this plant. American folklore states that carrying mustard seeds while on journeys guards you from accidents.[46]

Magical uses: The seeds of this plant are used to make the familiar spicy mustard sauce. Mustard is wonderful for promoting protection and courage, if it's eaten with visualization. Large amounts aren't necessary; simply use a bit of the prepared mustard, or add a few seeds to other foods.

Nutmeg

(Myristica fragrans)

Planet: Jupiter

Element: Fire

Energies: Psychic awareness

Magical uses: This powerful spice can be added in small amounts to psychic-awareness foods. Sprinkle some onto a glass of eggnog. While visualizing, drink to open your psychic awareness.

Eating large amounts of nutmeg will produce vomiting, so the tiniest fraction of a teaspoon will do.

Oregano

(Origanum vulgare)

Planet: Mercury

Element: Air

Energies: Peace

Magical uses: This common Italian culinary herb is a wonderful peace-inducer. Sprinkle onto foods, especially cheese pizza, to give them a peaceful energy. (Using oregano on a pizza that contains meat will cancel its effect.)

Parsley

(Petroselinum sativum)

Planet: Mercury

Element: Air

Energies: Protection, sex, money

Lore: Parsley has long been linked with the mystic arts. Even today, Mexicans wear a sprig of the herb over an ear to cure a headache.[115] Gardeners in Europe are still told that, to ensure proper germination, curses should be sown into the soil with parsley seed.

Magical uses: Why do chefs still place sprigs of parsley onto plates of food? Today, this is done for decoration. But at one time, the herb guarded food from contamination by "evil" before the meal could be eaten.

Parsley is a nutritious as well as a protective herb. Grow or buy fresh parsley and munch a small amount every day to strengthen your own natural psychic armor. Or, add the fresh (or dried) herb to protective foods to strengthen their powers.

In France, parsley has a reputation for stimulating sexual desire. This idea dates back to the time of Dioscorides, who stated in his ancient Greek herbal that parsley "provokes venery and bodily lust."

Contemporary magical practitioners in Louisiana pre-scribe magical parsley baths to attract money.[67] Place about two cups of fresh parsley (or three-quarters cup dried parsley) into a large square of doubled cheesecloth. Tie the cloth tightly to trap the herb inside and add to the bath. Visualize as you soak.

Peppermint

(Mentha piperita)

Planet: Mercury

Element: Air

Energies: Sex, purification, healing

Magical uses: Peppermint tea seems to have been used since the days of ancient Greece for stimulating interest in sexual activity. While many feel that it has more of a cooling effect, it's certainly worth a try.

Peppermint tea is drunk as part of personal purification rituals. Put one teaspoon of the dried herb into a teacup while visualizing purification. Add nearly boiling water, steep for thirteen minutes, and drink. The same tea can be used for healing.

Spearmint (that bright green herb that is usually sold simply as "mint") can be substituted for peppermint.

Poppy
(Papaver spp.)

Planet: Moon

Element: Water

Energies: Fertility, love

Lore: Poppies were known to humans as far back as the Stone Age. They seem to have been sacred to the Cretan mother goddess and they certainly were sacred to Demeter, Ceres, and Spes.[78] In Europe, poppy seeds were once used to create invisibility. Did it work? I don't know—those who tried it dropped out of sight.

It takes 900,000 of the tiny black seeds to make one pound.[71]

Magical uses: Though abuse of the latex extracted from ripening poppy seed pods (which is used to create opium, morphine, and heroin, among other drugs) continues, black poppy seeds are standard culinary and magical substances. Since the latex never reaches the seeds, they're neither illegal or narcotic.

If physical fertility is a concern, eat poppy-seed buns or other poppy-flavored foods with visualization. For love, add the tiny, round seeds to your favorite love-inducing foods. Or make a poppy-seed cake.

Rose

(Rosa spp.)

Planet: Venus

Element: Water

Energies: Love, happiness, psychic awareness

Lore: In India, a few wandering tribes of mystics are said to live solely on roses, abstaining from all other foods except the queen of flowers.[15] Roses have been eaten for thousands of years, and rose water is still an important part of Middle Eastern cooking.

Magical uses: Eat roses as a part of love diets. For a tasty treat, fresh rose petals can be sprinkled onto vanilla ice cream. Or, add rose water to dishes such as whipped cream, apple pie, and other appropriate foods. Rose water is available in gourmet cooking shops and a few grocery stores. Make sure that it is genuine rose water, not an artificially scented water.

Roses can also be eaten to induce happiness. Crystallized roses are fine for this purpose. Eat rose-flavored foods for psychic awareness.

Never eat flowers that have been sprayed with pesticides or that show insect damage! Check before you munch.

Rosemary

(Rosemarinus officinalis)

Planet: Sun

Element: Fire

Energies: Protection, conscious mind, healing, love

Lore: Rosemary, which thrives to this day on Mediterranean shores, was sacred to Venus and to many other goddesses. It was considered the flower of Mount Olympus. Rosemary was used in many ancient religious and magical ceremonies.

Magical uses: Add rosemary to protective foods, especially those utilizing tomatoes. Drink the tea or use in dishes designed to increase mental alertness and the ability to think clearly. If you're having trouble following a recipe, smell fresh rosemary.

Rosemary is also useful in diets designed to maintain good health and to stimulate the body's natural healing abilities. This tasty herb is also added to a variety of love-inducing foods.

Saffron

(Crocus sativus)

Planet: Sun

Element: Fire

Energies: Happiness, spirituality

Lore: In the ancient world, saffron was a sacred flower. Phoenicians baked saffron-flavored crescent cakes in honor of Ashtoreth. The tiny red inner portions (stigmas) of the flowers were used to dye garments and to flavor foods for the tables of the very rich.

Today, saffron is still the most expensive spice traded. Each flower produces only three stigmas, and it takes 13,000 of them to make up an ounce of the spice[71] Fortunately, only small amounts are ever needed for use in cooking. Saffron foods are perfect for Wiccan ritual feasts, particularly those linked with the sun.

Magical uses: Eat saffron-flavored foods (such as paella) to induce happiness. The saffron rice recipe given in chapter 26 is another fine happiness food. Saffron also induces spirituality.

Sage

(Saivia officinalis)

Planet: Jupiter

Element: Air

Energies: Longevity, health

Lore: Dedicated to Zeus by the Greeks and to Jupiter by the Romans, sage has been used in cooking, medicine, and magic for at least 2,000 years. The Latin name derives from the word *salvus,* "safe," due to its healing qualities.

Magical uses: Use sage in your cooking to enjoy a long life. This stems from an ancient belief as summed up in the words:

> *"Eat sage in May*
> *and live for aye" [ever]*

Sage is also an important part of healing diets. Visualize as you cook and eat. Rather strangely, one authority states that drinking sage tea reduces the desire for sex.[101]

Thyme

(Thymus vulgaris)

Planet: Venus

Element: Water

Energies: Love, psychic awareness, purification

Magical uses: Since the days in which it was used to cleanse Greek temples, thyme has always played a role in spirituality and religion. It was and is a popular seasoning as well.

Place one teaspoon of mixed thyme and marjoram into a tea cup. Add one cup hot water. As it brews, visualize yourself enjoying a satisfying, two-sided relationship. Sweeten with honey if desired and drink the tea, continuing to visualize.

Add thyme to psychic foods or drink the tea to gain control over your psychic awareness. Thyme is also used in purification diets.

Turmeric

(Curcurma domestica)

Planet: Mercury

Element: Air

Energies: Purification

Lore: Hawaiians use turmeric in purification ceremonies. It is mixed with sea water and flicked around the area with leaves.[77]

In India, turmeric is burned to detect the presence of demons, who are said to detest the smell. If a demon (in the disguise of a human being) is in the room, she or he will leave when turmeric is burned.[61]

Magical uses: We know turmeric from its use as a coloring agent in dill pickles, which it turns a greenish-yellow color (artificial colors are also used for this today). Pickling spices usually include turmeric.

For internal purification, eat a pickle with visualization. Or, add a small amount of turmeric (no more than one-eighth of a teaspoon) to your favorite nonsweet purification food.

Vanilla

(Vanilla planiflora)

Planet: Venus

Element: Water

Energies: Love, sexuality

Lore: Vanilla is one of Mexico's gifts to the world. The cured fruit of an orchid, vanilla was created long ago by a divine act.

In the distant past, when goddesses and gods still walked the Earth, Zanat, the young daughter of the fertility goddess, furiously loved a Totonac youth. Unable to marry him due to her divine nature, she transformed herself into a plant that would provide pleasure and happiness. Xanat became the vanilla orchid so that She could forever belong to her human love and to his people.[91]

This beautiful legend speaks of the respect that early Mexicans gave to this orchid and to its fermented fruit, which we know as the vanilla bean. The Totonac Indians may yet celebrate the Vanilla Festival in late spring with dances and feasts. Among them, the flower of the vanilla orchid is still known as *xanat*.[91]

Native to Central America, the plant is now grown in Mexico and other parts of the world.

The vanilla is the only orchid that is regularly used for food purposes.[71] The Aztecs, who knew it as *tlixochitl*, used it to flavor their chocolate, which they imbided in the form of a spicy, unsweetened liquid.[94] Vanillin—an artificial form of vanilla—is still used to flavor chocolate by American confectioners.

Vanilla was introduced to Europe via Spain in the late 1500s. Soon the French were using it to flavor chocolate and to scent tobacco. Eventually, it won out over rose as the favored flavoring material and became widely popular.[104]

Magical uses: Because vanilla is linked in Totonac mythology with love, and due to its pleasant smell and taste, it follows that it is one of the prime love flavorings. Vanilla ice cream, vanilla pudding, and all foods that are flavored with vanilla are fine for use in love-expanding diets. For a simple vanilla-charged sweetener, place a whole vanilla bean in a sugar jar or canister. Let it sit until the sugar has absorbed the scent of the vanilla. Add to love foods.

Though the story of Xanat isn't widely known, it's curious that American woman once dabbed vanilla extract behind their ears as a magical love perfume to attract men.

Sexual activity in a loving relationship may also be enhanced by the addition of vanilla-flavored foods to the diet.

As much as I love Mexico, I must give one warning: do not use the "vainilla" extract commonly sold there at extremely low prices. This is made from tonka beans *(Dipteryx odorata),* not vanilla, and is toxic. Do not take internally!

Additionally, only real vanilla extract (or the beans them selves) should be used in magical cooking. Artificial vanilla extract, which may cost all of a dollar or two less, is magically inert and will have no effect.

CHAPTER THIRTEEN

Honey, Sugar, Chocolate, Carob, & Maple Syrup

You may try to eat right. You may be a vegetarian, avoid processed foods, and never darken a fast-food restaurant's doors. But sweets still haunt you. A bit of honeyed herbal tea. A dish of ice cream made with real sugar. Even—horrors!—that chocolate bar that you've been craving for several weeks.

The full story of the religious and magical uses of these substances down through the ages would fill several volumes. In this chapter we'll discuss honey, sugar, chocolate, carob, and maple syrup—and the ways in which you can gleefully utilize them with moderation in your magical diet.

Honey

(product of *Apis mellifera*)

Planet: Sun

Element: Air

Energies: Purification, health, love, sex, happiness, spirituality, wisdom, weight loss

Lore: The world's first sweetener, honey has been gathered since humans lived in European caves some 10,000

years ago. Ancient rock paintings depict humans gathering honey from hives.[71]

All early honey-using cultures attached myths and legends to the divine substance. Most employed it for magical and ritual purposes as well as for food.

According to one Egyptian myth, the god Ra wept. The tears that dripped from His eye turned into the bees that produced the first honey.[23] Honey was a favorite offering to Min, the Egyptian god usually depicted with an erection, who oversaw—among other things—human fertility.[23] The Egyptians also used honey in medicine; indeed it is both antiseptic and antibiotic.[50]

Honey's high cost in earlier times probably contributed to its divine status. In Egypt, Sumer, Babylon, Greece, and Rome, honey was used in offerings to the goddesses and gods. Assyrians dripped honey on to foundation stones and walls of temples as they were being built.[84] Honey was offered to Anu, Ea, Shamash, Marduk, Adad, Kittu, and almost every other Babylonian and Sumerian deity.[24]

The Greeks used honey as an elixir to restore and maintain youth. Aristotle called it "dew distilled from the stars and the rainbow."[84] Honey cakes were made and offered to sacred snakes in the Acropolis in Athens. Honey was also offered to the dead.[71]

The Romans believed honey was a magical substance that endowed those who ate it with poetry and eloquence. Pliny instructed his readers to eat it every day for good health and long life.[84]

In ancient Rome, a special drink was created at the completion of the harvest. It was made of honey, milk, and poppy juice. This was said to induce euphoria, happiness, and dizzy optimism. Not surprisingly, sleep usually followed.[84]

Throughout Europe, honey was associated with the Great Mother, who was also the provider of milk. Demeter, Artemis, Rhea, and Persephone are just a few of the goddesses associated with honey.[71,78] These two substances—honey and milk—are the only two items in our diet that are specifically created for food.[29]

The Indian love-god Kama's bowstring was purportedly made of very cooperative bees. In India, a newborn child's tongue is smeared with honey. Also in that country, milk and honey is presented to guests and to the bridegroom during wedding ceremonies. Hindu novices often fasted from honey (among other foods) because of its supposed aphrodisiac properties.[81]

In Central America and Mexico, honey was deemed sacred. The Maya so highly esteemed this substance that they made offerings of corn meal when removing honey from the hives.[109]

Throughout Europe and in many other parts of the world, honey was made into mead, an alcoholic beverage that is still enjoyed by many. Mead is a favorite drink among some Wiccan groups.

Honey may have been so honored because it is produced by bees, which is rather miraculous in itself. It can be eaten as food, used as medicine, or distilled into an intoxicating brew. A substance with so many properties must surely be divine.[22]

In the Middle Ages, when sugar was still unavailable, honey continued to be used for sweetening and for medicine. It was prescribed for "grumbling guts" and used to cleanse wounds.[104]

As previously mentioned in this book, Pagan Germanic tribes baked and ate honey cakes on the night of the winter solstice. The mystic power of honey was probably consumed to lend energy and strength to the celebrants for the hard winter months ahead.

These extraordinary records of the uses of honey point to the high regard in which it has been held. In earlier times, sweet foods in general were rare, and for many millennia honey was the most widely used sweetener. Though India had sugar cane, the ancient peoples who lived there seemed to prefer honey. In the Middle East, date syrup, fig syrup, and grape juice were all used to sweeten foods, but honey was the most favored.[104]

Surprisingly, the first inhabitants of the United States didn't eat honey, for the native bees produced only a vile-tasting, unhealthy variety. It wasn't until after the introduction of the honey bee by the colonists in 1625 that honey became a popular sweetening agent in the United States.[74]

We still cling to at least one vestige of honey's fabled history in our own culture. Honey has long been used at weddings, and the honeymoon honors two ancient traditions. Its purity was thought to protect the couple from evil,[84] and honey was also symbolic of love and wisdom—certainly two welcome attributes at marriages.

The term "honeymoon" refers to the old European custom in which a newly married couple drank mead (honey wine) for one lunar month following their wedding. The honeymoon was originally the period in which mead was shared by the newlyweds.[31]

Magical uses: Here's a quick list of some of the magical uses of honey. If you've decided to substitute honey for sugar, a wealth of opportunities await you.

Purification

Health and healing

Love

Sexuality (the French may have thought that bee stings were powerful aphrodisiacs, but eating honey is simpler and far less painful)

Happiness (especially during weddings)

Spirituality (especially related to Goddess worship)

Wisdom

Weight loss (use in place of sugar)

Honey isn't habit forming. Easily assimilated by the body, it doesn't give the same rush and subsequent drop that sugar produces. We've been eating honey for thousands of years. Haven't we known something?

Sugar

(product of *Saccharum officinarum*)

Planet: Venus

Element: Water

Energies: Love

Lore: As we've seen, honey was worshipped in the past. Many humans of today are likewise devoted to sugar, the most popular sweetener in the world.

Sugar originated in either New Guinea[6] or on the Indian subcontinent.[104] It was grown in gardens in India as early as 1400 B.C.E., and the stalks were used in medicine and for chewing.[6] The peoples of India may have first produced crudely refined sugar in about 500 B.C.E.[71] China had the knowledge and raw materials to refine sugar around 100 B.C.E.[23]

An admiral of the fleet of Alexander the Great, after a historic voyage to India, brought sugar back to Rome.[81] Pliny, who described the substance as "a kind of honey that collects in reeds," wrote that it was "used only for medicine" in ancient Rome.[86]

Though we're not quite sure how the Polynesians first came into contact with sugar, they spread the plant throughout the Pacific Ocean during the migrations from island group to island group.[6] Sugar was widely cultivated throughout the Pacific islands.

In Tahiti, sugar cane was thought to have been formed from the human spine, probably due to the appearance of its stiff, jointed stems.[77] The origin of human beings was also ascribed to this miraculous plant. In the Solomon Islands, a stalk of sugar cane produced two knots. When these burst open, a man and a woman stepped out of them. They were the parents of all who came after them.[77]

Many of us associate sugar with Hawaii, due to the aggressive advertising of C & H products. It seems certain that the Hawaiians brought sugar cane plants with them when they migrated to those volcanic islands.[6] Soon, the Hawaiians were hybridizing sugar, producing at least forty distinct varieties.[77] Sugar there was used for food, religion, medicine, and magic.

A myth states that Kane (pronounced KAH-nay), a benevolent agricultural deity worshipped throughout the Pacific, brought sugar cane to Hawaii. The plant was not only sacred to Him but was also a physical manifestation of the god.[47] A certain species of sugar, *manulele* (flying bird), was chewed in Hawaiian rituals to renew a wife's love for her husband.[77]

As recently as five hundred years ago, sugar was still a costly substance in Europe. Only the extremely wealthy could afford it. Courtiers offered small lumps of plain sugar, housed in silver boxes, to favored women. We continue the custom by giving presents of candy.[104]

About 1580, sugar came into more general use in Europe. We wouldn't recognize this early version, which was poorly refined, almost black, and smelled of molasses.[81] After the discovery that fruit and flowers could be preserved in sugar, much of it was used for these purposes.[104] Jam was probably first made in the 1700s.[104]

Sugar was severely rationed on the home front during World War II. Many Europeans and Americans dreamed of the days when it could be purchased in quantities and used for everything from canning to pickling to preserving.

Today, sugar is a firmly established part of our lives. Though nutritionists warn of its dangers, the artificial sweeteners that food scientists have created to replace it are usually more hazardous than sugar itself. Honey is the sole healthy alternative.

Magical uses: Ruled by Venus and by the element of water, sugar is a natural love-inducing food. Sweets of all kinds can be ritually prepared and eaten with visualization to bring love.

Don't misunderstand. While eating small amounts of sugar-sweetened foods can be an important part of love diets, sugar binges aren't magical. Control the amount of sweets that you eat or you'll be so saturated with sugar energy that you'll love only it—not yourself, not others. This isn't the best condition in which to look for a relationship with another human being.

As we know it, sugar is in a highly refined state. Small, plastic-wrapped pieces of sugar cane, however, are sometimes sold in grocery stores. Though they've been processed (to pass agricultural inspection), they're the closest available version of sugar in its natural state. To taste what the ancients knew as sugar, slice off the tough peel and chew the inner, light-brown middle of the stalk. It is sweet, but not overpoweringly so.

Today, sugar is produced from both cane and from the sugar beet. Sugar experts claim that no difference in taste between the two can be detected. It is curious that beets have long been used to promote love.

Sugar from either plant can be used with equal results, but cane sugar has a longer magical history behind its graceful, tasseled stalks.

Chocolate

(a product of *Theobroma cacao*)

Planet: Mars

Element: Fire

Energies: Love, money

Lore: Ahhh! Chocolate. Dark. Sweet. Dense. Chocolate cheese cake. Chocolate milk. Hot-fudge sundaes. Chocolate-covered strawberries. Chocolate two-layer cakes with chocolate frosting. Chocolate ice cream. Chocolate truffles. The plant from which these culinary wonders spring was aptly named *Theobroma,* meaning "food of the gods."[116, 120]

The trees are probably native to South America,[71] and were probably brought to what is now Mexico by the Mayas prior to C.E. 600.[71] Cocoa trees were extensively cultivated by the Aztecs and the Toltecs.[71]

The forerunner of today's chocolate milk was enjoyed by the Aztecs centuries ago. Then as now, cacao beans were fermented and dried for several days until they had developed the characteristic color and taste of chocolate. The beans were ground and placed in water with vanilla, chili peppers, and other flavorings. Annatto was added to produce a reddish color, and the drink was whipped with a wooden instrument made especially for this purpose. What was missing? Sugar, which was unknown to the Aztecs, as well as milk. [104, 120]

This beverage seems to have been drunk only by men of the upper classes, who could afford it. Women were probably forbidden to drink it, due to its legendary ability to arouse sexual desire.

Cacao beans (our word "cocoa" is actually a corruption of the word "cacao") were highly regarded among Mesoamerican peoples. The beans were used as money. They were an accepted medium of exchange and could be traded for everything from food to slaves.[71, 91, 120]

Among the Mazatec peoples of Oaxaca, Mexico, cacao beans represented wealth. Prior to a magical healing, the shaman bundled together a few cacao beans, an egg, some copal (a resin incense), and parrot feathers in bark cloth. The shaman then buried this package outside the home, probably as a sacrifice to the deities that had granted her or him healing powers.[109]

Once cocoa beans were introduced into Europe, the recipe for chocolate beverages changed. It was the Spaniards who added sugar to cocoa and made the drink popular among the nobility of that country. By the late 1600s, chocolate had become a popular drink in western Europe. The clergy soon attempted to stamp out the "sinful" practice of drinking chocolate, trying to link chocolate with the "sorceries" of the Aztecs who had created it. Fortunately, they didn't succeed.[71, 120]

In the 1800s, the first solid chocolate was produced. This "eating chocolate," rich, solid, and delicious, was the forerunner of the sweet substance as we know it today.[104]

Chocolate is produced from cocoa (the ground, dry powder); cocoa butter (which is removed from the seeds during processing and then added to the cocoa); sugar (to counteract the bitterness); and several other ingredients, depending upon its intended use and country of origin. Milk, vanillan, salt, and nuts are the other major ingredients.

The chocolate bar wasn't introduced until about 1910. During World War II, millions of Hershey's chocolate bars were packed into D-rations. The familiar brown bar reminded the soldiers and sailors of home and sustained them through days of continuous fighting. [71]

Today, chocolate is known and loved around the world. We all know "chocoholics," those people who can't seem to get through the day without eating their favorite food. Recently, psychiatrists have speculated that many people, particularly women, eat large amounts of chocolate in an attempt to heal themselves from the effects of emotional trauma. Chocolate contains phenylethylamine, a substance that lifts us from depression and that produces effects similar to those of amphetamines.[71] (This is why chocolate should never be eaten at night by those who suffer from insomnia.)

Magical uses: When summing up the historical, magical, emotional, and scientific information concerning chocolate, its role in magical diets becomes clear. Chocolate foods, in any form, can be used to increase our ability to give and to receive love. Chocolate is also suitable for increased money and prosperity.

Use this potent food with visualization. As you cook, do so with visualization. Spoon or slice with visualization. Eat with visualization. Limit your daily intake of chocolate for the best magical results.

Today, chocolate is a multibillion-dollar business. Whole magazines and books are devoted to the subject. Cocoa futures are a popular item in the commodities markets. We're deluged with advertising singing the wonders of chocolate. Chocolate-scented pencils, erasers, and even perfumes are available.

Many of our peers see chocolate as an indulgence or, to use a Christian term, even a sin. To the food magician, chocolate is but one of many tools that we can use to improve our lives. A delicious one, true, but simply one among hundreds of others.

Some people don't eat chocolate, and these words aren't meant to convince them to begin consuming the food of the gods. If you enjoy chocolate, however, isn't it pleasant to realize that every delicious bite can be a union of energies, and that a slice of chocolate cake can be an effective partner in a private magical ritual?

Carob

(Ceratonia siliqua)

Planet: Venus

Element: Water

Energies: Love, money

Lore: Carob, a chocolate substitute that has found favor among health-food aficionados, isn't new. Its pods were used to produce a sweet beer in ancient Egypt.[69] Carob seeds, which are remarkably uniform in size, are said to have once been used as a standard unit of weight. The jeweler's "carat" (as in a one-carat diamond) may have originally been the weight of one carob seed.[29, 64, 90]

In American and European folk magic, carob (also known as St. John's bread) was used to attract money and to guard health.

Magical uses: Carob doesn't taste much like chocolate. True, when the powdered pods (minus the seeds) are ground and made into various dishes, the foods look much like chocolate, but its taste will give carob away. However, carob is much more nutritious than chocolate, has less fat, and doesn't contain caffeine.[90]

Those who enjoy carob's intensely sweet flavor can use it in love-attracting diets. Eat carob-flavored foods with proper visualization.

Carob can also be consumed to draw additional money. Look in health-food stores for carob powder and many carob-flavored foods.

Maple Syrup

(Acer saccharum)

Planet: Jupiter

Element: Earth

Energies: Money, love

Lore: Maple trees are native to both Europe and America, but the Europeans never tapped the sweet sap of the tree or used it as a sweetener.[124]

Things were different here. Long before Christopher Columbus arrived on our shores, many American Indian tribes, including the Ojibway, the Iroquois, and the Algonquin, possessed myths concerning the maple tree and its sweet syrup.[71] Lacking honey, Native Americans used maple sugar and, where the maples don't grow, fruit juice for sweetening foods.

By the 1700s, the settlers were using maple syrup as a medicine, particularly for colds and rheumatism.[111] Thomas Jefferson so liked maple syrup that he planted a grove of the trees and used no other sweetener.[111]

Magical uses: Maple syrup and maple sugar are now more expensive than sugar. Two hundred years ago, sugar was the more costly. Most maple syrup is still produced by hand in the United States and Canada.

Both maple syrup and maple sugar are fine sweeteners for use in money-attracting diets. Before adding the syrup to a recipe (or putting it on to your morning cereal), pour it on to a clean place in the shape of a dollar sign, while visualizing. Scrape it off with a spatula and then enjoy your food.

Maple sugar and syrup are also powerful love-stimulants.

There are many "maple" syrups on the market today. Most of these contain less than 10 percent maple syrup and all are artificially preserved. For true maple magic, use genuine, 100 percent pure maple syrup. This is sold in small bottles at fairly high prices. Maple sugar (available in health-food stores) can also be used.

CHAPTER FOURTEEN

Nuts & Alleged Nuts

I once despised nuts. To the young kid that I once was, they were dry, hard to chew, and came in difficult-to-open packages. I eventually realized that there were other varieties besides walnuts (which I still don't relish), and that even cracking them could be fun.

The title of this chapter refers to foods often mistaken for nuts (brazil nuts) as well as at least one substance (sesame) that, though a seed, has a nutty flavor.

It is curious that one contemporary slang term for insanity is "nuts," as in, "That politician's gone nuts." In the past, these crunchy foods were thought to bestow wisdom, not mental derangement.*

In any case, nuts are gifts from trees, the largest vegetable life forms on our planet. Trees were once worshipped as deities, or as the abodes of divine beings and spirits; nuts, the fruits of these trees, were sacred and magical.

Generally speaking, all nuts were thought to be useful for promoting physical fertility—the ability to produce children. Heart-shaped nuts were carried to promote love,

---

*Then again, wisdom and insanity are often subjectively determined.

while all double nuts (those rarities in which two nuts are formed within the shell) were considered to be the luckiest of all.

Today, we're rediscovering the importance of nuts in our diets. Here are some reasons why we should eat more of them.

Almond

(Prunus dulcis)

Planet: Mercury

Element: Air

Energies: Money, healing

Lore: In the past, five almonds eaten before drinking were believed to prevent intoxication. They probably would—if the taste of the nut changed one's mind about imbibing.[120]

In what was once known as Persia (modern-day Iran), almonds were used to cure insomnia, to stimulate lactation in nursing mothers, to relieve headache, and to guard against the evil eye.[120] Today, candied almonds are given as presents to the guests at Italian weddings.

Magical uses: Eat fresh almonds, roasted almonds, or other almond dishes to bring money into your life. Or, crunch these delicious nuts to stimulate health and to speed the body's healing processes. Eat with visualization!

Marzipan, an Arabic invention,[104] can also be eaten for these uses.

Brazil Nut

(Bertholletia excelsa)

Planet: Venus

Element: Earth

Energies: Love, money

Magical uses: This food, which is technically a fruit, is a delicious addition to love-inducing diets. Make banana bread with chopped brazil nuts for a potent love loaf.

Brazil "nuts" can also be used to bring increased money and prosperity. To do this, draw a small five-pointed star on the "nut" with visualization and eat.

Cashew

(Anacardium occidentale)

Planet: Sun

Element: Fire

Energies: Money

Magical uses: These nuts can be eaten to increase your income. Tasty Yuletide cookies created with cashews are perfect for this use, as is the Chinese dish of "cashew chicken." Or, eat them right out of the bag.

Chestnut

(Castanea spp.)

Planet: Sun

Element: Air

Energies: Love, conscious mind

Lore: At one time, Europeans left chestnuts on the table after eating supper on Samhain (November 1) to nourish the poor deceased souls of the dead.[61]

Magical uses: Roasted chestnuts, immortalized in the classic Nat King Cole song, are an excellent inducement to love. Though you might be tired of reading this, do remember to eat them with visualization. Chestnuts are also consumed to strengthen the conscious mind.

Coconut

(Cocos nucifera)

Planet: Moon

Element: Water

Energies: Spirituality, psychic awareness, purification

Lore: The coconut is one of the world's most useful trees. As many as three hundred products can be made from the fruit, husk, flower stalks, leaves, and trunk. Found in tropical areas around the world, it was probably spread from its currently unknown place of origin by ocean currents and by the migration of humans.

In ancient Hawaii, coconut was offered to many deities, including Kane. Coconut groves were worshipped as spiritual places linked with the divine.[7] Throughout the Pacific, Hina, goddess of the moon, is linked with the creation of the original coconut.[7]

Magical uses: This white, round nut would naturally have lunar symbolism, with all that implies—moistness, love, spirituality. Eat fresh coconut before or during rituals designed to boost your spiritual awareness. It is also a fine psychic-awareness food. Coconut is also useful for inner purification, if eaten with the proper visualization.

Whole coconuts are kept in the kitchen for power. Fresh coconut is best for magical and culinary purposes, but the shredded, packaged kind will do in a pinch.

Hazelnut

(Corylus spp.)

Planet: Sun

Element: Air

Energies: Wisdom, conscious mind, fertility

Lore: This tree, and its round, delicious nuts, played important roles in European folklore and folk religion. Linked with deities of the sky, the hazel was considered a guardian against lightning, damaging storms, and fire.[37] Hazelnuts were once placed into small bags and given to the bride on her wedding day.[114]

Magical uses: The hazelnut is thought to bestow wisdom on those who eat it. Wisdom isn't merely the accumulation of knowledge; it is the ability to correctly assimilate and utilize information. Hazelnuts stimulate the conscious mind in order to bring us closer to wisdom.

The nuts are age-old symbols of fertility, and so can be eaten with visualization if this is a problem.

Macadamia

(Macadamia spp.)

Planet: Jupiter

Element: Earth

Energies: Money

Lore: There is little ancient lore concerning macadamia nuts. Native to Australia, they have become quite popular in the United States in the last fifty or so years. The best crops are grown on the Big Island of Hawaii.

Magical uses: Nutritionists describe the macadamia as "the richest nut." Though high in calories, the macadamia has an unmatched taste. Eat macadamias—plain, made into candied brittle, or in pies—to manifest increased money in your life. But be prepared to pay handsomely for these yellowish-brown treats.

Peanut

(Arachea hypogaea)

Planet: Jupiter

Element: Earth

Energies: Money

Lore: Peanuts have an ancient history. Native to South America,[71] they were extensively cultivated by the Aztecs and the Mayas.[120] Soon after the conquest of Mexico, the Spaniards and the Portuguese brought the peanut to Spain, Africa, the Philippines, Java, China, and Japan. It soon became an important food crop around the world.[71]

Here in the United States, however, peanuts were looked down upon as a food of slaves and of slaveowners.[120] If not for the untiring efforts of the Afro-American botanist, statesman, chemist, and educator George Washington Carver, we might not be enjoying peanut butter sandwiches, ice creams, and brittle today.

Magical uses: This is another nut that is not (a nut, that is). Peanuts are actually seeds that grow underground.[71]

Raw or roasted peanuts are powerful money attractants. They can be eaten in any form, with visualization, to increase prosperity. Peanut butter.and grape jelly sandwiches are an excellent money food, particularly if made with oat bread.

Pecan

(Carya illinoensis)

Planet: Mercury

Element: Air

Energies: Money, employment

Magical uses: The word *pecan* is Algonquin.

I've always admired the exquisite gooiness of pecan pie. I was introduced to the wonderful flavor of pecan cake on my second visit to New Orleans, and have added this treat to my roster of magical foods.

Both of these dishes, as well as pecan pralines, pecan butter, pralines-and-cream ice cream, or anything else made with pecans, can be eaten as a part of money diets. The plain nuts themselves can also be enjoyed by themselves.

Eat pecans when seeking employment.

Pine Nut

(Pinus spp.)

Planet: Mars

Element: Air

Energies: Money, physical strength, love

Lore: Pine seeds were an important part of the diets of many American Indian tribes, for whom these "nuts" were a major food source.[33] They were also known and eaten throughout the Mediterranean region.[61] To the Chinese, they symbolize friendship and constancy. Pine nuts are actually naked seeds.

Magical uses: Visualize and eat pine nuts for money. Or, eat them for physical strength, as the ancient Romans did. Pine nuts can also be used to promote all forms of love.

Pistachio

(Pistachia vera)

Planet: Mercury

Element: Air

Energies: Love

Lore: Native to Asia, the pistachio has been consumed since at least 7000 B.C.E.[71] I find it curious that processed foods containing pistachios, such as puddings, are artificially colored green, while the shells themselves are often dyed red.

Magical uses: Eat pistachios for love.

Sesame

(Sesamum indicum)

Planet: Sun

Element: Fire

Energies: Sex, fertility, money, protection

Lore: Sesame was known in Egypt since at least 200 B.C.E., and possibly earlier.[23] Grecian brides received sesame cakes as symbols of fruitfulness. In ancient Athens, the seeds may also have been connected with serpent worship. In Rome, sesame was sacred to Hecate, goddess of the crossroads and of the Waning Moon.[35]

Ancient Babylonian women ate *halvah,* a sweet food made of sesame seeds and honey, to encourage the desire for sexual relations and to enhance their sexual attractiveness.[15]

An old ritual of unknown origin: "So men know not the evil that you do, mix eleven grains of wheat with sesame seed and wine and the juice of a (nonpoisonous) yellow flower and drink it daily."

Magical uses: Sesame was once known as the most fruitful of all plants. Women can follow the example of their ancient Babylonian counterparts by eating the seeds to stimulate sexual feelings. Sesame is also useful for encouraging conception.

Sesame-flavored foods can be eaten, or sesame seeds can be sprinkled onto foods, to draw money. With proper visualization, the seeds are also used for protection.

Walnut

(Juglans regia)

Planet: Sun

Element: Fire

Energies: Conscious mind, protection

Lore: Walnuts are native to North America, Asia, and Europe.[71] The ancient Greeks believed walnuts to be one of the foods eaten by the goddesses and gods.[64] Walnuts were used to treat problems of the brain in European folk medicine (because of this nut's remarkable resemblance to this organ).

These are the nuts that I didn't enjoy as a child. I still don't like them, but many people do. These furrowed nuts can be eaten for increased intellectual abilities. Alternately, walnuts can be added to protective diets.

CHAPTER FIFTEEN

Salt, Vinegar, Soup, & Noodles

Okay, okay. So maybe these subjects don't have much in common. I just couldn't find any other place for them.

Salt

(a mineral, sodium chloride)

Planet: Earth

Element: Earth

Energies: Grounding, stopping psychic awareness, protection

Lore: In the ancient world, salt was created by three processes: mining in the earth from long-dry ocean beds; boiling the water collected from salty springs until only the mineral was left; and evaporating sea water in flat lakes or salt pans.[104] This last method is still in use throughout the world and, indeed, the Morton Salt company has just such an operation less than twenty miles from where I sit writing this. Salt pans, carved from volcanic rock at the edge of the Pacific Ocean, can still be seen in many coastal areas of the world.

In the past, salt was one of the most sought-after substances. Human life is not possible without some salt in the diet, for the body cannot produce salt on its own. One theory suggests that our dependence upon salt is a vestige of the past. A popular theory (now somewhat disputed) states that all life emerged from the salty, briny sea.[23]

Those peoples far from the sea or from salt deposits had to be content with eating naturally salty foods and meat.[104] The salt trader's cargo was more precious than gold, and they were constantly subject to attack.

Salt played important roles in early religions. Some priests and priestesses of ancient Egypt were forbidden to eat salt due to its connection with the god Set.[23] Other sects, however, did use salt. The Greek historian Herodotus records that during one Isian festival, which included lamentations at the death of Osiris, lamps were lit after being filled with a mixture of oil and salt.[23]

Though the Greeks didn't add salt to their sacrifices until a rather late date,[23] they and the Romans dedicated salt to Poseidon and Neptune. Tiamat, the ancient Sumerian goddess of the sea, was also offered salt in ritual.[23] These uses are obvious acknowledgements of the link between salt and the ocean.

Roman soldiers were paid "salaries" with salt, and the substance was so precious that anyone caught selling it to the enemy was put to death.[23]

The Finnish sky god, Ukko, was credited with creating salt. He threw a spark of heavenly fire into the sea, thereby making the once-sweet water salty.

There are few records of salt use in the New World, but we do know that the Aztecs worshipped Huixtocihuatl, the salt goddess.[80]

The sacralness of salt lives on. While cooking, some Arab women throw pinches of salt across soups and stews with the belief that it will blind and drive away any demons that may be hovering over the food.[57] In contemporary Iran, a frightened person pushes a finger into salt and then puts it on to the tongue to remove fear.

The Japanese dispel unwelcome guests by sprinkling salt over the house entrance. Every morning, some restaurant-owners place small piles of salt at the entrance to their businesses, one on either side of the door. This attracts prosperity and customers to the business.[54]

Spilling salt is a negative omen throughout the English-speaking world, though this superstition is slowly disappearing.

One of the greatest teachers of our era, Mahatma Gandhi, began India's peaceful independence movement by publicly marching with many of his followers to Dandi. There he made salt—an illegal activity for private citizens.[104]

Magical uses: In magic, add salt to grounding diets if you've kept your head in the clouds for too long. Small amounts are sufficient to effect a refocus from the spiritual to the physical world.

Salt is useful in shutting down psychic awareness, so avoid eating salted foods if you're trying to accomplish just the opposite.

Small amounts of salt are added, with visualization, to protective and money-attracting foods. An overabundance of salt in the diet, however, will cause serious physical problems. The disease or ill health that will result greatly diminishes psychic protection. Eat salt moderately!

Vinegar

Planet: Saturn

Element: Fire

Energies: Purification, Protection

Lore: The first vinegar consisted of wine that had "turned." According to contemporary American folklore, giving away vinegar is tantamount to giving away "luck."[46]

Magical uses: We know this tangy, acidic liquid from its use in pickling and salad dressings. But vinegar is quite useful in magical diets. (Use only apple-cider vinegar. White vinegar shouldn't be used internally.)

Folk magicians wash quartz crystals in a mixture of water and vinegar to purify them. Similarly, a few drops of vinegar placed in a glass of water (or added to such foods as salad dressings) are used to purify our bodies, minds, and emotions.

Fill three small, shallow vessels with vinegar. Place these around the house to remove negativity. Drain the bowls and refill as necessary.

Vinegar is also protective. For a potent protective food, slice one raw onion. Place into a bowl and add equal amounts of vinegar and water to cover. Let sit, covered, in a cool place for twenty-four hours. Eat the onions as a zesty, protective relish during meals.

Soups

Generally speaking, soups are ruled by the moon and by the element of water. Here are two famous soups and some of their magical lore.

Bird's-Nest Soup. Many Westerners have heard of this Chinese delicacy. The price for the raw nests is currently around one thousand dollars a pound, due to the increasing difficulty in collecting them. The birds (a certain kind of swallow) build their nests in virtually inaccessible cliffs in China, Malaysia, Thailand, Indonesia, and Vietnam. Demand always outstrips supply, for there are many throughout Asia who love a good bowl of bird's- nest soup.

This tempting delicacy isn't made from sticks and twigs, as I once thought, but from the hardened strips of the birds' saliva, which they use to build their nests. The substance is washed and cleaned of extraneous matter until it is a mass of white, sponge-like material.

Bird's-nest soup can be eaten for pure enjoyment (though crab, shrimp, and ham are often added to the thirty-five-dollar bowl of soup to enhance its taste). Usually, however, it's consumed for magical purposes.

The soup is believed to provide youth and health to its diners, to clear women's skin, and to remove all forms of blemishes. Bird's-nest soup is eaten before important examinations in order to ensure success. Regularly eating bird's-nest soup is thought to maintain health, and it is also considered to be a potent sex arouser.[29]

Few of us will ever eat it, but it's an intriguing food that had to be included here.

Chicken Soup. The ancient peoples of Harappa, in the Indus Valley, were probably the first to domesticate the jungle fowl. This once-wild bird eventually became the chicken, and spread throughout the world.[104]

One of our favorite cures for the common cold, chicken soup has been proven in scientific tests to have some benefits. Drinking hot chicken soup clears the sinuses and relieves stuffiness.[21] This is thought to eventually kill the viruses that cause colds.

A pregnant woman in Chad (an equatorial African country) is warned not to eat chicken. If she does, she'll suffer a painful childbirth, and the child itself may even be deformed.[29]

In contemporary Egypt, the exact reverse is believed. Pregnant women eat chicken to supply the extra strength needed during the birthing process. Egyptian men eat chicken soup to promote virility. A man about to be married will down gallons of the stuff for several days before his marriage, so as not to have a disappointing wedding night.[23]

Noodles

I've already mentioned soba, the buckwheat noodles that the Japanese eat for money (see chapter 8). Noodles almost certainly originated in ancient China and spread from there to India, the Middle East, and finally to Europe.[104] Some claim that Italy created them, but this is doubtful. It is curious that many Italian and Chinese dishes that utilize noodles are somewhat similar. Spaghetti is popularly believed to have been introduced into Italy by Marco Polo upon his triumphant return from the Far East (but I'm *not* getting into this argument).[104]

Noodles are a staple food throughout China and Japan. In rural Japan, every town has a noodle shop. Running water may be provided by pierced bamboo poles that divert a stream right through the store. Farmers flock to these shops to eat the hot, nourishing noodles.

In China, noodles are symbols of long life. They are eaten on special occasions, such as anniversaries and birthdays, to bring success and good fortune. deTraci Regula, a friend of mine, says that to eat a long noodle on the Chinese New Year's Day brings only the best of "luck" during the coming year.

CHAPTER SIXTEEN

Food from Sea & River

The ocean has always been worshipped by peoples living near its great expanses. Deities rode the waves or lay submerged, far beyond where human eyes could see them. As late as the 1600s, unearthly monsters were believed to live in the sea's briny depths, and early maps were marked "Here Bee Monsters" across lonely expanses of the ocean.

The foods of the sea continue to feed millions of people today, as they have in the past. Though we would probably find many of these species repulsive (such as the sea worms that are considered delicacies throughout the South Pacific), many kinds of fish have been eaten for thousands of years.

Fish

Lore: The Egyptian god Ra was reputedly guided on his journey into the underworld by a fish. Naturally, this specific type of fish was eaten to relieve blindness in ancient Egypt.[23] The Egyptians offered fish to Isis, Amon, Aten, Ra, Amon-Ra, Khnum, Hapy, and many other deities. Priests dedicated to Osiris didn't eat certain kinds of fish due to their mythological entangle-ments.[23] Thousands of mummified fish have been found in Egyptian tombs and temples.

Fish were sacred to Ishtar in ancient Babylon and probably also to her predecessor, Inanna, in Sumer.[12] In Assyrian myth, one of the finned creatures pushed an egg from the Euphrates River onto the shore. The goddess Atargatis hatched from it. This divine act caused all fish to be worshipped and spared from the cook's art.[79]

In Greece and Rome, fish were sacred to oceanic deities such as Poseidon and Neptune, to Venus, and to other god-desses and gods—but they were eaten by all.

The old Hawaiians saw similarities between some of their deities and the astonishing fish that swim and flip around their islands. Kane and Pele were both linked with the *oopu* (a freshwater fish). It was hazardous to eat fish that were sacred to the family's particular deity.[7] There are many "fish stories" in Hawaiian mythology, such as the following.

A man from the island of Molokai caught some oopu fish, tied them up in the leaves, and set them on to a fire to cook. The fish suddenly spoke to him (because he wasn't supposed to eat it), and the poor man ran away in terror.[7]

Fish hooks, once the most important food-gathering device, are symbols of good fortune in Hawaii, where they are still worn. An Omnimax/Imax film, *Beyond Hawaii,* is centered around a fish hook that takes a Hawaiian youth on a trip into his people's past. In the night skies over Hawaii, the constella-tion Scorpio is thought to be Maui's fish hook.

In China, fish are thought to be transformed birds, while birds are fish that have gone through a transmutation. The fish is a symbol of freedom, harmony, and emancipation. Two fish are given to a newly wedded couple in the belief that the finny creatures will bring them joyous sexual union.[3]

The sacralness of the fish seems due to its ability to live in complete harmony with its environment, to its prolific egg-lay-ing capability, and to our early dependence on it for food. The Mediterranean goddesses connected with love were usually also associated with water and the ocean, which explains why fish were also used for courtship and marriage rituals in Europe.

Magical uses: Fish swim in the sea, in rivers, and in lakes. Water magically strengthens psychic awareness. Fish are also easier to digest than meat. These factors indicate that fish are fine for those wishing to increase psychic awareness. Poached fish, fish stews, and soups are particularly potent for this purpose.

Due to their long association with love, fish are also excellent foods to consume in order to expand your ability to give and to receive love.

Caviar and fish have also been thought to be aphrodisiacs. If interest in sexual activity is a problem, eat fish and visualize.

To close this section, here's a Victorian folk ritual that seems to have been popular in England a hundred years ago: on Halloween night, just before going to sleep, eat a raw or roasted salt herring. Don't drink any liquid with it. Don't even brush your teeth. Go to bed. As you sleep, you'll have a dream. In that dream, the man or woman who is to become your husband or wife will come to you with a glass of water to quench your thirst. To many young Victorians, such a ritual must have offered a tantalizing glimpse of the future.

Crab

Lore: These bizarre creatures have always been viewed with suspicion and a bit of awe. Their shells and unusual manner of walking are striking. I once read with shivers about some coral atolls in the South Pacific that are periodically covered with crabs. The strange creatures walk across the islands from one side to the other, scrambling over everything in their path.

To the Japanese, crabs were magical. Dried crab shells were often nailed over doorways of Japanese homes. This wasn't for decoration, but was meant to drive away evil and to keep those who lived within the house healthy and free of disease.[54]

One type of crab, known as *heike-gani,* is especially revered. The unusual markings on the crab's shell roughly resemble the outlines of a human face. The Japanese believed that these crabs were the incarnations of warriors who were defeated and drowned at Dannoura in the Inland Sea.[54]

Magical uses: Crab is another food said to have aphrodisiac properties.

Shellfish

Lore: We've all heard the stories of the gigantic clams *(Tridacna noa)* of the South Pacific. A diver accidentally pushes a leg between the calm's massive shells. They close around the leg, and the diver is subsequently drowned by the fierce, treacherous clam.

These are myths, of course. The clams aren't dangerous. It's impossible to trap a leg or arm between their "jaws." It'd be dangerous to have one of the shells thrown at you, but that's the extent of the clam's possible hazards.

Throughout the world (in the South Pacific, the Americas, in the Middle East, Asia, and elsewhere), clam shells have been used as money, for decoration, and as ritual implements.*

Disc-shaped beads of hardshelled clams, known as *wampum,* were used as money, as a tool of ceremonial exchange, and to send messages by Indians of the eastern coast of the United States. Wampum grew in favor until, in the 1600s, it became a legal form of currency in both English and Dutch colonies in America.

Magical uses: Like all seafoods, shellfish have long been eaten to induce the desire for sexual activity. Clam chowder is perhaps a bit heavy for this purpose, but any other form is fine. Shellfish can also be eaten as a part of psychic-awareness diets.

---

*A wonderul book on this subject is *Spirals From the Sea: An Anthropological Look at Shells* by Jane Fearer Safer and Frances MacLaughlin Gill. New York: Clarkson N. Potter, 1982.

Sushi

I'll admit that I've never been to a sushi bar; never eaten sea urchin (*uni*); never spent fifty to a hundred bucks to stuff my face with small, exquisitely prepared foods. But I've read up on the subject, and many of my friends have been initiated into the wonders of this particularly Japanese form of food preparation.

Though sushi preparation is quite complex, it generally consists of seafood, seaweed, rice, and some fresh vegetables. These ingredients make sushi an excellent addition to psychic-awareness diets. (Tragically, I've heard that some of the newest foods being used in sushi preparation in Japan are the avocado . . . and Spam.)

One favored food often found in Japanese sushi bars has long been banned from being served in the United States. Recently, permission was granted for a team of Japanese chefs to fly from their island nation to the U.S., bringing with them a treasured cargo: *fugu*. Fugu is responsible for many deaths each year in Japan. This dish looks innocuous enough—thin, almost transparent slices of fish.

The blowfish, however, from which it is prepared, is poisonous. Only the most experienced sushi chefs are allowed to prepare fugu. They remove the most poisonous parts. Even so, the fish is said to produce a slight numbness in the diner. If incorrectly prepared, the fish causes death.[54]

In Japan, fugu is one of the most expensive dishes on the sushi bar. It is also the most hazardous. Even if I do go to a sushi bar, I doubt that I'll ask the chef for fugu.

CHAPTER SEVENTEEN

Beer, Wine, & Alcoholic Beverages*

The first alcoholic beverages were the result of accidents. A jar of honey, mixed with water, sat for too long and began to bubble. Grape juice went bad. Coconut sap was left for one day too many in a gourd. Bread dough seemed to come to life. It is likely—although by no means certain—that the first alcoholic beverage was produced from honey at least 10,000 years ago.

By 3000 B.C.E., alcoholic beverages were of enormous importance in Mesopotamia. Beer (wine arrived later), with its undeniable effects upon those who drank it, was a sacred liquid that was used in ritual as well as daily life.

In the Middle East, wine quickly grew in acceptance. Sake was created in Asia. The secrets of fermentation, so necessary to the production of bread, were used throughout the ancient world in creating alcoholic beverages.

While reading this chapter, keep in mind that all societies have approved of at least one or two substances that altered consciousness. The Siberians had *Amanita muscaria*; early Mesoamerican peoples used a different but still

*This chapter shouldn't be construed as a recommendation to drink alcohol. If you do, drink moderately, and let someone else drive home. If you don't drink, don't start.

potent variety of mushroom *(Psilocybe* spp.); a certain type of sage *(Saliva divinorum);* and Datura were used by various American Indian tribes. Throughout South America, hallucinogenic plants such as *ayahuasca (Banisteriopsis caapi)* were ritually consumed. Fermented beverages were favored in many parts of Africa, and Polynesians called upon the sacred *avá* or *kava (Piper methysticum)*. Early Europeans, as we shall see, drank beer, ale, and wine.[58, 123]

Though there have always been those who abuse consciousness-altering substances, such drugs were often restricted to specific religious and magical ceremonies. They weren't purely recreational tools.

In the United States, alcohol is the only legally accepted drug of this type. Chocolate, sugar, coffee, tea, and tobacco can also be classified as drugs, though they aren't considered to be in the same league as alcohol. Yet many other mind-altering "drugs" of chemical or vegetable origin, whether prescribed or sold on the street, haven't caused the damage that alcohol has in our society.

In direct contrast to earlier times, most present-day metaphysical and magical organizations in the West forbid the use of any form of intoxicants, including alcohol, prior to ritual. Many of them do drink wine during the festivities that follow, but rituals aren't excuses for drug use.

This chapter examines the religious and magical uses of some of the major forms of alcohol.

Beer

Planet: Mars

Element: Fire

Energies: Purification

Lore: Beer was probably first deliberately made in Neolithic times.[104] Women almost certainly invented it along with raised bread, which was likewise dependent upon fermentation.

The earliest Mesopotamian civilizations drank and revered beer. Predynastic Egyptians enjoyed this beverage as early as 5000 B.C.E. Sumerian tablets dating to 2800 B.C.E. mention nineteen different types of beer.[29] The first public beerhouse ("bar") seems to have been established in Egypt in 1913 B.C.E.

Later, Isis was thought to have taught Her children the secrets of beermaking.[23] Hathor, the goddess of drunkenness, was also believed to have invented beer.[23] In ancient Egypt, inebriation was a source of mirth and may have been related to religious ecstasy.[23]

Beer was an integral part of Egyptian life, and even had a place in dream interpretation. Dreaming of drinking beer made of wheat foretold joy, while dreams of drinking barley beer meant the dreamer would continue to live.[23]

Aside from its use as a food, medicine, and ritual offering, beer was also utilized in magic. To prevent disturbing dreams, certain herbs were moistened with beer; the wet leaves were then rubbed on the dreamer's face while an incantation was spoken.[23]

The Sumerians, Egyptians, and Babylonians brewed beer with wheat and barley, but barley beer was their preferred beverage. It was the most popular drink for both humans and their deities in the ancient world—until wine took its place.

Magical uses: Today, beer is used in folk magic to purify the mind, body and soul. Add a half a cup of beer to a tub of water and soak.

Or, drink a bit of it (just that much, a bit) to purify yourself from the inside out. Hold the glass with both hands and visualize before drinking.

Some physicians recommend drinking a glass of beer or ale after meals to promote digestion. Because proper digestion is essential to our health, and because *small* amounts of beer are healthy for most individuals, beer can also be added to health diets. (Small here doesn't refer to a six-pack. Six *ounces* is fine.)

Guzzling beer was once accepted as a religious practice. However, drunkenness is no longer construed to be sacred in any meaning of the word.

Wine

Planet: Sun, (red wine); Moon (white wine)

Element: Fire

Energies: Celebrations

Lore: Beer was once the favored drink in ancient Mesopotamia, but people soon learned to produce wine by fermenting dates, sesame seeds, and other foods.[117] Later, grape wine was created. Countless bottles of wine were poured out as offerings to the gods and goddesses.[23]

The earliest wine deities were female. Goddesses lurked among the grapes and offered their fermented delights to humans. Among these early deities was Gestin, the Sumerian goddess of the vine.[117]

Around 3000 B.C.E., evidence suggests that the city of Kish was the home of a famous female wine merchant. Her name, Azag Bau, was also that of a queen, and the two personages may have been one and the same. A thousand years later, priestesses attached to various temples still made and sold wine.[117]

The wine goddess Pagat, who was worshipped in Ugarit circa 2000 B.C.E., apparently helped Danel, her father, to cultivate grapes and therefore to produce wine.[117]

Wine was a most acceptable offering in the days of old Mesopotamia. Ishtar was offered twelve vases of wine every day, and Nana, ten. The god Anu was given eighteen gold vases of beer and wine. Nebuchadnezzar poured out rivers of wine to Marduk, according to his scribes. The goddesses and gods, who were patterned after their human worshippers, were thought to enjoy drinking and even drunkenness.[117]

By 3000 B.C.E., the Egyptians had associated Osiris with wine. One of his many titles was "Lord of Wine at the Innundation,"[117] and Osiris is thought to have taught the people of Egypt the cultivation of grapes." Horus was also linked with wine. Red wine represented the right eye of Horus, white the left.[117]

In the earliest Egyptian dynasties, wine was reserved solely for the higher classes. It was also used during temple rituals. Priests (and priestesses) grew the grapes and produced the wine. Commoners apparently didn't drink the divine liquid until rather late in Egypt's long history, perhaps around 1000 B.C.E. [104]

In ancient Egypt, circa 1500 B.C.E., the presence of the snake goddess Renenutet ("giver of plenty") was invoked during wine making. On or near the wine press, in which grapes were transformed into juice, were shrines or small figures of Renenutet.[117]

As popular as grape wine became, however, the rich of ancient Egypt continued to enjoy a variety of wines, including those made from dates and, in the last dynasties, pomegranates.[117] Wine was a favored offering in this land. Ramses III reportedly offered 152,103 jars of wine to temples in Thebes, Heliopolis, and Memphis.[23] Wines of all types were placed among the grave goods left to nourish the dead pharaoh,[23] with the hope that he would continue to enjoy the beverages in the next life.

Wine was used in libations to the gods in ancient Greece, and was appreciated by the populace as a beverage. Like the Romans who followed them, the Greeks drank wine diluted with water to avoid the specter of Mothon, the goblin of drunkenness. (Unless, of course, they were busy worshipping the Greek deity of wine and drunkenness, Dionysius.)[117]

Wine was just as popular in ancient Crete. It was offered to the Cretan deities, including both Poseidon and Dionysius prior to the introduction of their worship into Greece.[117]

Ancient Rome had some curious ideas concerning wine. For the first few years after the founding of Rome, women were forbidden to drink wine in that city. Any caught doing so could be executed.[117] Wine continued to be a popular sacrificial libation, but only for certain deities. For others, wine was proscribed.[117]

Roman wines became famous in the second century C.E. Rome sold wine to Gaul and to Britain, where previously only ale and mead were drunk. After Rome invaded Britain, wine became an accepted drink there.[117]

Roman wines were made with grapes and flavored with various flowers and herbs. Roses, violets, myrrh, wormwood, and pepper, as well as honey, were all added to change the taste of the drink. To add further flavor, the vats in which wine was made were fumigated with rosemary, myrtle, bay, and myrrh.[117]

The Roman god of wine, Liber (or Liber Pater), never achieved a great following. Bacchus was the Roman version of Dionysius but, like Liber, didn't ascend to the vine-covered throne which Dionysius had once occupied.[117]

Wine continues to play an important religious role. Most notably, it is used in the Catholic Church as part of its most holy ceremony, during which wine is mystically transformed into the blood of Jesus.

Wine is also drunk as a part of a ritual meal in contemporary Wiccan ceremonies. Wine and crescent-shaped cakes are passed among the participants. The wine and cakes represent the bounties of the Goddess and God, and the ritual (sometimes known as Cakes and Wine) "earths" the power that was raised during the ceremony that preceded it. Such ritual imbibings date back centuries prior to the Christian era.

Magical uses: In general, white wines are associated with the moon, and red with the sun. Wine is a wonderful relaxant for the body, and a glass a day won't harm anyone who is in good health.

Don't drink alcohol prior to performing any sort of magical ritual. Too much alcohol will dull reflexes and mist the brain. Alcohol prevents the success of a magical ritual. Wine's best use is during celebrations following all sorts of magical rites and religious observances.

Other Alcoholic Beverages

Absinthe. This dangerous beverage was once quite popular, until it was found that drinking the liqueur (which was flavored with wormwood, *Artemesia absinthium,* among other plants) caused permanent damage to the body and nervous system.[28] Brain cortex lesions were apparently common among heavy absinthe drinkers.[1] Absinthe has been banned in the United States and in several European countries since 1915,[1] but some still seek it out as an aphrodisiac beverage. It is too dangerous to consider drinking.

Anisette. Sometimes drunk for purification.

Apricot brandy. Sometimes drunk to instill the desire for sexual activity.

Blackberry brandy. Can be drunk for money and for sexual arousal.

Brandy. Contemporary Mazatec shamans offer brandy to the "spirits" during rituals.[109] Brandy was also an ingredient in Renaissance magical incenses.

Chartreuse. Because this green liqueur contains basil, it is sometimes used as an aphrodisiac.

Cognac. This is said to induce love—as are all other alcoholic beverages. Cognac probably has as much of an effect as the rest of them, but "love" here should be read as "lust."

Creme de cacao. Sometimes drunk for love and money.

Creme de menthe. A purificatory liqueur.

Gin. A common contemporary offering to Pele, goddess of volcanoes, who lives in Halemaumau on the Big Island of

Hawaii. This is a modern version of the items once thrown into the crater—flowers, fruit and sometimes animals—but no living human beings. Pele took human lives by sending lava, smoke, and ash to quench them.

Kirsch. This cherry-flavored liqueur is sometimes drunk for love.

Kummel. The German liqueur, often served after heavy meals, is flavored with caraway. Small amounts can be sipped—with proper visualization—for health and protection.

Mead. Honey wine is still available. It is drunk as a part of love diets or during post-ritual celebrations with others.

Mezcal. A potent alcoholic beverage distilled from the fermented juice of the *maquey,* or century plant. Bottles of true mescal often contain an agave worm.[90] The worm, when eaten, is alleged to have hallucinogenic effects. Some Mexicans say that mezcal itself is an aphrodisiac.

Orange curacao. Love, purification.

Pernod. Can be drunk in small quantities for purification.

Pulque. Pulque was an honored drink in preconquest Mexico. Mayauel was the goddess of pulque.[78] She was once mortal, but the goddesses and gods took her as one of themselves.[10] She was considered to be both the bringer of intoxication as well as the ender of life. Pulque was probably used to stimulate warriors prior to battle,[78] and may have been first made by the Toltecs around 1000 C.E. The drink was used as an offering to the goddesses and gods by the Aztecs, Toltecs, and other Mesoamerican peoples. Pulque was also a favored offering during weddings and funerals, and was thought to have medicinal qualities.[109]

Rum. Used in contemporary Voodoo rituals for protection and to induce lust. It is a favorite offering to the *Orishas* (deities) in several Afro-Latino religions, such as Yoruba and Santeria. Rum was also used by shamans in Mexico to purify quartz crystals.

Sake (also spelled *saki*). Made from fermented rice (and technically a beer), sake was originally offered in Japan to deities
and to ancestral spirits. Afterward, the worshippers would
drink what the deities had not consumed. Sake still plays an
important role in contemporary Japanese society.[29] Marriages
may be consummated by drinking sake, and bottles of sake
are offered at shrines to deities and to revered ancestors, especially on the New Year.[54]

Strega. The label for this Italian liqueur is graced with a picture of a Witch. It is a potent addition to purification diets
(in moderation, of course) and is said to have been originally
formulated by Italian Witches.

Tequila. Used to promote the desire for sex. Mixtecs offered
tequila to their deities. Tequila and mezcal are made from different types of agave plants.

Whiskey. Widely used in American folk medicine, whiskey
also plays a role in contemporary American folk magic. A
piece of agar (a type of seaweed) is put into a jar of whiskey
and allowed to soak. This is done to attract "good spirits."
Toadstools are also soaked in whiskey, and the stem is used
to rub the bodies of those thought to be hexed.

Afterword

I feel it necessary to reiterate: don't let this chapter compel you
to drink. If you do drink, do so in moderation and let someone
else drive. If you don't drink, don't start!

You'll receive no power or wisdom from getting drunk. Alcohol doesn't open doors to psychic or magical development—in
fact, it closes them. Any substance that takes control of our
minds and bodies (such as alcohol) is detrimental to magical
mastery.

The information in this chapter is presented for historical
interest. I've never drunk many of these beverages and have no
intention of so doing!

CHAPTER EIGHTEEN

Tea & Coffee

Tea and coffee are among the world's most popular beverages. Cultivated in many far-ranging locations, these beverages have had a marked effect on contemporary societies.

Tea

(Thea sinensis)

Planet: Mars

Element: Fire

Energies: Conscious mind, money, courage

Lore: Probably native to northern India,[120] tea was introduced to China before C.E. 500.[71,76] By that date, tea was already an established Chinese article of trade.[3] In the tenth century, tea was considered the ideal drink; green tea was once called "liquid jade."

Some tea-growers in China may still worship Lu Yu, who wrote a book known as Tea Classic before his death in 804 C.E.[3,76] The art of tea-drinking was introduced to Japan during the thirteenth and fourteenth centuries.[3]

There are many legends and myths associated with tea. According to one, a holy man who wished to continuously meditate was plagued with sleep. He cut off his eyelids, which fell to the ground and were transformed into the first tea plants.[76]

Tea was sacred to Buddha.

The beverage was brought to England fairly early, and by the 1600s tea-drinking had been condemned by English clergy. Why was this innocent drink linked with evil? Because, these ministers felt, it led to a lack of morality and injured the health. As usual, the religious zealots had little effect.[120] Tea is still the most popular nonalcoholic beverage in England, though coffee is gaining.

Tea-leaf reading has been popular since at least the 1600s in England and elsewhere, and it continues to be a delightful act of divination.[82] A cup of tea is drunk. Usually, the drinker leaves a bit of tea, just a few drops or so, in the bottom of the cup. She or he then places the cup upside-down on the saucer, turns it around three times, and turns it right-side up again. The reader uses the symbols created by the randomly scattered tea leaves to contact the psychic mind and to form a link with the drinker. Teabags prevent the reading of the signs; loose tea is necessary.

Magical uses: Drink tea to stimulate the conscious mind (its high caffeine content will assist you in this). Tea is also drunk to bring money (hold the teabag, or the leaves themselves, in your hands and visualize prior to brewing); it also promotes courage.

Tea is a highly addictive substance. Use it with care and in moderation, as with all drugs.

Coffee

(Coffea arabica)

Planet: Mars

Element: Fire

Energies: Conscious mind, physical energy

Lore: Millions of Americans start their day with a cup of coffee. This ritual gives them a lift and prepares them to face the coming challenges. It also makes coffee growers, roasters, grinders, whole salers, and retailers happy.

Coffee probably originated in Ethiopia[104] or some other tropical African area.[71] The local people made the berries into wine, and also ate the beans as a stimulant.[71] Around C.E. 1000, Arabs in Ethiopia began making a hot drink from the beans.[71]

Coffee quickly moved across the Mediterranean. The first commercial coffee house was established in Turkey in 1554; England's first coffeehouse was opened in 1650.[104] Coffee became wildly popular in parts of the Middle East (Turkish coffee is one well-known variety), but was never fully accepted among the tea-loving Brits.

Coffee is grown throughout the temperate areas of the world. Much is produced in South America; coffee is also cultivated in the United States, on the Big Island of Hawaii. The coffee produced there—Kona coffee—is thought by many to be the best.

Coffee's wake-up effect has made it quite popular, but there are indications that caffeine alone doesn't lend the beverage its stimulating effect. Once caffeine has been ingested, it takes from thirty or ninety minutes for it to affect our central nervous systems.[41] Why does it seem that a sip or two of coffee will do the trick long before the caffeine can produce any physiological response?

There's speculation that the scent of fresh coffee triggers the conscious mind. Smelling the rich aroma every morning while we're trying to wake up sets a familiar pattern. After our morning routine begins, the smell automatically kicks us into wakefulness. Later, when this effect may have worn off, the caffeine does its work.

Coffee, tea, and caffeine remain controversial subjects. Some claim that caffeine is indeed a major health hazard. Others believe such reports are false. There's no doubt that caffeine is a powerful drug and shouldn't be given to babies or animals, who could suffer heart failure from large doses.[41]

Magical uses: Does coffee have "magical" effects? It can—if we don't drink twelve cups a day. Many become addicted to this bitter brew; but whenever we need a substance to get through the day, it can have no magical effects. Remember: moderation is the key to the successful use of any food or beverage.

However, small amounts of coffee (or tea) can be drunk to stimulate the mind and to energize the body. Brew and drink with visualization.

CHAPTER NINETEEN

The Mystic Egg

They come in all sizes, from the width of a fingernail to monstrosities nearly a foot long. Their showiest producers, birds, have always been linked with the skies and with the ancient deities that dwell there. As compact objects that contain the essence of life, eggs have been revered, cursed, collected, broken, eaten, buried, filled, and used in innumerable ways by humans desiring to tap their mysterious energies.

The earth itself is an egg. Life was created from a divinely produced egg. Eggs sustain human and animal life—much of which hatched from eggs.

Shiva created an egg out of which the earth and the sky were formed. Osiris, Aphrodite, Venus, and Eostra (whom we still revere today in the "Christian" festival of Easter) were all associated with eggs. Statues of Apollo show piles of eggs beside or beneath him.[79] In mythology throughout the world, eggs are intimately linked with the divine.

According to one belief, eggs are the perfect symbol of creation. Not only do they produce life itself (if they are fertilized), but the shell represents earth; the membrane air; the yolk fire; and the white water.[79] The "Akashic Egg," thus, contains not only the four elements but also the potential of manifestation.

Eggs once were substituted for humans during ritual sacrifices. Since at least Paleolithic times, eggs have been used in foundation rites to protect the home being built.[79] 10,000 years later, this rite is still practiced in India to protect houses and their future inhabitants.[79]

The "chicken," which originated in Asia, is the source of most of the eggs that are eaten today around the world. (The eggs of other birds are also consumed, but most of the folk magical uses included in this chapter refer to chicken eggs.) This mystical object has long been used in magical rituals of all kinds. Here are some of the ways in which people have used eggs.

Healing

In Jamaica, eggs are thrown against a "magic" tree as a sacrifice to the spirits who have brought illness to the sick. This ritual is accompanied by drumming and singing.[79]

Once Chinese grandmothers, on finding that their infant grandson or daughter was sick, took a bowl of rice, an egg, and two incense sticks to a street corner. The food was offered and the incense lit while the grandmother repeated the ailing child's name.[79] Some Chinese also attempted to prevent smallpox by eating dove's eggs.[76]

In Morocco, ill persons inscribed invocations on to hard boiled eggs and ate them to effect a cure.[79]

To maintain health, Germans once made small holes on both ends of an egg, blew out its white and yolk, and filled the egg with thirteen peppercorns and thirteen grains of salt. This egg was interred in the garden as a charm against fever (which is an indication of many types of infectious diseases).[79]

Protection

Eggs were thought to give protection, perhaps because so many of them are white—the color long associated with purity and divinity.

In ancient Egypt, eggs were apparently held in the hand while reciting protective invocations. This was done to protect those onboard ship from drowning and from attacks by hostile monsters of all kinds.[79]

Until recently, Germans customarily performed a special protective ritual on May Day. A fresh egg was buried under the threshold to guard the home from "evil."

To break the effects of the "evil eye," a Moslem living in India would wave salt, the herb turmeric, and an egg at the ailing victim. These three objects would then be thrown down at a crossroads.[79]

In Europe, eggs were hung up in homes for protection from hail, to deflect lightning, and to guard against the infestation of pests.[79]

Divination

The first egg laid by a hen has long been thought to possess special powers. Placing the first egg produced by a white pullet under the pillow was believed to produce a psychic dream of the sleeper's future mate.[82]

Records show that eggs have been used for divination in Europe since at least 1684.[82] One ritual was often performed on Midsummer. The small end of an egg was perforated with a pin. Several drops of the white were allowed to fall into a basin or a glass filled with water. The egg whites spread in the water and, from their shapes, the future was discovered.[82]

Similar practices continue throughout the world. For example, in contemporary Mexico, a sick person's body is stroked with a fresh egg, herbs (including rosemary and pepper tree leaves), and a "magical" cologne known as *siete machos*. The egg is broken into a glass of water. If it foams or is "dirty," the person has been subjected to bewitchment. There are many other ways of reading the egg's message.[121]

Another such divination: the healer rubs a sick child with a freshly laid egg while praying. The egg is then placed under the child's bed overnight. If, in the morning, the egg is found to have been "cooked," the child will surely recover.[42]

Simply dreaming of eggs, according to contemporary dream-interpretation folklore, can predict the future. Many eggs presage wealth; a few, its absence.[79] Double-yolked eggs have always been seen as signs of an impending wedding to the lucky finder.

Sex

Lore: In Morocco, women wouldn't eat eggs while their husbands watched, because it was indecent.[79] Caviar (fish eggs) has long been celebrated as a stimulant of sexual desire, as is a raw egg, drunk or swallowed straight down.

Jewish women once attempted to cure sterility by eating double-yolked eggs. The fertilizing symbolism is quite plain.[79]

Various uses: When a child was thought to be bewitched (and this was a serious consideration three hundred years ago), an egg was thrown into a lake or pond. If the egg sank, the child had been bewitched.[79] In the recent past, Russian peasants made offerings to their dead ancestors by throwing fried eggs over their shoulders.[79]

When business is slow and money isn't coming in, shopkeepers in India may rise early in the morning and walk to a crossroads with some salt and an egg. Words are uttered and the two mystic items are waved in the air. After breaking the egg and throwing its yolk and white onto the ground, the shopkeeper takes the shell and the salt back home (and/or to the shop) and burns them in the fire.[79]

Magical uses: Eggs are, indeed, mysterious objects. We eat them. Children still collect bird's eggs and nests. They are a powerful addition to a spirituality diet. They can be eaten in any form for this purpose. They're also fine for protection and grounding diets (due to their high protein content), and to encourage physical fertility.

I remember walking out in the shivering cold of an Oregonian morning with my grandmother. My head barely reached the top of the cloth-covered basket that swung over her arm as we went to the chicken coop. Morning after morning, during those summer weeks spent at my grandparents' farm, I'd find eggs that had mysteriously appeared under the feathered creatures.

The modern world has stripped away much of the magic of this basic food. Eggs, like our politics and morals, now come prepackaged. Many of us have little sense of their origin, and even less of the magic that humans once believed resided in them.

Until we find a double-yolked egg.

Stories occasionally hit the wire services of a chicken that has produced blue, purple, or red eggs. Public interest is often aroused by such seemingly miraculous events, and once more eggs (or at least, a representative few) are seen in all their former Pagan glory as symbols of creation, life, and the hidden forces behind nature.

I've been having breakfast while writing this chapter. What was on the menu?

Scrambled eggs.

CHAPTER TWENTY

From the Dairy

Milk

Planet: Moon

Element: Water

Energies: Love, spirituality

Lore: In about the year 8000 B.C.E., humans began domesticating animals. No longer willing to follow roaming herds across the countryside, they built pens and began feeding and watering their stock.

This revolutionary practice certainly ensured food supplies, but the domestication of animals may have religious origins. Milk, both human and animal, was strongly associated with the birth of young. Birth was associated with life and with deity. What better offering than the food of life could be made to the Mother Goddess, the source of all fertility? At least one food historian believes that the early domestication of animals may have sprung from the need for a regular supply of milk for use in religious rituals.[29]

Though human infants have always drunk human milk, several thousand years of genetic change were necessary before we could successfully drink the milk of animals. Today, a large percentage of the human population still lacks the enzyme necessary for the digestion of animal milk.[29]

Both cow's and goat's milk have been linked with deities and with religion. The famous Egyptian goddess Hathor, usually depicted with the head of a cow, provided milk to deceased pharaohs as well as to the living. The cow was revered as her symbol.

Many statues of a seated Isis holding her son Horus to her breast have survived from antiquity. These are often thought to have inspired similar representations of the Virgin Mary and her son.[23] The symbolism is the same: woman (the Goddess) during the act of nourishment.

Milk was a prime offering to the deities in ancient Egypt. Tutmose III placed gold and silver jars of milk on the altar to Amon. The divine liquid was also offered to Min, the ancient Egyptian deity of fertility.[24]

In Greece, goat nursemaids provided milk to Zeus, Dionysius, Asclepius, and many other deities. In his infancy, Zeus was attended by nymphs and by Almathea, the goat who fed him. Goats were thus honored as sustainers of life and bringers of food. Zeus created the *cornucopeia* (horn of plenty; cornucopia) when he presented one of the horns of Almathea to the nymphs.[88]

Though most milk today is pasteurized, it still retains some of its magical qualities. Contemporary Wiccan Esbats (Full Moon rituals) may include the serving of milk as a physical symbol of the Mother Goddess. In this way, coven members gain life from her, both symbolically and in reality.

Magical uses: Not surprisingly, milk is usually classed as a moon food, under the additional rulership of the element of water. It is a loving food, effective for strengthening your ability to give and to receive love.

As a major source of nourishment to billions of humans and to billions of animals, milk is linked with the endless Mother Goddess, provider of fertility. It's a fine food for use in diets designed to promote spirituality.

Those concerned with healthy eating prefer unpasteurized goat's milk over cow's milk. For those steeped in Egyptian lore, however, the cow's mythic connection with Isis and Hathor may suggest the use of cow's milk. This depends on the drinker's personal taste.

Butter

Planet: Moon

Element: Earth

Energies: Spirituality

Lore: Humans have been consuming butter for thousands of years. In ancient Mesopotamia, butter was offered on the altars of Ea, Shamash, Marduk, and other deities.[24] During the days of classical Greece and Rome, butter was deemed by the upper class to be a food fit only for barbarians such as cattleherders, who would certainly possess great quantities of it. For cooking purposes and for moistening bread, olive oil was preferred.[104] Since olive oil was expensive, the rich who could afford it looked down upon those who could not.

In India, ghee (clarified butter made from the milk of yaks) is poured on to images of the goddesses and gods as an act of worship and sacrifice.

Churning, the process whereby cream is separated from fresh milk, has long been an uncertain practice. With the hopes of "bringing" the butter, elder twigs were attached to the churn, or a bullet was placed in the milk itself. Chants, usually of quasi-Christian origin, were often said as well. This is a typical specimen:

> *"Come, butter, come!*
> *Come, butter, come!*
> *Peter's standing at the gate,*
> *Waiting for a buttered cake.*
> *Come, butter, come!"*

Magical uses: Butter, as a dairy food, is useful in spirituality diets.

Yogurt

Planet: Moon

Element: Water

Energies: Spirituality

Lore: Though its use in the American diet was once extremely limited, yogurt can now be found in virtually every food store in the country. This explosive growth in the popularity of yogurt began in the late 1960s. An ancient food, yogurt probably first appeared by accident: milk was left to sit for too long, the proper bacteria found their way into it, and a fermentation process created the yogurt.[71] Later, this nutritious food was deliberately produced to add a valuable new dish to the human diet.

Yogurt (also spelled *yoghurt*) is eaten around the world wherever herds of cows are maintained. In India, yogurt is offered to the goddesses and gods. Like butter, it is sometimes poured over small statues of the deities.

Frozen yogurt, an innovation of the 1970s, has by now fully penetrated the American "pop-food" market. It is available in a wide variety of flavors. Some brands are now fat-free and quite low in calories.

One company recently introduced a line of canned, yogurt-like milk products that contain no acidopillus cultures. Without the traditional "bite" of the genuine item, and with an extended shelflife, this new food cannot be classified as a yogurt. It's closer to a pudding.

Magical uses: To be of any magical benefit, yogurt should be plain or naturally flavored and colored. Honey-sweetened is best. Frozen yogurt or the more conventional kind can be used. For best results, eat plain yogurt. This food is fine for stimulating a greater awareness of the spiritual.

Cheese

Planet: Saturn

Element: Earth

Energies: Various (see below)

Lore: Cheese, a mildly odorous, solid or semisolid food created from milk, has been both adored and despised. We've had plenty of time to decide whether we like it or not—cheese has been around for as long as 5,000 years. Cuneiform tablets found at Sumerian and Babylonian archaeological sites mention cheese,[70] and the remains of what was probably cheese were discovered in an Egyptian tomb dating from as early as 3000 B.C.E. The tomb, incidentally, was that of a woman.[23, 104]

In Greece, Aristaeus, the son of Apollo, was credited with "giving" cheese to humans. Greek children ate cheese just as some children today eat candy. It was a favored food for the general populace and made up the basic diet of athletes training for the Olympics.[70] In parts of ancient Greece, wedding cakes were usually cheesecakes, made by pounding and straining cheese, mixing this with honey and flour, and baking the lot.[70]

There are many varieties of cheese. Some, such as Roquefort, have been known for over a thousand years.[70]

Magical uses: Cheese is generally ruled by Saturn and by the element of earth. However, semihard cheeses such as cheddar, jack, and others can be used in a variety of ritual applications.

Cut cheese into slices. As you cut, visualize your need. Using a sharp knife, cut each slice into a two-dimensional magical symbol that represents your goal. Infuse each slice with personal power, visualize, and eat.

The range of useful symbols is endless: pentagrams for protection, circles for spirituality, squares for money, hearts for love. See Symbols, page 341, for more ideas.

White cheese can be cut into crescent-moon shapes for Wiccan Esbat rituals, or for spells involving the moon.

Pasteurized processed cheese "foods" (such as American cheese) and cheese substitutes have no magical value whatsoever. These false cheeses shouldn't be eaten.

Ice Cream

Planet: Moon

Element: Water

Energies: Various (see below)

Lore: In the United. States, more than nine billion dollars of ice cream was sold in 1987. The national consumption for that year was estimated at a record 905 million gallons. Recently, premium ice creams (with a higher butterfat content) have swept into the stores, and ice cream is one of our favorite dessert foods.

No one knows for sure who invented ice cream. Alexander the Great is usually given credit. It was he (or, rather, his chefs) who concocted a chilled, jellied dessert then known as *macedoine*. In the first century C.E., Nero sent teams of runners into the mountains to bring back snow for his ice desserts.[124]

Marco Polo is said to have brought a recipe for what seems to be sherbet to Italy upon his return from Asia. Apparently, this iced dish evolved into ice cream in the 1500s in Italy.

Until 1777, ice cream was still rare in the United States. With the invention of insulated icehouses, the delicious dessert gained national popularity. Less than one hundred years later, the invention of hand-cranked home ice cream makers brought the cool food within the reach of millions.[124]

Magical uses: Flavor determines the magical uses of ice cream. Here's a list of specific flavors and their uses:

Blueberry cheesecake: Protection

Butter pecan: Money, employment

Cherry vanilla: Love

Chocolate (chip, fudge ripple, etc.): Money, love
Coffee: Conscious mind
Cookies and cream: Money
Macadamia nut: Money
Neapolitan: Love, money
Peach: Love, health, happiness, wisdom
Peanut butter: Money
Peppermint: Healing, purification
Pumpkin: Healing, money
Praline: Money
Strawberry: Love
Swiss almond: Money, healing
Vanilla: Love

magical
food diets

Foods with similar energies should be eaten together to gain the greatest effect. The combination of their energies has a far greater possibility of manifesting desired change than does eating a single food only occasionally. Therefore, I've devised several magical diets, each designed to create a different change within yourself and your life. This information is based on extensive research and personal experimentation.

Don't misunderstand: these aren't diets as most people understand them. Except for one, they aren't designed to create weight loss (what the Brits call "slimming"). And they certainly aren't all-inclusive. In most cases, these foods shouldn't be eaten to the exclusion of all others. The best practice is to simply add some of them to each meal.

Though there are some recipes here, I haven't included those that can be found in any good cookbook. Some of these foods don't have to be cooked and, indeed, they are most effective when eaten in a raw state. Your personal tastes will determine the form in which you eat these foods.

When using this section, remember these things:

All meals and snacks can be magical; but this doesn't mean that they must be. Still, it's best to include at least one of the suggested foods in every meal.

Cook and eat with visualization and with firm, solid purpose.

Use in moderation. I've listed salt for grounding, sugar for love, chocolate for money, and beer for purification. Is this license to overload your body with these substances and foods? No. Good health is the best starting point for all magical rituals and for personal transformation. "Binging" is anti-magical.

Eat balanced meals. Nutritional guidelines are in a state of flux at the time of this writing, but your daily meals should consist of fresh fruits and vegetables, protein, grains, and dairy products. If you're working on manifesting money, don't plan magical meals consisting solely of banana cream pie, candy, marzipan, and chocolate ice cream, even though these foods are suffused with money energies. If none of the nonsweetened foods in the "Money" chapter appeal to you, have a regular meal and make the dessert magical.

Eat foods that you enjoy. Piling your plate with steamed broccoli and brussels sprouts for protection is fine—unless you detest these foods. If you truly don't enjoy certain foods, they'll be ineffective magical tools precisely because of your lack of interest in them. This will result in the diet's failure.

Attune with all food before eating. Even if every dish doesn't fit into your magical diet, sense the food's energies and prepare yourself to absorb them. This is one of the side effects of prayer before meals (though you need not pray): it thanks the provider of the food and prepares the diner's body to receive the food.

Consult your physician or an alternative health practitioner before making drastic changes in your diet, and before fasting or embarking on any weight-loss program. This is just common sense.

Avoid foods that cause allergic reactions. There's no reason to brave an outbreak of hives just to gain the magical properties of strawberries. Substitute a dish with similar energies.

Write up a weekly diet plan. This makes it easier to determine how the foods linked with your need will fit into your meals. You can deviate from this, of course.

Do not use any magical diet in conjunction with an outside weight-loss program. The two usually don't mix. Weight-loss programs are designed for one reason: to drop pounds. Magical diets are designed for many other purposes.

Use one diet at a time. Concentrate on creating changes step by step. You can, of course, eat foods listed in other diets. Simply don't empower them, and they'll have little magical effect.

Don't switch diets from one day to the next. Allow the diet a proper amount of time to manifest your needed change. This might occur in a few days, a week, or a month.

Finally, give something back. Those of us who view food as a ritual tool acknowledge its sacredness. We regularly donate food to local charities. Not only does it give us a good feeling, it also helps those who, at present, can't eat without our assistance. The most needed items usually include: peanut butter, canned beans and corn, full-strength (not condensed) canned soup, powdered milk, and other nonperishable, easily prepared foods. Check your local social service agencies for the location of nearby food banks and assistance organizations.

On with the diets!

CHAPTER TWENTY-ONE

Love

There are many forms of love. Most of the foods mentioned in this chapter can be used for love in all of its manifestations: self-love, love among family members, friendship, love in small group situations—yes, even for that love which one human being blindly flings at another while hoping to receive love in return.

All love starts from within. We cannot and must not give love to others before we have respect and love for ourselves. Except out of compassion or pity, who would love us if we don't even like ourselves?

One of the physical manifestations of self-love is taking care of ourselves. Food, which certainly affects our bodies, also affects our emotions. It can be a powerful tool in creating self-love and, once this has been accomplished, to bring us into a loving, multifaceted relationship with another person.

The old saying "The way to a man's heart is through his stomach" is certainly true, even if sexist. In the early stages of a relationship, preparing meals for your love is an outward manifestation of your feelings. You not only care enough to cook for him (or her), you're also directly contributing to that person's survival by offering him or her the food necessary for life.

On the other hand, eating food specifically prepared for you by another is not only a gratifying, nourishing experience, it also shows your trust in that person (at least, your trust that she or he won't deliberately poison you).

Candlelit dinners in a small restaurant, with splits of champagne and tasty food, are designed to create emotional and physical intimacy between the diners. Dining out is an accepted part of the "dating" process, and can certainly be continued with good effect during magical diets.

To gain the magical effects of these love foods, however, they should be prepared and eaten at home. If you've already established a relationship with another person, prepare the dishes together. This implies an equal, harmonious relationship. Simply eat these foods and visualize if you're not currently enjoying a relationship. You soon will be.

In the folk magic tradition of many cultures, food is prepared and served to another person with the sole purpose of magically "forcing" him or her to fall in love with the cook. This is common in folk magic even today. You will find no such magic in this chapter because such rituals are manipulative. The first rule of folk magic is to respect all other persons' rights as human beings with free will. When we trespass on that free will and attempt to force someone to do something, we're practicing negative ("black") magic.

Besides, it's impossible to force another person to fall in love with you. Love is much more magical than that. This powerful emotion can't be created out of thin air, no matter what you may read in cheap spellbooks. When contemplating a ritual of this kind, ask yourself this question: would you want someone that you simply don't like to serve you love-charged foods?

If you're preparing and serving love-energized foods to your longtime mate, matters become simpler and yet more complex. You've already established a relationship, which implies not only trust but also a measure of give and take. Serving him or her a love-charged meal won't trespass on free will as long as you announce what you're doing. Saying something like "Oh, by the way, this dish is said to increase love" as you bring it to the table is sufficient. For a relationship that has worn at the seams, involve your partner in your cooking. Fully explain what you're doing and why.

He or she just may get into the spirit.

Remember: start with love for the self, then branch out in search of another. If you already have another, deepen the relationship with these foods.

Don't make the common mistake of believing these foods will produce a desire for sex. These are *love* foods, after all. See chapter 25 for more information along this line.

Spices and Herbs

Anise	Ginger
Basil	Licorice
Cardamom	Marjoram
Chicory	Poppy seed
Cinnamon	Rose
Clove	Rosemary
Coriander	Thyme
Fennel	Vanilla

Add these spices to soups, fish, and other love-inducing foods. Use fresh herbs when available. Combine with other foods listed below, for potent love-inducers. Visualize as you grind the herbs and spices, or snip the fresh leaves. Visualize as you add them to the food. Visualize as you eat.

What do you visualize? Yourself as a loving, accepting person. *Don't* visualize yourself involved with another person *unless you're already involved with him or her.*

Vegetables

Beet	Sweet potato
Pea	Tomato
Rhubarb	Truffle

Serve warmed to stimulate the warmth of love.

Fruits and Seeds

Apple	Nectarine
Apricot	Orange
Avocado	Papaya
Banana	Passion fruit
Carob	Peach
Cherry	Pineapple
Guava	Quince
Lemon	Raspberry
Lime	Strawberry
Mango	Tamarind

Serve fresh fruit salad. Carve a heart into the peel of an apple and eat, or share the apple with a lover. In making pies with any of these fruits, trace a heart with a knife on the upper crust (or lower, if one-crusted). Or, cut steam vents in the shape of a heart. Visualize!

Nuts

Brazil nut	Pine nut
Chestnut	Pistachio

Place a bowl of nuts on a table. Sit before it. Hold a nut in your hand, visualize love, and eat the nut. Repeat nine times. Any dishes that contain these nuts, such as pesto (the basil-pine nut treat), are also effective love-enhancers if they're prepared (or eaten) with visualization.

Desserts

Apple pie (flavored with cardamom)
Brownies
Carob bars (obtain at health-food stores)
Cherry-vanilla ice cream
Chocolate cake
Chocolate ice cream
Gingerbread
Ginger ice cream
Fudge ripple ice cream
Lemon chiffon pie
Key lime pie
Neapolitan ice cream
Strawberry ice cream

Also, pies made from any of the fruits listed above.

Beverages

Creme de cacao
Dessert wines
Kirsch
Lemonade
Limeade
Milk
Orange curacao
White wine

Other Love Foods

Carob
Chocolate in all forms
Dill bread
Fish
Honey
Maple syrup
Pickles

Rye bread

Strawberry jam

Sugar

Preparing and Cooking Love Foods

Burn a pink candle. in the kitchen while preparing foods. Chop vegetables and fruits into round, flat shapes, or use a melon ball tool to create spheres (circles and spheres are symbols of love). Or, cut into heart shapes.

Combine the foods in various ways:

—avocado and tomato sandwiches on rye

—cinnamon toast served with chicory coffee and fresh, sliced strawberries (naturally heart-shaped)

—a love shake of milk, vanilla ice cream, and a melted chocolate bar

—fruits in juice or nectar form

Recipes

Oranges of Love

2 ounces soaked and strained gum arabic*

1 cup orange flower water

1 ounce powdered sugar

2 egg whites

1 ounce granulated sugar (colored orange with food coloring)

While strongly visualizing love, mix together the softened gum arabic and orange flower water with enough powdered sugar to form an elastic paste. Set aside. Blend together egg whites with the orange-colored sugar and the remaining powdered sugar.

---

*Gum arabic is available at herb stores and through some mail-order suppliers.

Make small balls of the orange mixture; cover with the egg-white mixture and set on waxed paper.

Fruit Salad Spell

> *Fruit of mango, fruit of pine,*
> *let the one I love be mine.*
> *Fruit of apple, fruit of peach,*
> *bring him [her] close within my reach.*
> *Fruit of banana, fruit of cherry,*
> *let his [her] love for me not vary.*
> *As I work my magic spell,*
> *warmly in his [her] heart I dwell.*
> *I now invoke the Law of Three:*
> *this is my will, so mote it be!*

The "fruit of pine" can be either pine nuts or pineapple.

Make a salad of the above-mentioned ingredients, concentrating on the love you wish to share. Chant the spell as you chop and slice. Mingle the fruits and place your hands on either side of the bowl, while visualizing you and your loved one building a life together. Then serve the salad. (Courtesy Morgana of Hawaii.)

Cheese of Love

½ pound cottage cheese

½ handful of at least three of these fresh, minced, mixed herbs: dill weed, lemon thyme, chives, basil, marjoram, thyme, rosemary

Visualize as you gently mix the herbs into the cottage cheese. Serve by the light of pink candles with a lettuce and tomato salad and crisp pickle chunks.

Love Philtre

5 hazelnuts

1 teaspoon lavender flowers

1 clove

Dash ginger

Dash cinnamon

Place in a mortar and pestle. While visualizing, powder together until finely reduced. Add very small portions to food to increase love.

CHAPTER TWENTY-TWO

Protection

We are surrounded by unseen, nonphysical energies that are naturally produced by other human beings. Most of these energies are benevolent, or at least neutral, in their effects. Some, however, can be disturbing to our psyches and health. Others (negative thoughts or energies deliberately sent our way) can be harmful. We also face the possibility of physical dangers to our bodies, minds, emotions, and possessions. This is a fact of life.

To prevent the intrusion of such energies into their lives, and to prevent dangerous physical encounters, folk magicians have always called upon a large array of natural tools such as herbs, stones, metals, candles, and specially designed jewelry. One of the least-known magical defensive tools is—you guessed it—food.

Our natural sense of self-survival provides us with a "psychic armor" of built-in protection against negative energy. This is what sustains us. In time of need, we can boost our psychic armor. The foods listed in this chapter are useful in increasing our internal protective systems.

Don't misunderstand these words. I'm not saying that negative energies are spirits, ghosts, or demons. In the large majority of cases, demons and spirits are products of the human mind that have no real existence.*

Nor am I stating that we're open to psychic attack at any time, or that such nonphysical attacks will be effective. These are rare (usually the product of an egotistical and/or ego-deficient person) and amount to little more than a ceremonial blowing off of steam.

I've written about the practice of "psychic attack" in many of my books. I've always stated that such rituals are almost never performed. When they are, they're usually not effective. But I still receive letters from readers who believe they've been "cursed." A review of their recent lives may seem to back them up, but this can be misleading.

The psychic armor that I mentioned above usually guards us from negative energies. If we *believe*, however, that we've been attacked and are powerless to defend ourselves, that belief in our vulnerability can erode our psychic armor and allows any negative energy that passes by to affect us. If we believe it, a "curse," even if none has been performed, will be effective. We've cursed ourselves.

When I first studied magic, I was solemnly warned that I could be subjected to all sorts of occult dangers. Evil spirits would surely notice me. They'd hang around to throw a few astral wrenches into my rituals and through the spokes of my life. While this notion would make a great television movie, it's completely false. As long as your magic is positive and nonmanipulative, there is no danger in practicing it. None! If, however, you perform magic to harm or to control another human being, beware of reaping the destructive fruits of destructive magic.

Still, when an individual begins sensing and moving energies (which is the essence of magic), she or he naturally becomes more aware of energies of every kind. With expanded consciousness, one can sense and feel things that were previously elusive or

---

*Some humans who are confronted with nonphysical energy lack the means to accurately identify it. Thus, a force of coldness is a "ghost" and a sinister energy is a "demon." The latter is particularly true if the observer is the product of a conventional religious upbringing.

invisible. Most of these energies—such as those within stones, plants, and the earth itself—are positive and shouldn't be avoided. Some are negative and shouldn't be invited inside ourselves. A few of my early magical teachers were actually warning me about these nonspecific, negative energies (which they labelled "evil spirits"). The daily life of a magician isn't a constant struggle between the forces of light and darkness. Rational folk magicians don't spend half their time chanting protective spells and the other half wearing charms to guard themselves from evil. However, we all have periods when we sense the need for protection. This chapter gives you some delicious ways to guard yourself.

A protective diet can also be useful for staving off physical danger. Naturally, if someone's trying to mug you, you won't be able to drink a cup of cranberry juice or munch a slice of garlic bread to halt the robbery. If you live or work in a crime-ridden neighborhood, however, or if you've been attacked before, or if you simply think that you should smooth out a few kinks in your psychic armor, add these foods to your diet.

A few words on domestic violence: if you're a battered wife, lover, child, or (yes, indeed) husband, don't eat protective foods. Call your local police station. Leave—right now—with your children if you have any. Move into a shelter or stay with friends who'll understand. Don't go back to the person who attacked you! Love may have blinded you in the past, but now it's time to open your eyes.

Spices and Herbs

Basil	Horseradish
Bay	Marigold
Black pepper	Mustard
Cayenne	Paprika
Clove	Parsley
Fennel	Rosemary
Garlic	

Add to food for increased protection. Before using any dried, ground herb or spice in protective cooking, sprinkle it onto a flat plate or a square of waxed paper. With your index finger, trace this symbol (or one of the protective symbols, pages 341–344).

Visualize protection as you trace. Know that the protective energies within the spice have been aroused by your ritual. Add to the food as usual.

Protective herbs and spices can be added to just about any food, even if the dish isn't protective in nature. Their strong energies are also linked with other powers, such as love, health, and purification.

Vegetables

Artichoke	Jalapeno
Bamboo shoots	Kohlrabi
Bean sprouts	Leek
Bell pepper	Mustard
Bok choy	Onion
Broccoli	Poke
Brussels sprouts	Potato
Cabbage	Radish
Cauliflower	Rhubarb
Chili peppers	Shallot
Chives	Soybean sprouts
Collard greens	Sunflower sprouts
Corn	Tomatoes
Horseradish	Watercress

Slice vegetables at sharp angles or into long, pointed spear-like shapes. Visualize them as daggers of protective energy. Lightly steam the vegetables, add a small quantity of salt (for its protective qualities, not its flavor), and eat.

Make a pizza. Put basil, black pepper, and parsley in the tomato sauce (all protective foods). Place five chives into the shape of a pentagram on top of the sauce; add bell peppers, cheese, and any other items. Visualize as you make the pizza. Bake and eat for potent protection.

Fruits

Blueberry	Plum
Carambola	Prickly pear
Cranberry	Quince
Mango	Raspberry
Pineapple	Tangerine

Eat these fruits fresh or baked into dishes. Sprinkle salt on to pineapple to cut its acidity and to increase its protective qualities.

Nuts and Seeds

Almond	Sunflower seed
Sesame	Walnut

Eat with visualization.

Desserts

Bell-shaped cookies	Pineapple pie
Blueberry coffee cake	Rhubarb pie
Cranberry sauce	Star-shaped cookies

The sweetener added to such foods increases your self-love, which is so necessary for survival.

Beverages

Cranberry juice cocktail
Rum

Drink with protective meals.

Other Protective Foods

Chili	Rice
Curry	Salsa
Eggs	Szechwan foods
Fried foods	Soy sauce
Garlic bread	Spicy, hot foods
Hot foods	Tofu
Meat	Tortilla
Nachos	Twisted breads
Olive oil	Vinegar
Pretzel	

Eat a diet heavy in proteins. If you're vegetarian, load up on tofu, cheese, beans, and corn as well as the protective vegetables mentioned in an earlier list. Grounding yourself through the ingestion of protein foods closes you to outside influences and increases the effectiveness of your psychic armor.

Preparing and Cooking Protection Foods

Burn white candles in the kitchen while cooking. Eat with the certain knowledge (not faith) that the food will strengthen your own psychic protection and will ward off negative energies. Bless all food before eating in any way that seems appropriate. Serve protective foods in white or red dishes. These foods can be combined in many ways. Experiment!

Recipes

Fiery Protection Salad
½ head red cabbage
1 red bell pepper (or green, if red isn't available)
1 red onion
2 radishes
½ cup cider vinegar
¼ cup olive oil

1 tablespoon mixed, dried basil, parsley, and rosemary

⅛ teaspoon fresh, minced garlic

Black pepper to taste

Cut the onion in half. Rub the salad bowl with the cut side of one of the halves. Place this half on a paper towel under the kitchen sink to absorb negativity. (Remove the next morning and deposit outside of your home.)

Cut the other onion half into two pieces. Set aside one of these for use in other cooking and firmly mince the other, visualizing the powerful strokes of the knife driving away negativity. Smell the onion's protective aroma.

Core and shred the cabbage. Core and slice the bell pepper into long, pointed pieces. Thinly slice the radishes. Visualize!

Add the vegetables to the bowl.

Make the dressing by crumbling the dried basil, parsley, and rosemary between your fingers. Place in a small bottle with a tight lid. Add the cider vinegar and olive oil. Pour in the minced garlic. Shake well just before serving. Serve dressing over salad. Grind on black pepper before serving.

Pentagram Cookies

1 cup almonds, finely ground

1¼ cups flour

3 teaspoons almond extract

¼ teaspoon cloves, ground

½ cup confectioner's sugar

½ cup butter, softened

If necessary, grind the almonds in a blender or food processor until finely reduced. Combine almonds, flour, sugar, almond extract, and ground cloves. Work in butter and egg yolks with the hands until well blended. As you work, visualize glowing golden pentagrams entering the dough.

Chill the dough for 20 to 30 minutes or until cold, yet pliable. While the dough is cooling, grease 2 cookie sheets and preheat oven to 325°F (163°C).

Pinch off a piece of dough. the size of a walnut. Using your fingers, flatten onto the greased cookie sheet. With a toothpick or a small knife, lightly carve a pentagram on the cookie (see diagram).

Strongly visualize as you draw.

Repeat the entire process until the dough is used up. For even cooking, ensure that all cookies are approximately the same thickness.

Bake at 325°F (163°C) for about 18 to 20 minutes or until golden brown. Cool on racks.

Eat with power.

CHAPTER TWENTY-THREE

Health &
Healing

These two subjects are intimately linked. If we're successful in maintaining good health, healing won't be necessary. During a period of illness, we naturally wish to regain a state of good health. Thus, the goal common to both of these subjects is health itself.

Nutritionists have always recognized the importance of a balanced diet in maintaining good health. Many MDs don't accept this, but they're in the business of restoring health, not preserving it. Medical doctors have little training in the role that nutrition can play in creating bodily health.

There are many nonoccult methods of achieving this state. Eat four or five small meals per day, not two or three large ones. Never skip breakfast. Eat more vegetables, grains, and fruits than meat. Cut your intake of fat, sodium, and white sugar. Increase the "fiber" (roughage) in your diet by eating less processed food and more whole grains, fresh vegetables, and fruits. Regularly exercise for at least twenty minutes a day.

Many guidelines to maintaining health have been published. Check the library or your local bookstore for recent, authenticated books. Avoid all fad diets.

Because this is a book of magic, you'll find no more nutritional information in this chapter. I'll be suggesting foods, however, that you can add to your diet to regain or to maintain good health. Such foods must be part of a balanced, sensible diet or they won't be effective.

At the risk of being repetitive—see your doctor before starting one of those "miraculous healing" diets.

Healing

No doctor, herbalist, psychic, magician, or Witch can heal you. There are no miraculous cures that others can perform on your body, mind, or emotions. No spells or rituals can create instant health.

Still . . . doctors, massage therapists, chiropractors, herbalists, psychics, magicians, and even Witches can boost the body's healing process. They can help you to overcome disease and negative conditions. This is accomplished by sending energy to you by one of two methods:

—through prayer, laying-on of the hands, massage therapy, and simple magic (the projection of healing energy into our bodies).

—through the administration of energies in physical form such as herbs, tinctures, teas, Bach flower remedies, essential oils (through aromatherapy), as well as certain prescribed medicines.

If you're sick, consult a qualified, experienced health practitioner of your choice and follow her or his instructions. Eat some of the foods in this chapter, visualizing health as you prepare and consume them; eat nothing that would interfere with the advice of your health practitioner.

Spices and Herbs

Allspice	Peppermint
Garlic (*not* garlic salt)	Sage

Charge before adding to health-giving foods. Use garlic in place of salt for seasoning dishes.

Vegetables

Cucumber	Sprouts
Olive	Tomato
Pumpkin	

Eat fresh with visualization.

Fruits

Apple	Pineapple
Lemon	Watermelon
Peach	

Other Health Foods

Almond	Kummel
Apple cider vinegar	Marzipan
Cider	Walnut
Honey	

Foods to Avoid

Canned foods
Deep-fried foods
Fast food
Fatty foods
Processed foods
Preserved foods
Salt
Sugar
Very heavy desserts of all kinds

Preparing and Cooking Health Foods

Just before cooking or preparing foods, place a pinch of dried, ground sage into a spoon. Using a potholder if necessary, hold the bowl of the spoon over one of the stove's gas jets or a candle flame until the herb smoulders and releases its healing scent.

Burn a blue or purple candle while cooking, visualizing health (or healing).

Bake a loaf of whole-grain bread. Just before you put the bread into the oven for baking, use a sharp knife to cut an equal-armed cross on the top of the loaf. Bake and eat.

Such dishes as these are most appropriate:

—a salad of cucumbers, tomatoes, and sprouts with a dressing of olive oil and apple cider vinegar mixed with powdered rosemary and sage.

—an apple pie sweetened with concentrated (frozen) apple juice and cinnamon—no sugar.

—unsweetened applesauce (make at home or buy unsweetened).

—small amounts of marzipan, fashioned into equal-armed crosses.

Recipes

Healing Apple Crisp

2 cups apples, peeled and sliced

1 teaspoon lemon juice (freshly squeezed)

½ cup honey

½ to ¾ cup graham crackers, crumbled

2 tablespoons butter, melted.

Preheat oven to 375°F (190°C).

Visualize yourself in glowing, radiant health as you peel and slice the apples, squeeze the juice, and crush the graham crackers.

Turn prepared apples into a 9 x 9 baking dish. Mix the lemon juice into the honey and pour over the apples. (If the apples are very tart, use slightly less lemon juice and slightly more honey.)

Combine the crumbled graham crackers with the butter and sprinkle over the apples. Bake at 375°F (190°C) for 30 to 40 minutes (until the apples are tender). Serve topped with cream and a sprinkle of cinnamon.

Serves four.

CHAPTER TWENTY-FOUR

Money

Few of us couldn't use more money. No matter how much we make, it never seems to be enough. When embarking on a money diet, keep in mind that your attitude toward money is just as important as is the substance itself. Here are some tips:

Visualize yourself as a prosperous person. Retrain your thinking. Kill all thoughts of the "Gosh, I'm so broke!" variety. Concentrate on the feeling of having more money.

Budget each paycheck. Determine where your money is going every month. Spend wisely.

Know that, though money may solve some problems, it is no panacea. Some of the problems that we have without money will still be around when we have money.

Most of us don't want money; we want what money can buy.

Be prepared to work for money, even if just by putting personal power into your ritual.

Set realistic goals. A week-long money food plan won't make you suddenly find thousands of extra dollars in your bank account. Money diets are also virtually worthless for trying to win at lotteries, lotto, bingo, and gambling—simply because there are so many others trying to win, relying on all kinds of magic.

Wealth is a relative state of mind. A person making 30,000 dollars a year seems astonishingly wealthy to someone making 20,000 dollars, while an unemployed person may look with jealous eyes at the 20,000-dollars-a-year worker.

Accept money into your life. Know that you are a prosperous person deserving of extra income. Don't wish for it to happen; *allow* it to happen.

Give something back. When you notice a permanent or temporary increase of money, donate a percentage to charitable causes such as environmental protection groups, animal rights organizations, food banks, battered women's shelters, hospices, and other worthy groups. Give something back or you might not get any more.

As you eat the foods listed below, feel the money energy vibrating within them. Cook and eat with visualization!

Herbs and Spices

Allspice	Dill
Basil	Ginger
Cinnamon	Parsley
Clove	

Add to any foods, particularly money-attracting dishes.

Vegetables

Alfalfa sprouts	Lettuce
Bean	Pumpkin
Black-eye pea	Spinach
Cabbage	Tomato
Eggplant	

Fruits

Banana	Grape
Blackberry	Kumquat
Fig	May apple
Pear	Pomegranate
Pineapple	

Blackberry cobbler; fig newtons; banana bread; grape juice; strawberry tarts: all are money-attracting foods.

Grains

Barley	Millet
Bran	Oat
Buckwheat	Rice

Rice with cinnamon is an excellent money attractant.

Nuts

Almond	Peanut
Brazil nut	Pecan
Cashew	Pine nut
Macadamia	Sesame

Desserts

Banana cream pie	Gingerbread
Butter pecan ice cream	Macadamia nut ice cream
Blackberry pie	Maple sugar candy
Carob bars	Marzipan
Candy	Pecan pie
Chocolate	Pralines
Chocolate-covered bananas	Pralines and cream ice cream
Chocolate ice cream	
Whipped cream	

Other Money Foods

Blackberry brandy

Chocolate milk

Crème de cacao

Maple syrup

Milk

Oat bran muffins

Peanut butter and grape jelly sandwiches on oat bread

Rich desserts

Salt (in moderation)

Tea

Preparing and Cooking Money Foods

Burn a green candle in the kitchen. Cut vegetables into square shapes (to represent the element of earth). Use square pans to bake pies.

Heavy, rich, and sweet foods are ideal for money diets, but don't ignore nuts and vegetables, and never load up on ice cream and other desserts in place of more healthy fare. You will suffer physically from such an unbalanced diet!

Keep your pantry well stocked with foods of all kinds. In the past, as today, food was a sign of wealth. Keep some on hand at all times.

—Add bran to foods

—Have a snack of mixed cashews, almonds, and pecans

—Use only whole-grain breads (no white breads!)

Recipes

Money Trifle

(The amount of ingredients is determined by the size of the bowl used. This recipe is designed for a medium-sized mixing bowl, and will serve 5 to 6. If using a smaller or larger bowl, simply adjust the amounts accordingly.)

1 cup chopped bananas, fresh blackberries, chopped pineapple (sprinkled with salt), or thinly sliced pears

1 teaspoon lemon juice (optional; see below)

4 cups sponge cake (cut into ½-inch squares)

⅛ cup sherry

1 cup prepared custard (recipe p. 248) or banana pudding

1 cup whipped cream (freshly made)

Prepare fruit with visualization. See it bursting with money energy. (If using bananas, sprinkle lemon juice over them to prevent darkening.)

Place half of the cubed sponge cake into the bottom of a 1-to1½-quart bowl or soufflé dish. Sprinkle half of the sherry over the cake. Place all of the fruit over the cake. Place the remaining cake cubes on top of the fruit and sprinkle the remaining sherry over them.

Spread the custard or pudding over the cake. Finally, top with the whipped cream. Garnish with additional fresh fruits, if desired. (Lay blackberries or thin slices of banana into the shape of a pentagram on top of the whipped cream.)

Cover. Refrigerate overnight or for at least 6 hours.

Custard

      2 eggs
      1 egg yolk
      1¾ cups light cream
      ¼ cup granulated sugar

Beat eggs and yolk in a saucepan. Stir in cream and granulated sugar. Cook and stir until custard coats a metal spoon. Remove from heat; immediately place pan into a bowl of ice water. Cool, stirring occasionally. Spread half on to cake, store the rest in the refrigerator.

Note: This dessert is very heavy and luxurious. Eat small amounts, and visualize during every part of its preparation!

CHAPTER TWENTY-FIVE

Sex

This is the one type of food magic that is well known to the public—aphrodisiac foods! When eaten, these mystical, magical wonders are supposed to turn the most civilized of us into frothing, arousing animals.

As far back as the first civilizations, humans have used food to spark their sex lives. Both delicious and (to us) revolting foods of all kinds have been eaten with this hope. Some foods popularly thought to stimulate sexual desire are oysters, caviar, and champagne—perhaps the most famous of such foods. Some swear by celery soup; others use herbs such as saw palmetto and damiana. In Asia, the prosaic ginseng root, as well as more profound ingredients such as rhinoceros horns, are considered aphrodisiacs.*

The love potions of the past weren't designed to turn a person's head—they were used to heat the loins. Many of these foods are still used for this purpose—with the attendant dangers of infringing on the free will of others.

All of the foods mentioned in this chapter, if prepared and eaten with visualization, can create or increase sexual

---

*These horns have no effect other than a psychological one, but the demand has led to an uncontrollable slaughter of these animals by poachers and traders.

desire. Serving them to unsuspecting friends simply to get into bed with them would be an exercise in futility, for the diner must be prepared to accept the energies before they'll have any effect.

Instead, eat these foods to increase *your own* sexual appetite. This is especially beneficial if you're involved in a relationship that has lost some of its fire. Serve them to your loved one if you must, but only with the honest statement of the food's legendary ablities (visualizations shouldn't, um, be any problem here).

If you're experiencing difficulties engaging in or enjoying sexual contact, see a qualified professional. Foods have only so much power. They can be of help in overcoming some problems, but serious problems should be treated by a psychologist, a sex therapist, a gynecologist, or some other specialist.

Herbs and Spices

Caraway	Parsley
Cardamom	Peppermint
Coriander	Vanilla
Licorice	

Add small amounts to food. Touch with your index finger and visualize before using.

Vegetables

Carrot	Olive
Celery	Sweet potato
Endive	Truffle

Lightly cook, stir-fry, or steam these vegetables. Serve hot or warm for the best results. In this one particular diet, it's better not to eat these foods raw.

Fruits

Blackberry

Fig

Mango

To gain the most potency from these fruits, warm them.

Nuts and Grains

Barley

Sesame

Rice

Beverages

Apricot brandy   Plum wine

Chartreuse   Rum

Cognac

A small quantity (one glass) of any alcoholic beverage acts as an aphrodisiac. Too much kills the desire and, in men, can actually prevent the ability to engage in sex.

Other Sex Foods

Bird's-nest soup   Coffee

Caviar   Crab

Champagne   Eggs

Clam chowder   Fig newtons

Fish   Oysters

Halvah   Parmesan cheese

Honey   Shellfish

Omelets

Especially for Women

Fig

Oyster

Mango

These foods are traditionally thought to have more potent effects on women.

Especially for Men

Bean	Olive
Blackberry	Parsnip
Carrot	Papaya

These foods are traditionally thought to have a more potent effect on men.

Burn a red candle in the kitchen while cooking and preparing sex foods. Cook and prepare with the proper visualization. Cut foods into round and oblong pieces.

—rice with sugar and cinnamon

—stir-fried foods

Recipes

Sex Coffee

½ cup cold water

1 teaspoon decorticated (shelled) cardamom seeds

1½ cups hot, freshly brewed, double-strength coffee

While touching the cardamom seeds, strongly visualize your need. Place the cold water and the cardamom seeds in a sauce pan. Bring to a full boil; boil for 2 minutes. Strain liquid through a coffee filter. Pour into fresh, hot coffee, and stir. This recipe serves 2 small portions, so share it with a friend.

Note: Recent research seems to indicate that the consumption of coffee increases our interest in sex.

Mango Upside-Down Sex Cake

2 cups ripe mangos, sliced

2 tablespoon lemon juice

1 tablespoon butter

⅓ cup brown sugar

¼ cup shortening

¾ cup sugar

1 egg

½ cup milk

1½ cups flour

2 teaspoon baking powder

¼ tsp. salt

Preheat oven to 375°F (190°C).

As you slice the mangos, visualize yourself enjoying sexual activity. Place the sliced mangos in a bowl; pour lemon juice over them, toss and let stand for 15 minutes. Melt the butter in an 8-inch pan or casserole. Add the brown sugar; cover with a layer of the mango slices. In a bowl, cream together the shortening and sugar. Add the beaten egg. Sifting the dry ingredients, add alternately with the milk. Pour the batter over the mangos. Bake at 375°F (190°C) for 50 to 60 minutes or until done. Let cool slightly, and then invert the pan over a plate.

CHAPTER TWENTY-SIX

Spirituality

Spirituality can be defined as the human experience of, or interaction with, the divine.* This is the aim of every religion and the goal of those who sense something sacred within and beyond our three-dimensional world. Spirituality is an expansion of our awareness to greater things.

This isn't always a religious phenomenon. Many who haven't found a faith that speaks to them are spiritual. Those who don't recognize a holy book or spiritual teacher can tune into the unseen world. Spirituality is part of every religion, but it need not be.

When people find that their lives lack meaning or purpose, or discover that they're unsatisfied with material possessions, they sometimes turn to the forces they've always sensed but ignored. Developing an awareness of spirit often brings emotional fulfillment.

This leads some to enter a conventional, established religion. Others create their own personal relationship with a divinity unlike any other. Some spiritual persons may not

---

*Known as God; Mary; Buddha; the Great Mother; Osiris; Diana; Grandfather; Hina; and by many other names.

"worship" or revere this ultimate force(s), but their interactions with others, their outlook on life, even their forms of speech and living patterns, may change as a direct result of their spiritual experiences.

From a spiritual perspective, all food contains divine energies. After all, who created the food itself? Who gives it life? Who brings the rain? Religious persons *worship* the being(s) that created food and our world. Magicians *work with* the energy contained within these divine manifestations.

This is a book of magic, not religion. It's a guide to using the energies contained within foods as tools of personal transformation. If you wish to enhance your spiritual awareness, try the tips contained in this chapter. They have been designed to enable you to experience the spiritual reality in your everyday life. They can be used by persons of all religions, particularly those commonly termed "Pagan."

This diet won't make you a mystic, and it probably won't transform you into a religious zealot. But it might, just might, bring you a sense of peace. A greater understanding of the spiritual world that exists just behind the physical can be a powerful tonic to our lives.

Though I could have greatly expanded these lists (for all civilizations have linked food with deity), I've limited the selection to those foods that have been found to be particularly effective in producing a spiritual state.

Vegetables

Corn	Soy bean sprouts
Eggplant	Squash
Mung bean sprouts	Zucchini
Olive	

Corn-on-the-cob, corn chowder, eggplant parmagiana, sprout-rich salads, baked squash—these are all powerful stimulants to spirituality.

Fruits

Banana

Coconut

Date

Except for dates, eat the foods fresh for the best results.

Other Spirituality Foods

Butter	Saffron
Coconut cream pie	Tofu
Eggs	Tortilla (corn only)
Honey	Wine
Milk	Vegetarian foods
Olive oil	Yogurt

Most psychic-awareness foods are also appropriate (see chapter 27).

Foods to Avoid

Artificially flavored foods

Dried or dehydrated foods

Meat

Preserved foods

Root crops (such as potatoes)

Salt

These foods seem to "close down" our spiritual awareness. They should be eaten in small quantities. At every other meal, substitute tofu or dairy products for meat. Use spices and herbs for flavoring in place of salt.

Preparing and Cooking Spirituality Foods

Burn a white or purple candle while working in the kitchen. Visualize. As you handle, cut, peel and/or mix the food, sense the spiritual energies that are contained within it.

Immerse yourself in the energy exchange that takes place during the process of eating. Feel divine energy becoming part of your body, spirit, and soul. Pray before meals if you feel comfortable doing so.

Cut foods into circles or balls to represent the spiritual world. Cook lightly or eat the foods raw for the best results.

To externalize your spirituality, donate food to food banks and to shelters.

Recipes

Spirit Salad

        1 banana, ripe (i.e., with a browning peel)

        ⅛ cup coconut, shredded (fresh if available)

        1 8-ounce container plain yogurt

        1 teaspoon white wine

        1 tablespoon honey

Peel banana and cut into small slices. Place in a bowl with the coconut. Mix the wine into the honey. Sprinkle this mixture over the fruits; let sit for 1 minute.

Turn the plain yogurt into the bowl over the fruits. Mix with a spoon, stirring clockwise. Serves 1.

Saffron Rice

        1 tablespoon vodka or gin

        ¼ teaspoon saffron (true saffron)

        3 cups water

        1 cup uncooked (not instant) rice

        2 teaspoons salt

        1 tablespoon butter

Touch the saffron with the index finger of your projective hand (the hand that you use for writing) and visualize the precious herb's energies enhancing your spirituality.

Warm alcohol over very low heat. Add the saffron to the alcohol, remove from heat, and stir. Let sit until alcohol is colored.

Place the water, rice, and salt into a pot over medium heat. Add the butter to prevent overboiling. Pour in the saffron mixture, stir and cover.

Simmer over low heat for 15 minutes, or until the rice has absorbed all of the liquid.

CHAPTER TWENTY-SEVEN

Psychic Awareness

We're all born psychic. Unfortunately, as we mature, most of us lose this natural ability to tune into subtle energies. Magicians believe that we possess two minds. One of these can be termed the *conscious mind,* which is active when we think, remember something, work at our job, drive a car, or punch in a telephone number. The other has been called the *psychic mind,* in which we receive psychic signals.

In childhood, our two minds are linked. Information freely flows between them; thus, our conscious mind can "know" information that it has not received through the five senses. This is the point at which we are psychic.

However, as we mature, we're taught to slam a door of ignorance and disbelief on our "normal" consciousness and our psychic mind. If this training is successful, the free interchange of information between our two minds is functionally ended. Our psychic mind can then freely communicate with us only in dreams.

At times, our conscious mind gives way and allows a bit of information to come through from the psychic mind. This is the explanation for "hunches" and "intuition." These two words refer to psychic information unexpectedly (and unknowingly) obtained by the conscious mind from its submerged twin.

There are psychics among us, those who have free access to this source of information. These individuals have never lost their natural psychic talent, or have trained themselves to contact their psychic mind.

I don't know exactly how psychic awareness works, but I've seen far too many examples of it to deny its existence. Several years ago, I walked into my apartment in the afternoon. A friend of mine who was staying with me at the time looked at me, smiled, and told me that I'd just eaten lunch, where I'd eaten, and what I'd consumed. These weren't guesses. This was knowledge. And it was quite correct.

Though this may be a minor bit of psychic awareness, it's an example of why I've come to accept it as a real phenomenon of the human experience. Psychics can, indeed, know things that the rest of us do not.

That's fine for them, you may be asking yourself. But what about us? This chapter contains foods and dishes which, if properly prepared and eaten, will enhance your ability to tune into your psychic mind. They'll break down the barrier between your two consciousnesses, giving you access to a new source of information.

In order to enjoy the maximum benefits of this diet, attend courses on psychic development at nearby stores or learning centers. Or, read good books on the subject and practice the exercises that the authors give you.*

Another way to speed your development is to use psychic tools. Many find tarot cards to be a wonderful means of sparking psychic awareness. Work with a pack that you like; allow its symbolism to reopen the door to your psychic mind.

Remember: you were born psychic. Everyone is "gifted" in this way. If you wish to be psychic tomorrow, you must begin to work today. Eat these foods. Attend classes and read books. Slowly,

---

*An excellent book is *Practical Guide to the Development of Psychic Powers* by Melita Denning and Osborne Philips.

you'll discover a whole new world around you, and psychic awareness will once again be a natural part of who you are.

Spices and Herbs

Bay	Mace
Celery seed	Nutmeg
Cinnamon	Rose
Dandelion	Thyme
Lemongrass	

Add sparingly to food. Or, crumble a bay leaf between your fingers, visualizing yourself as a fully functioning psychic person. Smell its rich aroma and add to a soup.

Roses are a wonderful food. See the end of this chapter for recipes.

Vegetables

Bamboo shoots	Mushrooms
Celery	Soy bean sprouts

Stir-fry bamboo shoots, mushrooms, sprouts, and tofu. Add a bit of garlic for flavor. These make a wonderful psychic meal.

Other Psychic Awareness Foods

Coconut

Dandelion coffee (made from the roasted roots)

Fish

Fresh flowers

Fresh juices

Mulberry

Peppermint tea

Shellfish

Soup of all kinds (except potato)

Sprouted bread

Sushi

Tofu

Vegetable soup

Foods to Avoid

Alcohol

Caffeine products (colas, coffee, tea, chocolate)

Meat

Root crops (potatoes, peanuts, carrots, etc.)

Salt

Preparing and Cooking Psychic Awareness Foods

Burn blue candles in the kitchen. Cut food into circles or spheres.

It's best *not* to eat directly before contacting your psychic mind. Generally, eating "closes down" our psychic awareness. Eat after psychic work for best results, especially if you're eating nonpsychism-inducing foods; or eat lightly.

Recipes

Psychic Rose Ice Cream

½ cup fresh red rose petals

1 pint vanilla ice cream, softened but not melted

⅜ cup red wine

⅛ cup rose water

1 tablespoon powdered sugar

12 candied red rose petals (see following recipe)

Use roses that have not been sprayed with insecticides. Choose petals that are free of dirt and insect nibblings. Wash thoroughly in cold water. Drain on paper towels or bamboo racks.

Using a small pair of scissors, snip off the white base of each petal. Place prepared rose petals into a measuring cup; stop when you have half a cup. Visualize yourself as a psychic person as you work.

Place prepared rose petals, wine, rose water, and sugar into a blender. Process for one minute. Turn out softened ice cream into a bowl. Add red wine–rose water–sugar mixture to ice cream. While still visualizing, stir clockwise until blended.

Pour mixture into an icecube tray and set in freezer. Stir once or twice to mix during freezing process. Let freeze overnight.

To serve, scoop into glasses. Top each serving with candied rose petals:

Candied Rose Petals
>   2 cups fresh red rose petals
>   1 egg white
>   1 cup granulated sugar

Visualize throughout.

Wash rose petals. Snip off white bases. Drain and dry.

Slightly beat the egg white. Dip each rose petal into the egg-white until moistened. Next, sprinkle the sugar over each petal until evenly coated. Place on an ungreased cookie sheet. Repeat until all roses have been prepared.

Dry in the sun or in a warm oven of 250°F (120°C) until petals are stiff and crystallized.

Cut out pieces of waxed paper. Lay one in the bottom of a tin canister. Place one layer of rose petals on this. Repeat. Store in a cool, dry place.

Rose Honey
>   1 cup fresh rose petals (prepared as in Psychic Rose Ice
>   Cream)
>   2 cups honey

Visualize as you prepare the roses. Place the honey into a glass saucepan. Bring to a boil over medium heat. Reduce heat to low and add the petals. Simmer for about 9 minutes; remove from the fire. Cover with a cloth and let sit for 24 hours.

Bring to a boil again over medium heat. Strain through a coffee filter into a glass jar with a close-fitting lid. Tighten lid well. Let sit for 3 days.

Serve with sprout bread for a psychic-inducing food.

CHAPTER TWENTY-EIGHT

Peace & Happiness

We're all subjected to stress and to disappointment. Our jobs, our interactions with others, and the very structure of our civilization creates stress. When we drive (or run for the bus), when we open our mail, when we answer the telephone or ask our employers for a raise—we experience stress.

Many of us succumb to such pressures. We may experience depression, or "escape" into mind- and mood-altering substances.* Our bodies and our minds are telling us to slow down, to release, and to relax.

Stress is a part of our daily lives, but so too are its opposites—peace, happiness, and relaxation. Many of us meditate to release stress. Some exercise or see a massage therapist. A half hour of yoga does the trick for many individuals. But isn't there something else we can do to bring peace and happiness into our lives?

Yes, there is. We can eat foods that have traditionally been used to encourage happiness and to produce peace.

---

*If you are severely depressed or sense that you may have emotional troubles, consult a qualified therapist. Your doctor should be able to make a referral. If addiction in any form has taken over your life, seek help through organizations such as Alcoholics Anonymous, Narcotics Anonymous, and others. Check your phone book.

Naturally, a diet such as the one outlined in this chapter can't work in a vacuum. You, the eater, must allow these energies to take effect. You must take an active role in transforming the effects of physical, emotional, financial, and mental stress into peace and happiness.

Magicians know that we can't always be at peace, or forever remain happy. We're humans, after all. But the addition of certain foods to our diets—and a few other simple steps—can help in increasing our happiness and in producing peace.

Realize that happiness and peace come from within. No one else can give them to us. Though we may feel these emotions when we're with others, only *we* can bring ourselves to experience them.

Positive thinking is one avenue of change.* Instead of always searching for the negative aspects of everything you see or hear about, look for the positive. Alter your thought patterns. If you're used to seeing the world from a disgruntled, cynical viewpoint, change the way you think.

Certainly, if you're locked into a loveless relationship, work at a dead-end job (or no job at all), have few friends, and many bills, things can get pretty bleak. It's easy to get caught up in the unfairness of it all. It's easy to sit back and let circumstances step all over you.

But if you've decided that a change is in order, or if you've decided that your life isn't what it could and should be, then reprogram yourself and your energies. Charge them with positive thinking. Change your life—perhaps by cutting off deadening relationships, moving, or finding a more fulfilling job.

While you're taking the first steps toward finding peace and happiness in your life, spend five minutes every day to sit and think. Instead of dwelling on the negative aspects of your life, think of the positive ones. Visualize, if you wish, the glowing life that you will soon lead. These short "meditations" will begin to

---

*I'm forever indebted to my father for teaching me the basics of positive thinking in my formative years. I tend to be cynical, but I've learned the power of positive thinking.

alter your thinking and actually charge your personal power with positive energies.

The past is just that: past. We can certainly learn from it, but it isn't a map for our futures. We can create a depressing future or a happy future. Create your future today by taking control of your life. Happiness isn't in the prism of the past. It's our birthright, and we can achieve it now, today, by reprogramming ourselves to accept the peace and happiness that we deserve. To further speed the change from a sad life to a happy one, alter your diet as well. The following foods, correctly prepared with visualization, are another way in which you can empower your life with peace and happiness.

Herbs and Spices

Cumin	Oregano
Marigold	Rose
Marjoram	Saffron

Add small amounts of these ingredients to happiness and peace foods. Charge with energy by touching the spice with your index finger and visualizing. The rose recipes in chapter 26 can be used with good effect for happiness, but eat only small portions (these dishes have a high sugar content).

Vegetables

Cucumber

Lettuce

Olive

Don't eat any of these vegetables if you don't enjoy them. This will only depress you.

Fruits

Apple	Peach
Apricot	Persimmon
Passion fruit	Raspberry

A fresh, ripe piece of fruit can be a comforting food. Mark a circle intersected with an equal-armed cross on the fruit prior to eating it or cooking with it.

Other Peace and Happiness Foods

Celery soup

Cheese pizza (flavored with oregano)

Chocolate

Fish

Honey

Lemon pie

Lentil

Milk

Saffron bread

Saffron rice (see the recipe in chapter 26)

Wine

Foods to Avoid

Alcohol (in excess)

Coffee

Heavy foods

Meat

Root foods

Salt

Spicy foods

Tea

Eat more frequent, smaller meals. Avoid very heavy dishes and meals that rely solely on meat for protein. Eat less sugar. Once it has been ingested, it boosts the blood-sugar level, producing pleasant feelings. However, its effects soon wear off, leaving us in a dangerous, depressed state. Eat fresh fruit when you have the urge for something sweet. All love foods (save those heavy with sugar) can also be eaten.

Preparing and Cooking Peace and Happiness Foods

Burn one white or one light blue candle in the kitchen while cooking or preparing these foods. Cut the vegetables and fruits into round or ball shapes to stimulate peace.

Passion fruit is increasing in popularity as a flavoring for fruit drinks and "tropical"-style yogurts. Look in your grocery store for these products and add them to your peace-and-happiness diet. Passion fruit seed salad dressing may be available in your area; it can also be obtained through the mail.

Though I've listed many healthful foods above, some of you may zero in on two in particular: wine and chocolate. In small amounts (no more than a glass a day), wine can be a friend that soothes us after a hard day's work. Drinking any more than this will quickly turn it into an enemy. Watch yourself.

As stated in chapter 13, chocolate contains a substance that seems to cause the human brain to secrete chemicals that soothe and relax us. But chocolate eating can soon become chocolate addiction. As long as we're dependent upon a substance, we can never be truly happy. Again, eat in moderation.

Recipes

Perpetual Happiness Drink

½ cup apple juice

½ cup cherry juice

½ cup apricot juice (or nectar)

4 or 5 fresh raspberries

Blend together all ingredients for a few seconds. Pour into a glass, place your hands on either side of the glass, and visualize, arousing the peaceful energies that reside within the fruits.

Drink half a cup whenever you desire. Store the remainder in the refrigerator. Alternately, drink a cup of apple juice.

Peaceful Cider Cake

3 cups sifted flour

½ teaspoon baking soda

¼ teaspoon nutmeg, ground

¼ teaspoon cinnamon, ground

½ cup butter, softened

1½ cups sugar

2 eggs, beaten

½ cup apple cider

Preheat oven to 350°F (177°C).

Visualize yourself as a peaceful person while you measure the spice, flour, and baking soda. Sift together the first 4 ingredients and set aside.

Beat together the butter and sugar in a large mixing bowl. Add the eggs and mix. Alternately, add the flour mixture and the apple cider. Begin and end with the flour mixture.

Place the batter into a well-buttered loaf pan. Bake at 350°F (177°C) for one hour, or until a toothpick inserted into the center of the cake comes out dry.

CHAPTER TWENTY-NINE

Purification

At times, we don't feel like ourselves. We may have been brooding about something for several weeks. We may just be stepping away from an unsatisfying relationship. Or, perhaps, we simply realize that it's time for a change time to break an addiction or transform our lives.

If (and when) this is the case, a purification diet can be useful in creating a physical transformation. Adding these foods to your diet, preparing them with visualization, and eating them with power blows the cobwebs out of your mind, body, and emotions. The concept of purification not only includes removing the bad or the useless, but also means renewal. A purification diet can do both.

Some people may eat purifying foods while undergoing a major change in their lives, such as when halting a substance dependency. Such a diet may also be a part of spiritual quests. It is also useful before other types of magical diets in clearing the way for the change.

Purification foods bring a welcome change in our bodies and emotions. Try this diet for a week or so if you've been feeling hampered by the past, imprisoned by your emotions, or "unclean" due to the actions of others in your immediate vicinity.

This is also an excellent diet for psychics (not for those on a psychic diet, but for those among us who don't need to work at being psychic). This diet won't close you down, but it will purify you from the negative energies that you can sometimes easily pick up from others.

Eat purification foods for a week after following a heavy protection diet. Purification and protection diets can be alternated if necessary. Give it a try.

Herbs and Spices

Bay	Peppermint
Black pepper	Thyme
Horseradish	Turmeric

Fruits

Coconut	Lime
Grapefruit	Melon
Guava	Orange
Lemon	

Other Purifying Foods

Anisette

Beer

Creme de menthe

Flowers

Fresh juices

Honey

Lemonade

Lemon sorbet

Onion soup

Orange juice

Peppermint tea

Salt (in moderation)

Shellfish

Soups

Steamed foods

Vinegar

Water

Yeast products

These are some of the foods that you can enjoy during your purification diet. Water should, of course, be as pure as you can find it. Bottled spring water is ideal. We should drink eight glasses of water every day to maintain good health. To boost water's purifying properties, float a slice of fresh lemon in every glass.

Foods to Avoid

Canned foods

Dried foods

Meat

Preserved foods

Meat shouldn't be eaten in large amounts, if at all. Avoid processed foods and especially all artificially flavored, colored, or preserved foods. Fresh is best.

Cooking and Preparing Purifying Foods

At least one white candle should be burning in the kitchen. Cut foods into round or oblong shapes—but no sharp, julienned slices. Psychologically and magically, such shapes are less purifying than rounded ones.

A glass of beer each day after your last meal is purifying but, as with all alcohol, keep it to one or one-half glass. What do you do with the rest of the beer? Add it to your bath. It purifies from the outside. (Some people enjoy pouring warm beer on to their hair after shampooing—another possible use for the left-over brew.)

Salt is a purifying substance, but use it only in small amounts. Salt is an ancient symbol of purity; but we now know that consuming too much salt can be deadly.

Yeast products have been recommended because of the nature of yeast—an active, alive food. If you're on a no-yeast diet (as many are today), simply don't include yeast foods. Soups are fine purifying tools, as long as they don't contain meat.

Recipes

Winds of Change Drink

> 3 oranges
>
> 2 grapefruit
>
> 1 lemon
>
> 1 lime
>
> Honey to taste

Slice and juice the fruits, visualizing their purifying energies. Pour the juices into a glass. Add 1 teaspoon honey; stir well. Taste. If desired, add more honey. Enjoy as often as you wish during your purification diet.

Purification Mead (nonalcoholic)

> 1 quart water
>
> 1 cup honey
>
> 1 lemon (cut into slices)
>
> ½ teaspoon nutmeg
>
> Juice of ½ lemon
>
> A pinch salt

As you slice the lemon, smell its purifying fragrance. Visualize. Place the water, honey, lemon slices, and nutmeg into a stainless steel or glass pot. Boil. Scum will begin to form on the surface of the water. Skim this off with a wooden spoon as it rises. When the liquid is clear, add the salt and the juice.

Strain and cool. Drink at room temperature or cold. This is a nonalcoholic replacement for honey wine that's quite purifying.

CHAPTER THIRTY

Weight Loss

Millions of us are overweight, though the standards used to gauge our ideal weight vary and don't equally apply to all individuals. Some could stand to lose a few pounds; others are dozens or hundreds of pounds overweight. Some among us go crazy when finding that they've gained a pound; others don't care.

One thing seems clear—few of us are completely happy with our bodies. Print ads, commercials, motion pictures, and television programs are populated by people with perfect faces, perfect teeth, perfect hair, and perfect bodies. Those of us who don't share these attributes are exposed to such seemingly perfect beings day in and day out for our entire lives. The underlying message is that thin is not only in—it's natural.*

Weight-loss centers are mushrooming around the country. Hundreds of diet books are launched every year. Millions of dollars are spent on appetite suppressants, aerobics

---

*This is a recent phenomenon, of course. The success of the 1960s model Twiggy has received much of the blame for our current skin-and-bones ideal of a woman. Such thinness is largely determined by genetics. Dieting cannot create it without endangering the health, so don't try to achieve this look.

classes, and weight-loss support groups. Millions dream of dropping a few pounds and, more importantly, of keeping them off.

As I wrote in the introduction to part three, this isn't a "diet book." Most people think of the words "dieting" and "losing weight" as being synonymous. This isn't the case. There are many types of diets: low-salt, low-cholesterol, high-fiber, weight-loss, even weight-gain. The secret for success with any diet is to think of it in permanent terms. A "diet" isn't something that you do for a while; it should be a permanent change in eating habits.

This chapter isn't an all-encompassing diet. If these foods are added to your meals, and prepared and eaten with visualization, they can indeed be useful in lessening your pounds—but they aren't a mystical guarantee of weight loss.

Before trying to lose weight, consult a qualified doctor. Ensure that your problem isn't being caused by a biological condition. Once you've been cleared of such worries, begin to add these foods to your diet.

The basics of any weight-loss program are:

—Eat lots of vegetables

—Consume less fat and sugar

—Increase your exercise

—Never skip a meal

Here are some more ways to lose weight:

Do nothing but eat while you're eating. Don't read the paper, watch television, or perform any other activity. Sure, you can talk to the person on the other side of the table, but keep meal times for eating.

Don't reward yourself with food—unless it is one of those listed in this section. "Rewarding" yourself with a hot-fudge sundae is actually punishing yourself. See what I mean?

Don't celebrate with food. Choose other activities to serve as get-togethers.

Limit the number of meals that you consume out of the home. It's much harder sticking to any type of diet when you have little or no control over what you eat and how it's prepared.

Eat three large or four small meals a day. Don't skip breakfast. This has been proven to slow the body's metabolism and can actually *increase* your weight! It also raises cholesterol levels. If you follow this plan, you'll do wonders.

Herbs and Spices

> Chickweed
>
> Dill
>
> Fennel

Season foods with these herbs. Dill goes well with green beans. Fennel seeds can be pushed into pizza crusts (remember: no more than one or two pieces per meal). Eat a bit of fresh chickweed before meals if it's available.

Vegetables

Celery	Kelp (all seaweeds)
Chervil	Onion
Chives	

Actually, all salad greens are useful in weight-loss programs. Use an apple cider vinegar or tofu-based dressing; avoid dressings high in fats and oil.

Seaweeds, though not commonly eaten here, are wonderful helps in losing weight. Add them to soups and stews.

Other Weight-Loss Foods

> Apple cider
>
> Grape juice
>
> Honey
>
> Pickles

Fill a teaspoon with honey. Visualize yourself as a slimmer person. Eat the honey. Do this fifteen minutes or so before a meal. This reduces your appetite and certainly can kill cravings for sugar. Anytime you have the urge for sugar, eat a teaspoon of honey.

Or, drink half a glass of unsweetened apple juice or grape juice to stem sugar cravings.

Eat one pickle a day. This is an old weight-loss idea.

Foods to Avoid

> Fats
>
> Fried foods
>
> Salt
>
> Sugar

Is this a surprise? Also, avoid consuming dietetic foods. Research indicates that low-calorie, artificially sweetened foods often stimulate the appetite, leading people to eat or drink so much of them that they don't save any calories. Those "diet" drinks aren't.

Also, all artificial sweeteners are potentially dangerous. Honey isn't nutritionally superior to sugar to any significant degree, but it's less processed, has its own taste, and is available in a smaller number of foods, which limits your dessert possibilities.

If you must eat sugary foods, only eat those you prepare yourself—and then in small amounts.

Preparing and Cooking Weight-Loss Foods

Burn a yellow candle in the kitchen while cooking and eating to strengthen your conscious resolve.

Do eat some sort of dessert, but make it one sweetened with fruit juice or honey. And, once again, eat small portions. Would a four-inch-square piece of honey cake taste better than a two-inch-square piece? Of course not.

Eat slowly. Chew thoroughly. Be aware of everything that you put into your mouth. Affirm while you eat that food is nourishing and good for you, and that it will help you to lose weight.

CHAPTER THIRTY-ONE

Other Magical Food Diets

These are short descriptions of other magical diets that you can follow.

Physical Strength and Magical Power

All foods that lend the body strength also lend extra magical power. There's no difference between the two; there's only the purpose for which they are used.

Fruits

> Citron
>
> Date
>
> Fig
>
> Pineapple

Other Power Foods

> Chocolate
>
> Coffee
>
> Endive
>
> Flaming foods

Honey

Leek

Meat (lean)

Proteins of all kinds

Rum

Salt

Sautéed foods

Spicy foods

Spirulina

Tea

Tofu

Foods to Avoid

All those that lead to sleep, such as lettuce and grapes; very sweet foods that lull us into a half-conscious state directly after consuming them.

Preparing and Cooking Power Foods

Burn red or purple candles in the kitchen. Sautéeing foods adds to their energizing effects.

Though it's best not to eat directly before a magical ritual, a light meal two hours before the working is fine.

Fertility

Many couples are looking for ways to increase their chances of conceiving a child. If you've both been checked and neither is sterile, try adding these foods to your diet. Visualize!

Fruits

Fig

Grape

Mulberry

Pomegranate

Other Fertility Foods

Barley

Eggs

Egg breads

Hazelnut

Hot-cross buns

Milk

Poppy seed

Rice

Sesame

Watercress

Preparing Fertility Foods

Burn green candles while cooking or mixing. If possible, eat in bed with your lover. And keep trying!

Grounding

When you can't seem to concentrate, when you're psychic awareness is far too open, or when you can't come down to earth, a grounding food plan may be advisable. Eat these foods when you feel lost in a dream world, or when fantasies cloud your mind.

These foods are also eaten after heavy magical and spiritual ritual to get back in touch with the earth.

Vegetables

Beans (all types)

Carrots

Potatoes

Sweet potatoes

Other Grounding Foods

Crackers

Cheese

Cheese omelets

Eggs

Grains

Heavy proteins

Meat

Peanuts

Salt (in moderation)

Tofu

Foods to Avoid

Beer and all alcoholic foods

Flower foods

Psychic foods

Seafood

Sugar

Yeast (raised) bread and baked goods

Preparing and Cooking Grounding Foods

Burn a tan or brown candle in the kitchen. Cut foods into square chunks and serve on square dishes (if you have any).

Conscious Mind

These foods can help us better cope with problems such as balancing checkbooks, filling out forms, and studying for exams and tests. They stimulate the conscious mind.

Herbs and Spices

Dill

Rosemary

Nuts

Chestnut

Hazelnut

Walnut

Other Conscious Mind Foods

Coffee

Honey

Raisins

Tea

Watercress

Foods to Avoid

All psychism-inducing foods.

Preparing and Cooking
Conscious Mind Foods

Burn a yellow candle in the kitchen. Visualize your conscious mind operating at peak efficiency.

Luck

"Luck" is an ambiguous term, which is why I've enclosed it in quotation marks throughout this book. Some people believe that they have bad "luck" and want good "luck." I've defined "good luck" in the glossary of this book as:

"An individual's ability to make timely, correct decisions, to perform correct actions, and to place herself or himself in positive situations. 'Bad luck' stems from ignorance and an unwillingness to accept self-responsibility."

And so, positive or negative, good or bad, we create our own "luck." If you wish, add some of these foods to your diet. Prepare and eat them with visualization.

All the "luck" that we'll ever need is within ourselves. Perhaps eating these "lucky" foods will bring that point home.

Luck Foods

Bananas

Black-eye peas

Cabbage

Coconut

Coleslaw

Green foods

Hazelnut

Kumquat

Mincemeat pies (eat on New Year's Day)

Noodles (eat on Chinese New Year)

Nutmeg

Pancakes

Pear (eat on Thanksgiving)

Red beans and rice

Sauerkraut

Preparing and Cooking Luck Foods

Burn green candles in the kitchen.

scott's favorite recipes

INTRODUCTION TO SCOTT'S FAVORITE RECIPES

We are pleased to present a collection of recipes Scott had planned for a separate magical cookbook. Scott passed from this life before completing his magical cookbook, leaving the work unpublished. But now, the beginnings of his cookbook, and his favorite recipes, are here as a special feature. Delight in magical recipes ranging from "Love Pie" to "Sandwiches."

The recipes are divided into chapters by courses that are listed in alphabetical order: appetizers, beverages, desserts, main dishes, salads, soups, and vegetables.

Inspirational full-course meals are waiting for you in the following pages. Transform your kitchen into an enchanting household space and cook up a magical storm at the same time.

Give Scott's recipes a try, and enjoy the magic!

Llewellyn editors

CHAPTER THIRTY-TWO

Appetizers

The fresh chives, parsley, basil, and garlic in the following recipe charge this toast with superprotective energy.

Magic Herb Toast

8 French rolls, sliced horizontally into ¾-inch-
thick pieces

½ cup butter, softened

1 teaspoon fresh chives, chopped

1 teaspoon fresh parsley, chopped

½ teaspoon fresh basil, chopped

1 clove garlic, finely chopped

Cream the butter together with the chives, parsley, basil, and garlic until it forms a smooth, spreadable paste. Spread this on sliced French rolls. Broil until light brown.

Yield: 4 servings.

Magical uses: Protection.

Halloween is a popular holiday in both the United States and in Scotland, where it originated. Many foods have become associated with this magical night and, indeed, often seem to taste even better when made only on October 31. Foods specifically associated with Halloween are: apples, nuts (especially hazelnuts), ginger, and, of course, pumpkins—the pumpkin is the United State's addition.

Roasted Jack-O-Lantern Seeds

> 1 pumpkin
> Salt
> 1 tablespoon vegetable oil (optional)

Heat oven to 350°F (177°C). Slice open pumpkin and scoop out seeds. Wash seeds until all strings and orange insides have been removed. Pat seeds dry with a cotton dish towel. Spread seeds on an ungreased cookie sheet or shallow baking pan. Bake until a light golden brown, stirring every few minutes for even browning. Remove from oven, add salt to taste, let cool, and serve. Store any leftover seeds in a tightly covered jar.

> **Yield:** About 2 cups.
> **Editor's note:** Vegetable oil may be used to grease the cookie sheet to prevent the seeds from sticking to the pan.
> **Magical uses:** Festival food—Halloween/Samhain.

Most supermarkets and hardware stores sell special Halloween cookie cutters during September and October. These cookie cutters are usually shaped like bats, cats, Witches, brooms, cauldrons, owls, and other appropriate figures. The older cutters were made of metal; today, plastic is being used. No magical kitchen is complete without a set of these cutters, which are used in the following recipe.

Sandwiches

> 8 slices white or wheat bread (your favorite)
>
> 3 ounces cream cheese, at room temperature
>
> 1 peeled cucumber, thinly sliced

Lightly spread two pieces of bread with cream cheese. Generously cover one piece with cucumber slices. Place second piece of bread on top of cucumber covered slice. Press a Halloween-shaped cookie cutter (or simply star- and crescent-shaped cutters) into the center of the sandwich. Remove the outer bread and discard. Repeat with remaining ingredients.

> **Yield:** 4 servings.
>
> **Variation:** For children, you can make sandwiches out of any type of sandwich: bologna, peanut butter and jelly, and so on. Warning: these are known to disappear.
>
> **Scott's note:** I don't let the outer edge of the sandwiches go to waste; I always eat them.
>
> **Magical Uses:** Festival food—Halloween/Samhain.

CHAPTER THIRTY-THREE

Beverages

Madeira Quick Amatory Drink

> Madeira
> Sugar cubes
> Orange curacao

To a glass of good quality madeira, add two lumps of sugar and four drops of orange curacao.

> **Magical uses:** Love.

Apricot Brandy Quick Amatory Drink

> Apricot brandy

Add apricot brandy to any drink.

> **Magical uses:** Love.

The Drunken Pumpkin

> 1 pumpkin
> apple cider
> Cranberry juice cocktail
> Ginger ale
> Rum

Slice off the top of the pumpkin. Scoop out seeds and clean out pumpkin as thoroughly as possible. Pour roughly equal amounts of apple cider, cranberry juice cocktail, ginger ale, and rum into the pumpkin until full. Then pour liquids back out of the pumpkin and into a saucepan. Warm until just boiling. Refill the pumpkin with the liquids and serve immediately.

> **Scott's note:** Save the seeds, and use in the Roasted Jack-O-Lantern Seed recipe listed in the appetizer chapter on page 296.
>
> **Magical uses:** Festival food—Halloween/Samhain.

Samhain Cider

3 oranges

3 teaspoons whole cloves

1 gallon apple cider

1 teaspoon cinnamon, ground

1 teaspoon nutmeg, ground

1 cinnamon stick

1 cup orange juice (optional)

Wash the oranges well, then stud them with the cloves. Pour the cider into a large pot and warm over low heat. Add the studded oranges, cloves, cinnamon, nutmeg, and cinnamon sticks. Let simmer uncovered for 13 minutes. Add the orange juice, if desired. Serve in mugs.

> **Yield:** 10 servings.
>
> **Editor's note:** To stud oranges, first use an ice pick or nutmeg pick to puncture the orange peel. These holes will allow the whole cloves to easily slide into the orange peel.
>
> **Magical uses:** Festival food—Halloween/Samhain.

Mulled Wine

This drink is a real "warmer-upper" for a cold Halloween night. Let your adult friends give it a try.

3 bottles red wine

3 oranges

3 teaspoons cloves, whole

1 teaspoon cinnamon, ground

1 teaspoon nutmeg, ground

1 cinnamon stick

1 cup orange juice (optional)

Wash the oranges well, then stud with the cloves. Pour the wine into a pot and warm over low heat. Add the studded oranges, doves, cinnamon, nutmeg, and cinnamon stick. Let simmer for 13 minutes. Add the orange juice, if desired. Serve in mugs while warm but not hot.

Yield: 10 servings.

Editor's note: To stud oranges, first use an ice pick or nutmeg pick to puncture the orange peel. These holes will allow the whole cloves to easily slide into the orange peel.

Magical uses: Festival food—Halloween/Samhain.

Witches' Brew

This recipe was inspired by a delicious drink, served only during the month of October at the famous Cafe del Rey Morro restaurant at Balboa Park in San Diego, California. This is, at best, an approximation of the original drink.

1 10-ounce tulip glass

Crushed ice

¾ ounce light rum

¾ ounce dark rum

¼ ounce orange curacao

Sweet and sour

2 ounces orange juice

2 ounces pineapple juice

Grenadine

Pineapple wedges (fresh if available)

Maraschino cherries

Toothpicks

Fill the glass with ice. Add the light rum, dark rum, curacao, sweet and sour, orange juice, pineapple juice. Top with a dash of grenadine. To garnish, spear fresh pineapple and red cherries with a toothpick.

Yield: 1 serving.

Magical uses: Festival food—Halloween/Samhain.

Ginger Tea

Ginger is a wonderfully warm, fragrant spice. It is also a powerful money attractant. The cinnamon boosts the ginger's power. You may wish to try the following recipe.

5 cups water

⅓ cup fresh ginger root, peeled and thinly sliced

¾ cup sugar

½ teaspoon cinnamon, ground

Thinly slice the ginger and add to the water in a large saucepan. Boil for 20 minutes. Strain out the ginger. Add the sugar and cinnamon. Stir until sugar is dissolved. Serve hot in mugs.

Yield: 4 servings.

Magical uses: Love, money, and success.

CHAPTER THIRTY-FOUR

Desserts

Prosperous Banana Fritters

1 cup sifted all-purpose flour

2 teaspoons baking powder

1 teaspoon salt

¼ cup sugar

1 egg, beaten

⅓ cup milk

2 tablespoons melted butter

3 firm bananas

¼ cup cornstarch

Cooking oil

½ cup whipped cream

Heat 21 inches of oil in a deep frying skillet to 350°F (177°C). In a large bowl, sift together the flour, baking powder, salt, and sugar. Combine egg, milk, and butter in a separate bowl and then add to flour mixture. Mix together until a stiff, smooth batter forms. (If necessary, for dipping consistency add additional milk, sparingly.) Peel and cut each banana into 4 pieces crosswise. Roll each piece in cornstarch. With tongs, dip into fritter batter and coat all sides. Lower bananas gently into cooking oil to avoid splattering. Fry until golden brown, turning often. Serve with whipped cream.

> **Yield:** 3 servings.
> **Magical uses:** Prosperity.

Pineapple is a symbol of hospitality. It is also a powerful protectant. Combined with rum, its powers are doubled. The following recipes are quite refreshing and are for adults only. Because fresh pineapple can be difficult to prepare, I have included two versions of the recipe. Enjoy!

Tipsy Pineapple

> 1 fresh whole pineapple
> Light rum

Select a pineapple that can stand up by itself. Slice off the top of the pineapple. Using a long, sharp, flexible knife, cut down and around the fruit inside the shell, about ¼ inch from the sides. Try to bend the knife when you reach the bottom. If everything goes right, you should be able to lift out the entire inside of the pineapple, leaving the shell intact (you may have to tug a bit). Place the inside pineapple fruit on cutting board. Cut spears from the juicy fruit, removing the woody core. Return the spears to the pineapple. Pour enough of the rum over the fruit to cover. Replace the top of the pineapple. Place in the refrigerator overnight. Serve the next day, chilled, as a refreshing money attractant.

> **Yield:** 4 servings.
> **Variation:** If you do not wish to cut a fresh pineapple, drain 2 cans pineapple chunks. Place the chunks in a bowl. Pour rum over the fruit to cover. Tightly cover the bowl and refrigerate overnight.
> **Magical uses:** Protection, luck, and money.

Flaming Love

> 1 whole pineapple (or 2 cans pineapple rings packed in
>   juice)
>
> ½ cup butter
>
> ½ cup brown sugar
>
> ¼ cup light rum

Preheat oven to 350°F (177°C). If using a fresh pineapple, peel, core, and cut into half-inch rings. Place a single layer of pineapple rings in a shallow baking pan. Dot tops with butter and sprinkle with brown sugar. Place under the broiler until sugar and butter turn a light brown. Gently heat the rum in a small saucepan during the broiling. Remove the pineapple rings from the broiler when done and transfer them to a chaffing dish (or other heat-proof container.) Pour the heated rum over the top and ignite. Serve immediately.

> **Yield:** 4 to 6 servings.
>
> **Magical uses:** Protection, luck, and money.

Groundhog Day Cake

Candlemas (Groundhog Day) was in antiquity a time of praying for sun and a speedy end to winter. Today in the United States, Groundhog Day is a time for a popular form of "weather prediction." The following cake celebrates this holiday.

> 1½ cups water
>
> 1 cup quick oats, uncooked
>
> 1 cup semisweet chocolate chips (6 ounces packaged)
>
> 1½ cups flour
>
> 1½ teaspoons baking soda
>
> 1 teaspoon salt
>
> 1½ cups butter, softened
>
> 1 cup quick oats, uncooked
>
> 1 cup brown sugar, firmly packed

¼ cup granulated sugar

2 eggs

Frosting (your choice of flavor)

Preheat oven to 350°F (177°C). Heat the water in a medium-sized saucepan until boiling. Add the oats and stir. Cover, remove from heat, and let stand for stand 20 minutes. Melt chips over hot, not boiling, water in a double boiler. Stir and set aside. In a small bowl combine the flour, baking soda, and salt and set aside. In a large bowl, cream the butter, brown sugar, and granulated sugar. Beat in eggs, one at a time. Blend the oats and melted chocolate into the creamed mixture. Add flour mixture, blending just until mixed. Pour the batter into a greased and floured 13 x 9 x 1½ inch pan. Bake for 35–40 minutes. Remove cake from oven. Let stand for 5 to 10 minutes, then turn out cake onto a flat surface or serving tray. Cool completely and frost top and sides with frosting of your choice.

Magical uses: Festival foods—Candlemas/Groundhog Day.

CHAPTER THIRTY-FIVE

Main Dishes

M any types of fish are thought to be particularly suitable to induce love including salmon, mullet, hal-
ibut, herring, and anchovies. Lobster shares a similar claim.
Here's a simple recipe to prepare virtually any type of fish
to taste-tempting perfection.

Mermaid's Love

  1 fresh fish fillet (your favorite kind)

  3 tablespoons butter

  1 medium onion, sliced salt

  pepper

Preheat oven to 350°F (177°C). Place fresh fish fillet on a
large square of aluminum foil. Dot fish with butter and top
with onion slices. Season with salt and pepper. Fold up the
aluminum foil and seal. Bake 12 minutes or until done.

Magical uses: Love.

For untold centuries, humans have searched for foods,
potions, and exotic materials that would stir love or excite
the erotic senses. In this 4,000-year quest, several foods
have been found to have a greater effect than others.

Love Pie

> 1 dozen first-quality oysters
>
> 1 steak, trimmed and cut into 1-inch-wide strips
>
> Butter
>
> Flour
>
> ¾ cup beef bouillon
>
> ½ cup water
>
> 2 tablespoons cornstarch (optional)
>
> 1 pie crust
>
> 2 tablespoons milk

Preheat oven to 350°F (177°C). Cut oysters in half. Place each half in a strip of trimmed steak, add a pat of butter, and roll the steak around the oyster. Coat each roll with flour. Place in a pie pan. Pour beef bouillon and water over oyster/steak rolls. Cover with pie crust. Slit crust top to allow steam to escape. Brush crust with milk. Bake for 1½ hours.

> **Yield:** 6 servings.
>
> **Editor's note:** For a thicker pie sauce, mix 2 tablespoons of cornstarch into the water and bouillon and then pour the liquid over the oyster/steak rolls.
>
> **Magical uses:** Love.

Teriyaki Steak on Stakes

For nonvegetarians, beef represents one of the most effective protective foods available. The following recipe deliciously takes advantage of this energy, and boosts it with the added power of garlic.

> 2 pounds sirloin steak
>
> ½ cup soy sauce
>
> 1 tablespoon sherry
>
> 3 tablespoons sugar

⅛ teaspoon powdered ginger

1 clove of garlic, finely chopped

Skewers

Diagonally cut steak into 2 x 1 x ¼ inch strips. Combine the soy sauce, sherry, sugar, ginger, and garlic. Stir well. Pour over steak strips and marinate in the refrigerator for at least 30 minutes. Thread the meat slices on skewers. Grill or broil for 5 minutes or until done.

Yield: 48 skewers.

Magical uses: Protection.

Witches' Halloween Pie

The following is a variation on the classic English dish, shepherd's pie. This version is named Witches' Halloween pie, and it is certainly appropriate for Halloween night.

1½ cups charmed potatoes (see p. 319)

1 egg

¼ cup butter, melted

1 medium onion, finely chopped

1 clove garlic, crushed

1 pound chopped steak

½ cup beef gravy (fresh or canned)

¼ cup beef bouillon

1 bay leaf

2 teaspoons fresh parsley, chopped

1 teaspoon Worcestershire sauce

Salt

Pepper

Prepare mashed potatoes as in Charmed Potatoes (page 319) except add one beaten egg during the mashing process. Set aside. In a saucepan, sauté the onion and garlic in 1 tablespoon of the butter until light brown. Add the chopped steak and cook, stirring often, until done. Stir into the saucepan the gravy, bouillon, bay leaf, parsley, and Worcestershire sauce. Add salt and pepper to taste. Cook for 20 minutes, stirring occasionally. Turn out into a lightly greased 1½-quart casserole dish. Spread the mashed potatoes on top of the mixture. Brush with the remaining melted butter. Bake in a 400°F (202°C) oven for 20 minutes or until the potatoes are light brown. Serve hot.

Yield: 6 servings.

Magical uses: Festival food—Halloween/Samhain.

Cozido

This traditional recipe was originated by the Witches who live in the Basque area of Spain.

3 pounds beef rump or round, cut into cubes

4 quarts water

1 pound ham

1 large onion, quartered

3 tomatoes, peeled and quartered (or 1 cup canned, drained)

3 turnips, peeled and quartered

4 carrots, peeled and sliced

2 garlic cloves, finely chopped

1 bay leaf

1 tablespoon parsley, chopped

Salt, to taste

Pepper, to taste

1 pound garlic-seasoned smoked sausage

1 medium cabbage, cored, and cut into wedges

4 cups turnip greens, coarsely chopped

4 medium potatoes, peeled and halved

1 can chickpeas (garbanzo beans)

Place the beef in a very large pot with the water. Heat to boiling and remove the frothy residue from the water. Reduce heat and cook, covered, for 1 hour, stirring occasionally. Add ham, onion, tomatoes, turnips, carrots, garlic, bay leaf, parsley, salt, and pepper. Cook covered for another hour, stirring occasionally. In the meantime, fry the sausage. Drain sausage and add the cabbage, turnip greens, potatoes, and chickpeas. Add this mixture to the soup pot mixture. Simmer uncovered for about 30 minutes or until tender.

Yield: 6 servings.

Magical uses: Festival food—Halloween/Samhain.

Chicken Halloween

This recipe supposedly tastes best when it's cooked outdoors in a cauldron over a roaring fire. Considering what your neighbors might think of this, your own kitchen will suffice.

1 whole chicken, cut up

8 cups water

2 bay leaves

1 medium onion, chopped

3 slices of bacon, cooked, chopped

6 sausages (1½ inch long, with skin on)

1 stalk celery

Salt

Pepper

½ cups uncooked rice

Add chicken, water, bay leaves, onion, bacon, sausage, celery, salt, and pepper to a 6-quart pot. Cook about 1 hour or until chicken is tender, stirring occasionally. Drain broth into a bowl and set aside. Debone the chicken. Return chicken to pot. Add the rice and 3½ cups of your freshly made chicken broth. Cover and cook another ½ hour.

Yield: 6 servings.

Magical uses: Festival food—Halloween/Samhain.

CHAPTER THIRTY-SIX

Salads

The following rather peculiar salad is, indeed, ancient—it was approved of by such Roman poets as Ovid and Martial.

Ancient Roman Aphrodisiac Salad

Salad

1 head of arugula (or a small head of cabbage)

Dressing

2 tablespoons vinegar

4 tablespoons olive oil

1 teaspoon garlic, finely chopped

Salt

Freshly ground pepper

Tear the arugula into small pieces. Combine the vinegar, olive oil, chopped garlic, salt, and pepper. Pour liquid over rocket. Serve with other amorous foods.

Yield: 4 to 6 servings, depending on the size of the arugula or cabbage.

Note: If arugula is unavailable, cabbage can be substituted.
Magical uses: Love.

Love Salad

This salad is a potent start of any amatory meal.

Salad
½ head of lettuce, torn in pieces

2 tomatoes, cut into wedges

6 radishes, sliced (about ¼ cup)

2 stalks celery, chopped (about ¼ cup)

French Caper Dressing:
⅓ cup red wine vinegar

¾ teaspoon salt

¼ teaspoon pepper, freshly ground

1 cup olive oil

1 tablespoon capers, chopped

To make the salad: place lettuce, tomatoes, radishes, and celery in large salad bowl and toss together. To make the French caper dressing: in a separate bowl, beat together the vinegar, salt, and pepper while adding the olive oil. Add capers, stir, and pour over salad. Toss and serve.

Yield: 4 servings.
Magical uses: Love.

CHAPTER THIRTY-SEVEN

Soups

This soup really is green. Trust me, or try it yourself. Somehow, it seems perfect for Halloween.

Green Soup

1 cup fresh spinach

¼ cup butter

1 cup celery, finely chopped

2 tablespoons chives, chopped

½ teaspoon dried tarragon

4 cups chicken broth

½ teaspoon sugar

½ teaspoon garlic salt

1 lemon, sliced

Triple wash spinach and finely chop. Set aside. Melt the butter in a Dutch oven. Add celery and sauté on medium heat for 5 minutes, stirring occasionally. Add chives, spinach, and tarragon and sauté for another 3 minutes. Add chicken broth, sugar, and garlic salt. Simmer for 30 minutes. Strain broth through a sieve to remove all fibrous vegetable matter. Ladle into bowls. Float 1 lemon slice on each serving.

Yield: 4 servings.

Magical uses: Festival food—Halloween/Samhain.

Potatoes are not only nourishing, they are also an excellent protective food. Try this recipe.

Potato Soup

5 medium-sized potatoes, peeled and cubed

2 medium onions, finely chopped

2 teaspoons salt

2 cups water

1 tablespoon butter

½ cup flour

6 cups milk

5 slices bacon, chopped

Pepper

1 tablespoon dried parsley

In large saucepan place cubed potatoes and chopped onions. Add salt and cover with water. Cover, place over medium heat, and boil until potatoes are tender. Drain off water, replace cover, and set potatoes and onions aside. Melt butter in a Dutch oven over medium heat. Stir flour into melted butter. Slowly stir in the milk to make the sauce. Increase heat to high, stirring constantly until sauce is thickened. Reduce heat to low. Stir in potatoes and onions. Fry chopped bacon slices in a skillet until crisp. Drain on paper towel and stir into the soup, adding salt and pepper to taste. Serve in individual bowls and sprinkle with parsley flakes.

Yield: 6 servings.

Magical uses: Protection, and healing.

Money Soup

This Money Soup recipe is inspired by the rites often performed on New Year's Eve to attract money during the next year. This version, however, can be used at any time and is quite delicious. The silver object is not eaten, of course, but is retrieved after it has infused the cabbage with money-attracting energies. The same object can be reused as often as desired.

> 1 quarter or a small silver object
> 2 cups water
> 1½ tablespoons butter
> 1 large onion, minced
> 1 small head green cabbage, shredded
> 4 cups chicken stock
> Salt
> Pepper

Boil the quarter or silver object in the water to sterilize it; set aside. In a saucepan on low heat melt the butter. Add the minced onion and sauté until light brown. Add the shredded cabbage and cook until tender. Toss in the silver object. In a separate saucepan, bring the chicken stock to a boil. Add boiling chicken stock to sautéed vegetables. Reduce heat and simmer for 10 to 15 minutes. Add salt and pepper to taste.

> **Yield:** 6 servings.
> **Magical uses:** Money.

CHAPTER THIRTY-EIGHT

Vegetables & Side Dishes

The following recipe is actually a simplified version of an even more complex food ritual in which several charms were baked into a special Halloween cake. This was then served to unmarried, young men and women. The type of charm that each received determined that person's future: a coin, wealth; a horseshoe, good luck; a thimble, spinsterhood; a button, bachelordom; a wishbone, the heart's desire. This custom hasn't yet completely disappeared. In this much simpler version, we use mashed potatoes.

Charmed Potatoes

1 coin or charm

5 large potatoes, peeled and cubed

1 teaspoon of salt

Water to cover potatoes

¼ cup butter, melted

⅓ cup milk, warm

1 tablespoon salt

¼ teaspoon pepper

Boil the charm. Let cool, and if you wish, wrap it in waxed paper. Boil the potatoes in salted water until tender. Drain. Warm milk slowly in a saucepan. In a large bowl, mash potatoes until fluffy and free of lumps, slowly adding butter and milk. Add salt and pepper to taste. Arrange the potatoes in a serving bowl. Secretly insert the charm somewhere in the potatoes. The person who receives the charm will be quite lucky for the next month.

Yield: 4 to 6 servings.

Magical uses: Festival food—Halloween/Samhain.

Hearts of Artichoke Pie

Did you know that artichokes are thistles? The famous Scottish flower is in the same family. The following delicious recipe, which resembles a quiche, takes advantage of both the artichoke and the onions' protective natures.

1 can (14½ ounces) artichoke hearts
1 large onion, chopped
1 tablespoon butter
6 eggs
⅓ cup light cream
½ pound Monterey Jack or Swiss cheese, grated
salt
pepper
1 pie shell, 9 inch

Drain and chop artichoke hearts, reserving liquid. Sauté the onion in butter and reserved liquid. Set aside. Whisk together the eggs and light cream. Add the artichokes, grated cheese, and onion mixture. Add a dash of salt and pepper. Pour into pie shell. Bake for 40 minutes at 350°F (177° C).

Yield: 4 to 6 servings

Magical uses: Protection.

supplemental material

These tables summarize some of the information contained in part two. Additional foods here aren't mentioned elsewhere. For suggested foods related to magical changes, see chapters 21–31. For more complete information, check the index or look in part two.

Planetary Rulers

Sun

These foods are generally useful for healing; protection; success; magical and physical energy; strength; health; and spirituality.

Alcohol	Dried foods	Raisin
Bamboo	Grapefruit	Red wine
Bay	Hazelnut	Rice
Carambola	Honey	Rosemary
Cashew	Kumquat	Saffron
Chestnut	Lime	Sesame

Chicory	Marigold	Squash
Cinnamon	Olive	Sunflower
Citron	Orange	Tangerine
Corn	Pineapple	Tortilla
Date	Pretzel	Walnut
Dehydrated foods		

Moon

These foods are generally useful for stimulating psychic awareness; healing; purification; promoting sleep; love; friendships; spirituality; fertility; peace; compassion.

Blueberry	Grapefruit	Passion fruit
Broccoli	Ice cream	Poppy
Brussels sprouts	Lemon	Potato
Butter	Lentil	Pumpkin
Cabbage	Lettuce	Seaweed
Cauliflower	Melon	Soufflé
Chickweed	Milk	Soup
Coconut	Milk shakes	Soy
Cucumber	Mushroom	Watermelon
Egg	Omelet	White wine
Grape	Papaya	Yogurt

Mercury

These foods are generally useful for strengthening the conscious mind; divination; studying; self-improvement; communication; wisdom.

Almond	Fennel	Parsley
Bean	Marjoram	Pecan
Caraway	May apple	Peppermint
Celery	Mulberry	Pistachio
Chervil	Mung sprouts	Pomegranate
Dill	Oregano	Turmeric

Venus

These foods are generally useful for love; reconciliation; beauty; youth; peace and happiness; pleasure; "luck"; friendship; compassion; meditation.

Alfalfa sprouts	Avocado	Brazil nut
Apple	Barley	Cardamom
Apricot	Blackberry	Carob
Cherry	Persimmon	Sugar
Guava	Plum	Sweet potato
Licorice	Raspberry	Thyme
Nectarine	Rhubarb	Tomato
Oat	Rose	Truffle
Pea	Rye	Vanilla
Peach	Spirulina	Wheat
Pear	Strawberry	

Mars

These foods are useful for promoting protection; courage; aggression; physical and magical strength and sexual energy.

Artichoke	Chocolate	Mustard
Asparagus	Coffee	Pine nuts
Banana	Coriander	Poke
Barbecued foods	Cranberry	Prickly pear
Basil	Cumin	Radish
Beer	Flaming foods	Salsa
Black pepper	Fried foods	Szechuan food
Carrot	Garlic	Spicy food
Chili	Ginger	Tea
Chile rellenos	Horseradish	Tempura
Chives	Leek	Watercress

Jupiter

These foods are generally useful in promoting money; employment; and overall prosperity.

Allspice	Eggplant	Millet
Anise	Expensive foods	Nutmeg
Buckwheat	Endive	Peanut
Clove	Fig	Rich foods
Dandelion	Macadamia	Sage
Desserts	Mace	Spinach

Saturn

These foods are generally useful for a variety of magical changes (see part two).

Beet	Quince
Cheese	Vinegar
Tamarind	

Elemental Rulers

Earth

These foods are generally used to promote grounding; money and prosperity; fertility; healing; and employment.

Allspice	Macadamia	Pumpkin
Barley	Mace	Quince
Beet	Maple syrup	Rhubarb
Brazil nut	Millet	Rye
Buckwheat	Mushroom	Salt
Butter	Oat	Spinach
Cheese	Peanut	Soy
Eggplant	Potato	Wheat

Air

These foods are generally useful for strengthening the conscious mind.

Almond	Date	Parsley
Bamboo shoot	Endive	Pecan
Banana	Hazelnut	Peppermint
Bean	Honey	Pine nut
Caraway	Kumquat	Pistachio
Chervil	Marjoram	Rice
Chestnut	Mulberry	Sage
Chicory	Olive	Tangerine
Dandelion	Oregano	Turmeric

Fire

These foods are generally used for promoting courage; protection; aggression; sex; and health.

Alcohol	Coriander	Poke
Artichoke	Corn	Pomegranate
Basil	Cumin	Pretzel
Barbecued foods	Dill	Prickly pear
Bay	Fennel	Radish
Beer	Fig	Raisin
Black pepper	Flaming foods	Rosemary
Carambola	Garlic	Saffron
Carrot	Ginger	Salsa
Cashew	Horseradish	Szechuan foods
Celery	Leek	Sesame
Chili	Lime	Squash
Chile rellenos	Mango	Sunflower
Chili	Marigold	Tea
Chives	May apple	Tortilla
Cinnamon	Mustard	Vinegar

Citron	Nutmeg	Walnut
Clove	Onion	Watercress
Cocoa	Orange	Wine
Coffee	Pineapple	

Water

These foods are generally useful in promoting love; psychic awareness; peace and happiness; purification; healing; sleep and friendships.

Apple	Brussels sprouts	Coconut
Apricot	Cabbage	Cranberry
Avocado	Cardamon	Cucumber
Bagel	Carob	Grape
Blackberry	Cauliflower	Grapefruit
Blueberry	Cherry	Guava
Broccoli	Chickweed	Ice cream
Lemon	Peach	Strawberry
Lentil	Pear	Sugar
Lettuce	Persimmon	Sweet potato
Licorice	Plum	Tamarind
Melon	Poppy	Thyme
Milk	Raspberry	Tomato
Nectarine	Rose	Truffle
Papaya	Soups	Vanilla
Passion fruit	Spirulina	Watermelon
Pea	Steamed foods	Yogurt

Astrological Rulers

Plants have long been linked with the constellations of the Zodiac. In these tables, I've listed diets and some of the major foods which are "ruled" by the twelve signs.

Why include this information here? Many people wear colors and gemstones that are said to be related to their sign. In doing this, they hope to strengthen the positive aspects of their sun sign. These same persons may also choose to eat the foods suited to them, as governed by the stars above.

Aries

Allspice	Fried foods	Rhubarb
Artichoke	Garlic	Rice
Barbecued foods	Ginger	Salsa
Carrot	Gingerbread	Szechuan food
Cayenne pepper	Horseradish	Shallot
Chili	Mustard	Spicy food
Chives	Onion	Tea
Cinnamon	Pepper	Tempura
Clove	Pimento	Wine
Cumin	Poppy seed	
Fennel	Radish	

Taurus

Apple	Chestnut	Pie (generally)
Apple cider	Cookies	Pita bread
Apricot	Gooseberry	Raspberry
Avocado	Granola	Rhubarb
Banana	Guava	Rose
Barley	Guacamole	Rye
Bean	Kiwi fruit	Spinach
Blackberry	Mango	Sugar
Bread	Oat	Thyme
Buckwheat	Passion fruit	Tomato
Cake	Pastry	Tortilla
Caper	Pea	Vanilla
Cardamom	Peach	Wheat
Carob	Pear	
Cherry	Persimmon	

Gemini

Asian pear	Celery	Mint
Alfalfa sprouts	Dill	Parsley
Almond	Fennel	Pecan
Bean	Filbert	Peppermint
Brazil nut	Lemongrass	Pistachio
Caraway	Lentil	Pomegranate
Carbonated drinks	Marjoram	

Cancer

Bland foods	Crescent cakes	Mango
Breadfruit	Cucumber	Marinated foods
Cabbage	Egg	Mushroom
Cantaloupe	Frozen foods	Papaya
Cauliflower	Gazpacho	Poi
Cheese	Ice cream	Potato
Coconut	Kefir	Pumpkin
Cold foods	Lemon	Quiche
Crab	Lettuce	Sauces
Shellfish	Steamed foods	Watermelon
Shrimp	Squash	White foods
Soufflé	Taro	Uncooked foods
Soup (generally)	Tofu	Yogurt
Soy	Turnip	

Leo

Alcohol	Dried foods	Saffron
Barbecued foods	Grapefruit	Sesame
Broiled foods	Flaming foods	Shish kabob
Cashew	Honey	Sunflower
Chamomile	Nutmeg	Tangerine

Chocolate	Olive	Tea
Cinnamon	Orange	Vinegar
Citron	Pineapple	Walnut
Coffee	Raisins	Wine
Corn	Rice	Yeast
Curried foods	Rosemary	

Virgo

Almond	Endive	Peanut
Barley	Fennel	Pecan
Bean	Filbert	Peppermint
Caraway	Marjoram	Pistachio
Celery	Millet	Pomegranate
Chicory	Oat	Rye
Dill	Parsley	Salt

Libra

Apple	Cake	Gooseberry
Apricot	Candy	Granola
Avocado	Caper	Kiwi fruit
Barley	Cardamom	Mango
Bread	Carob	Oat
Broccoli	Cherry	Passion fruit
Buckwheat	Cookies	Pasta
Pastry	Raspberry	Tarts
Pea	Rose	Thyme
Peach	Rye	Tomato
Pear	Spearmint	Vanilla
Pizza	Strawberry	Wheat
Plum	Sugar	

Scorpio

Allspice	Coriander	Pepper
Artichoke	Cumin	Peppermint
Asparagus	Garlic	Pimento
Basil	Ginger	Pine nut
Beer	Horseradish	Shallot
Carrot	Leek	Szechuan food
Chili	Mustard	Spicy foods
Chives onion		

Sagittarius

Anise	Imported foods	Sarsaparilla
Champagne	Kona coffee	Sassafras
Clove	Maple sugar	Star anise
Endive	Root beer	Tea
Expensive foods	Sage	Truffles
Fig		

Capricorn

Barley	Frozen foods	Preserved foods
Beet	Jams and jellies	Quince
Bitter foods	Pea	Tamarind
Cheese	Pickled foods	Turnip
Corn	Potato	Vinegar
Cranberry		

Aquarius

Almond	Endive	Pistachio
Anise	Filbert	Rare foods
Bean	Hazelnut	Sage
Beer	Mace	Spearmint
Brazil nut	Marjoram	Star anise
Caraway	Mulberry	
Carbonated drinks	Parsley	
Citron	Pecan	

Pisces

Anise	Maple sugar	Shellfish
Bouillabaisse	Nutmeg	Sorbet
Chestnut	Root beer	Soup
Clove	Sage	Star anise
Endive	Sassafras	Syrup
Fig	Sauces	Sushi
Fish	Seafood	

This is a listing of some convenience foods that are available in grocery stores across the country. Name brands are frequently mentioned, but none of the manufacturers, their advertising representatives, or other organizations connected with these products make magical claims.

Ideally, we'd live in a world with plenty of time for food preparation. We'd eat only wholesome, freshly prepared dishes with little added salt and no artificial preservatives, flavorings, or colorings.

The reality is quite different. Few of us haven't reached for a frozen dinner or a can of vegetables at one time or another. Healthy and organic prepared foods are now becoming commonplace (such as frozen dinners, soup mixes, candy bars), but can be difficult to find. Most of the dishes mentioned here are neither healthy nor organic. Look at the product's label before buying; avoid anything that contains MSG (monosodium glutamate), sodium diosinate, sodium guanylate, sodium nitrate, potassium sorbate, BHA, BHT, very high levels of sodium (salt), or other food adulterants. Some foods are available in low-salt or low-sugar forms; check the "dietetic" section of your grocery store.

If you must occasionally eat these foods, choose them with their magical properties in mind. Prepare as directed on the packaging. Then, just before you're ready to eat, visualize and empower the food with energy.

I've only included selected foods here. I'm sure you'll be able to think of others to add to each list.

Grounding

Frozen quiche

Frozen pepperoni pizza (check label to ensure that it contains real cheese, not "mozzarella cheese substitute"; most frozen pizzas contain no real cheese!)

Stouffer's Salisbury Steak frozen dinner

Love

Dole Pineapple (canned in pineapple juice)

Kellogg's Frosted Flakes

Haagen Dazs Mother's Lemon Pie Ice Cream

Hershey's Kisses

Ocean Spray's Mauna Lai Passion Fruit Drink

Pepperidge Farm's Chocolate Cake

Sarah Lee Cherry Cheesecake (and anything else by Ms. Lee)

Magical and Physical Energy

Canned chili (the hotter the better)

Coca-Cola

Pepsi

Lea and Perrin's Tabasco Sauce

Money

General Mills' Cheerios

Kellogg's Rice Crispies

Marie Callendar's Blackberry Cobbler

Puffed Rice Cereal

Welch's Grape Jelly

Peace

Bottled, unsweetened applesauce

Kern's Apricot Nectar

Progresso Lentil Soup

Protection

Bottled artichoke hearts (drain before eating)

Frozen garlic bread

Knorr's Leek Soup mix

Pepperidge Farm's Onion Soup

Laura Scudder's Hawaiian Kettle Potato Chips

Psychic Awareness

Cinnamon bread

"Gourmet" frozen fish filet dinners

7-Up

Purification

Canned, sectioned grapefruit (unsweetened)

Frozen orange-juice bars

Minute Maid Lemonade

Sex

Kern's Mango Nectar

Nabisco's Fig Newtons

Rice cakes

Note: I don't advocate a steady diet of such foods! If you must, eat them with fresh milk, fresh fruit juices, and fresh vegetables.

The Magical Uses of Fast Food

(If you thought that the last section was bad, don't even read this one.)

Fast food has revolutionized American eating habits. It's now an established part of our way of life. The food is often only passable in taste and quality, and often abysmal when it comes to levels of fat, sugar, and salt; but it can come in handy.

Several years ago a truly natural, organic, and vegetarian fast-food restaurant opened in San Diego. It even had a driveup window. I remember their excellent vegetable soup and the tasty avocado, sprouts, cheese, and tomato sandwiches. Unfortunately, it soon closed, unable to compete with the junkier neighbors nearby.

Here—with a shudder—is a list of a few of the basic fast foods and their magical qualities.

Warning! Eating from the four food groups doesn't mean alternating between Burger King, McDonald's, Wendy's, and White Castle. If eaten at all, fast food should be a change of pace—not a steady diet! (In these days of ecological awareness and concern for our planet, it's best to avoid patronizing restaurants that package food in Styrofoam containers.)

Banana split: Love

Broccoli and cheese: Protection

Baked potato: Protection

Fish sandwich: Psychic awareness

French fries: Grounding, protection

Hamburgers: Grounding, protection (see chapter 5)
Iced tea: Physical and magical energy, conscious mind
Onion rings: Protection

Shakes
Chocolate: Love, money
Strawberry: Love
Vanilla: Love

I have to stop; I can't write another word about fast food . . .

These are both old and new symbols that can be used in your magical cooking to add specific energies to the foods. Use foods appropriate to the symbols. Vegetables can be cut into these shapes; pizza dough carefully stretched and smoothed according to the symbols; cookies cut; pastries iced; and breads inscribed. Slices of solid cheese are another possibility. Use your imagination in inventing new ways to utilize these magical symbols.

This is just one magician's list, of course. Use other symbols if you feel comfortable with them and if they seem to allow you to generate more energy.

Little or no magic resides within these symbols. It is the magician drawing them who gives them power.

Love

Protection

Psychic Awareness

Purification

Money

Peace

Spirituality

Weight loss

Sex

Fertility

Most of the food items mentioned in this book are available in supermarkets and at larger grocery stores. Even exotic foods such as kiwi fruits, carambola, and mangos are now being shipped throughout the country. Crystallized ginger, saffron, fresh herbs, and Asian food specialty items can be found in many supermarkets. Nuts, whole grains, seaweed, fresh juices, and tofu are available in health food stores.

But some ingredients can be hard to find, so I've included this appendix. These establishments sell herbs, spices, food products, and prepared foods by mail. Catalog prices and information were accurate as of the time of this writing, but changes do occur.

Please note: none of these businesses make magical or "supernatural" claims for their products, and you need not mention what you'll be doing with them.

For updated information regarding mail-order sources of exotic foods and spices, see the latest issues of the food magazines listed below. Most bookstore chains such as Barnes & Noble, B. Dalton's, and Waldenbooks carry most of them. If you can't find these titles, write directly to the magazines for current subscription information.

Magazines

Bon Appetit
Chocolatier
Cook's
Gourmet
Chile Pepper Magazine

Mail Order

Aphrodisia
282 Bleeker St.
New York, NY 10018
Dried herbs and spices.

Bueno Food Products
1224 Airway Drive, S.W.
Albuquerque, NM 87105
Blue corn products.

Enchantments, Inc.
341 E. 9th St.
New York, NY 10003
Enchantments sells herbs and spices.

Hawaiian Plantatians
1311 Kalakaua Avenue
Honolulu, HI 96826
(800) 367-2177
Passion fruit (*liliko'i*) jelly; guava jelly; exotic mustards and honeys; papaya seed dressing; macadamia nuts; cookies, fudge, and desserts.

Jaffe Bros.
Valley Center, CA 92082
Natural foods, untreated dried fruits, nuts, seeds grains, unrefined oils, beans.

Mauna Loa Macadamia nuts
S.R. Box 3, Volcano Highway
Hilo, HI 96720
(808) 966-9301
Macadamia nuts in every conceivable form. Pick some up while you're in Hawaii.

Pendery's
304 East Belknap
Fort Worth, TX 76102
(800) 533-1870
Pendery's offers a large selection of spices and herbs (including saffron), chili peppers, kitchen accessories, and unique blends.

Spellbound
455 Broad St.
Bloomfield, NJ 07003
Herbs, spices, candles, and many other magical items.

Spice Merchant
Box 524
Jackson Hole, WY 83001
(307) 733-7811
Offers unusual and hard-to-find Chinese, Japanese, Thai, and Indonesian food ingredients. Also has bamboo shoots, true saffron, sliced mango, coconut milk, and many other exotic foods.

Bold words within each discussion refer to other related entries in this glossary.

Akasha: The fifth element; the omnipresent spiritual power that permeates the universe. It is the energy out of which the elements formed.

Aphrodisiac: An organic substance thought to produce sexual excitement.

B.C.E.: Before Common Era; the nonreligious equivalent of B.C.

C.E.: Common Era; the nonreligious equivalent of A.D.

Conscious mind: The societally controlled, intellectual, theorizing, materialistic half of the human mind that is at work during everyday activities. Compare with psychic mind.

Curse: A conscious direction of negative energy toward a person, place, or thing. Contrary to popular belief, curses are rare. Also known as "psychic attack."

Divination: The magical act of discovering the unknown by interpreting seemingly random patterns or symbols through the use of such tools as clouds, tarot cards, flames, or smoke. Divination contacts the **psychic mind** by tricking (or drowsing) the **conscious mind** through **ritual** and the observation of, or the use of, tools. Divination isn't necessary for those who can easily attain communication with the psychic mind, though they may practice it.

Elements: Earth, air, fire, and water. These four essences are the building blocks of the universe. Everything that exists (or that has the potential to exist) contains one or more of these energies. The elements hum within ourselves and are also at large in the world. They can be utilized to cause change through **magic.** The four elements formed from the primal essence, or power—**akasha.**

Energy, energies: A general term for the currently unmeasureable (but real) power that exists within all natural objects and beings—including our own bodies. To many, this energy stems from the divine source of all that exists. It is used in **folk magic** rituals.

Evil eye: The glance said to be capable of causing great harm (even death) that was once almost universally feared. It is supposedly an unconscious curse.

Folk magic: The practice of using **personal power** as well as the energies within natural objects such as food, crystals, and herbs to cause needed change.

Food magic: The utilization of the **energies** naturally inherent in foods to manifest specific personal transformations. Certain foods are chosen for their energies, and are ritually prepared and eaten to introduce these energies into the magician's body. **Visualization** is necessary to activate the energies inside the foods, as well as to prepare the diner to accept them.

Great Mother, The: The timeless female source; the creatress; the nurturing, nourishing, fertile force of the universe. One form of the Goddess, linked with agriculture and the bounties of the earth.

Grounding: The process of temporarily shutting off psychic awareness and reorienting the awareness to the material world.

"Luck, good": An individual's ability to make timely, correct decisions, to perform correct actions, and to place herself or himself in positive situations. "Bad luck" stems from ignorance and an unwillingness to accept self-responsibility.

Magic: The movement of natural **energies** (such as **personal power**) to create needed change. Energy exists within all things: ourselves, foods, plants, stones, colors, sounds, movements. Magic is the process of "rousing" or of building up this energy, giving it purpose (through **visualization**), and releasing it to create a change. This is a natural, not supernatural, process, though it is little understood.

Meditation: Reflection, contemplation, turning inward toward the self or outward toward deity or nature. A quiet time in which the practitioner may dwell upon particular thoughts or symbols, or allow them to come unbidden.

Pagan: From the Latin *paganus,* a "villager," a "country-dweller." Today, the word is used as a general term for followers of Wicca as well as other shamanistic, polytheistic, and magic-embracing religions. Pagans aren't Satanists, dangerous, or "evil."

Pentagram: The basic five-pointed star, visualized with one point upward. The pentagram represents the five senses; the elements (earth, air, fire, water, and akasha); the hand, and the human body, among other things. It is a protective symbol known to have been in use since the days of old Babylon. Today, it is frequently associated with Wicca. The pentagram is also a symbol of the element of earth and, hence, of money.

Personal power: The energy that sustains our bodies. We first absorb it from our biological mother within the womb, and later from food, water, sunlight, and other natural objects.

We release personal power during movement, exercise, sex, conception, childbirth, thought, and magic.

Psychic attack: See **Curse.**

Psychic mind: The subconscious, or unconscious, mind in which we receive psychic impulses. The psychic mind is at work when we sleep, dream, and meditate. **Divination** is a ritual process designed to contact the psychic mind. Intuition is a term used to describe psychic information that unexpectedly reaches the conscious mind. **Psychism** describes the state in which information from the psychic mind is available to the conscious mind.

Psychism: The act of being consciously psychic.

Ritual: Ceremony. A specific form of movement, manipulation of objects, or inner process designed to produce specific results. In religion, ritual is geared toward union with the divine. In magic, it is a series of simple actions (both external and internal) that allow the magician to move energy toward needed goals. A spell is a magical ritual.

Visualization: The process of forming mental images. Magical visualization consists of forming images of needed goals during **ritual.** Visualization is also used to direct **personal power** and natural **energies** during **magic** for various purposes. It is a function of the **conscious mind.**

Wicca: A contemporary **Pagan** religion with spiritual roots in the earliest expressions of reverence for nature as a manifestation of the divine. Wicca views deity as Goddess and God; thus it is polytheistic. It also embraces the practice of **magic** and reincarnation. Many Wiccans identify themselves with the word **Witch.**

Witch: Anciently, a European practitioner of the remnants of pre-Christian folk magic, especially herb magic. One who practiced **Witchcraft.** This term's meaning was later deliberately altered to denote demented, dangerous, supernatural beings who practiced destructive magic and who threatened Christianity. This was a political, financial, and sexist move on the part of organized religion. Though this negative meaning is still currently accepted by many non-Witches, it doesn't describe Witches themselves, who simply practice nonthreatening, love-charged **folk magic**. The term Witch is also used by members of **Wicca** to describe themselves.

Witchcraft: The craft of a Witch; magic, especially magic utilizing **personal power** in conjunction with the energies, within foods, stones, herbs, colors, and other natural objects (See **folk magic**). From this definition, Witchcraft isn't a religion. Many followers of the **Pagan** religion of **Wicca,** however, use **Witchcraft** and **Wicca** interchangeably to describe their religion.

Numbers preceding each work are those used in notes throughout this book. This is a partial list of the most important sources consulted during the research portion of the preparation of *Cunnigham's Encyclopedia of Wicca in the Kitchen*.

1 Abel, Ernest L., *Alcohol: Wordlore and Folklore*. Buffalo: Prometheus Books, 1987. A fascinating excursion into the surprising etymologies of common words and their connections with alcohol. Historical backgrounds of alcoholic beverages.

2 Abella, Alex, *The Total Banana*. New York: Harcourt, Brace and Jovanovich, 1979. A compendium of banana lore: its history, ritual and culinary uses. Printed on yellow paper.

3 Aero, Rita, *Things Chinese*. Garden City (New York): Dolphin, 1980. Rituals and lore associated with Chinese foods.

4 Bailey, Adrian, *The Blessings of Bread*. New York: Paddington Press, 1975. The history of bread from antiquity to the present. Very well illustrated and researched.

5 Baker, Margaret, *Folklore and Customs of Rural England.* Totowa (New Jersey): Rowman & Littlefield, 1974. General English food magic.

6 Barnes, A. C., *The Sugar Cane.* New York: John Wiley and Sons, 1974. This exhaustive study of sugar cultivation begins with a chapter discussing the history of sugar.

7 Beckwith, Martha, *Hawaiian Mythology.* Honolulu: University Press of Hawaii, 1979. Ancient symbolism of Hawaiian and Polynesian foods, including fish, coconuts and bananas. Food rituals and superstitions.

8 Best, Michael, and Frank H. Brightman (editors), *The Book of Secrets of Albertus Magnus of the Virtues of Herbs, Stones, and Certain Beasts.* London: Oxford University Press, 1973. Food magic is scattered throughout the text.

9 Bunzel, Ruth, "Psychology of the Pueblo Potter" in *Primitive Heritage,* edited by Margaret Mead and Nicolas Calas. New York: Random House, 1953. Ritual uses of clay pots.

10 Burland, C. A., *The Gods of Mexico.* New York: Putnam's, 1967. Corn and pulque information.

11 Burkhardt, V. R., *Chinese Creeds and Customs.* Four volumes bound as one. Golden Mountain Publishers: Taipei (China), 1971. Reprint. Hong Kong: South Morning China Post Ltd., 1982. A glorious introduction to Chinese ritual and beliefs, well-spiced with food lore.

12 Busenbark, Ernest, *Symbols, Sex and the Stars in Popular Beliefs.* New York: Truth Seeker Company, 1948. Speculations regarding the religious uses of food in the ancient world. Not entirely reliable.

13 Carpenter, Edward, *Pagan and Christian Creeds.* New York: Harcourt, Brace and Company, 1920. Vegetative deities and pre-Christian food magic.

14 Clebert, Jean-Paul, *The Gypsies.* Harmondsworth (England): Penguin Books, 1967. This intriguing look at continental Gypsies includes some food lore.

15 Clifford, Terry, and Sam Antupit, *Cures*. New York: Macmillan, 1980. Various foods are mentioned in this book of traditional healing practices, many of which are magical.

16 Cochrane, Peggy, *The Witch Doctor's Cookbook*. Sherman Oaks (California): Sherman Press, 1984. I love the title of this work, a collection of exotic recipes from around the world. No magic, lore, or mythology is included.

17 Connell, Charles, *Aphrodisiacs in Your Garden*. New York: Taplinger Press, 1966. A tongue-in-cheek guide to growing and using purportedly aphrodisiac plants.

18 Corum, Ann Kondo, *Folk Wisdom from Hawaii*. Honolulu: Bess Press, 1985. A charming compilation of Polynesian, Asian, and Hawaiian folklore, some of which is food related.

19 Cost, Bruce, *Ginger East to West*. Berkeley: Aris Press, 1984. An exhaustive look at ginger, this work contains numerous recipes as well as Chinese ginger folklore.

20 Culpeper, Nicholas, *The English Physician*. London: 1652. Lore relating to some plants used as food can be found in this classic, though medicinally unreliable, source.

21 Cushing, Frank Hamilton, "Zuni Breadstuff" in *Primitive Heritage*, edited by Margaret Mead and Nicolas Calas. New York: Random House, 1953. Zuni lore concerning corn and pots.

22 Daniels, Cora Linn (editor), *Encyclopedia of Superstitions, Folklore and the Occult Sciences of the World*. Three volumes. Detroit: Gale Research Co., 1971. The magical dualities of food are included in this massive work.

23 Darby, William J, Paul Ghalioungui, and Louis Grivetti, *Food: The Gift of Osiris*. Two volumes. New York: Academic Press, 1977. An exhaustive study of food in ancient Egypt. Documented in formation regarding specific foods and their use in Egyptian religion and magic. The ultimate source in this area.

24 Delaporte, L., *Mesopotamia: The Babylonian and Assyrian Civilization*. New York: Knopf, 1925. Food offerings.

25 De Lys, Claudia, *A Treasury of American Superstitions*. New York: Philosophical Library, 1948. The chapter entitled "Give Us This Day" examines food superstitions.

26 Diamond, Denise, *Living With the Flowers*. New York: Quill, 1882. Flower cookery and much else of interest.

27 Emboden, William A., *Bizarre Plants*. New York: Macmillian, 1974. Truffles.

28 Emboden, William A., "Plant Hypnotics Among the North American Indians" in *American Folk Medicine*. Ed. Wayland D. Hand. Los Angeles and Berkeley: University of California Press, 1976. Absinthe.

29 Farb, Peter, and George Armelagos, *Consuming Passions: The Anthropology of Eating*. Boston: Houghton Mifflin, 1980. An indispensible look at food throughout history. Numerous food rituals are included. Fascinating.

30 Ferm, Vergilius, *A Brief Dictionary of American Superstitions*. New York: Philosophical Library, 1959. Food customs and lore.

31 Fielding, William J, *Strange Customs of Courtship and Marriage*. New York: Permabooks, 1949. Wedding cake and culinary plant symbolism.

32 Flower, Barbara, and Elisabeth Rosenbaum (translators), *The Roman Cookery Book: A Critical Translation of The Art of Cooking by Apicius*. London: George G. Harrap & Co., 1958. The oldest extant cookbook, filled with unusual and somewhat unappetizing Roman recipes. Of interest simply to show that food fashions do indeed change. Aphrodisiacs.

33 Ford, Richard I., "Communication Networks and Information Hierarchies in Native American Folk Medicine: Tewa Pueblos, New Mexico" in *American Folk Medicine.* Ed. Wayland D. Hand. Los Angeles and Berkeley: University of California Press, 1976. Corn meal, tamales and pine nuts.

34 Fox, Helen Morganthau, *Gardening with Herbs for Flavor and Fragrance.* New York: Macmillan, 1933. Herb cookery and lore.

35 Friend, Hilderic, *Flower Lore.* 1883. Reprint. Rockport (Massachusetts): Para Research, 1981. Intriguing legends and rituals of diets.

36 Gerard, John, *Gerard's Herbal: The Essence Thereof Distilled by Marcus Woodward.* London: Spring Books, 1964. Magical properties of foods are included in this condensed version of Gerard's classic herbal.

37 Goldsmith, Elizabeth, *Ancient Pagan Symbols.* New York: G. Putnam's Sons, 1929. Reprint. New York: AMS Press, 1973. Foods and ancient divinities.

38 Gonzalez-Wippler, Migene, *Rituals and Spells of Santeria.* Bronx (New York): Original Publications, 1984. Foods associated with various Santerian deities.

39 Gordon, Jean, *The Art of Cooking With Roses.* New York: Walker and Company, 1968. A useful guide to this pleasant art.

40 Gordon, Lesley, *The Mystery and Magic of Trees and Flowers.* Exeter (England): Webb and Bower, 1985. Plant lore is included in this ritzy little book.

41 Goulart, Frances Sheridan, *The Caffeine Book: A User's and Abuser's Guide.* New York: Dodd, Mead and Company, 1984. This indepth survey of the use, abuse, and physiological effects of caffeine includes valuable information relating to coffee, tea, and chocolate.

42 Granger, Byrd Howell, "Some Aspects of Folk Medicine Among Spanish-Speaking People in Southern Arizona" in *American Folk Medicine*. Editor Wayland D. Hand. Los Angeles and Berkeley: University of California Press, 1976. The magical uses of eggs.

43 Graves, Robert, *The White Goddess*. New York: Farrar, Straus and Giroux, 1976. Food lore and magic is interspersed throughout this poetic study of the eternal Goddess.

44 Haining, Peter, *Superstitions*. London: Sidgwick and Jackson, 1979. Food superstitions and rituals.

45 Hand, Wayland D., (editor), *American Folk Medicine: A Symposium*. Los Angeles and Berkeley: University of California Press, 1976. These proceedings from the UCLA Conference on American Folk Medicine cover a wide range of topics related to food magic. An intelligent and immensely satisfying "read."

46 Hand, Wayland D., Anna Cassetta, and Sondra B. Theiderman (editors), *Popular Beliefs and Superstitions: A Compendium of American Folklore*. Three volumes. Boston: G. K. Hall, 1981. Various aspects of food lore and culinary superstition are included in this monumental work.

47 Handy, E. S. Craighill, and Mary Kawena Pukui, *The Polynesian Family System in Ka-u, Hawaii*. Rutland (Vermont): Tuttle, 1972. Sugar magic and lore in old Hawaii.

48 Hansen, Barbara, "An Earthly Delight." *The Los Angeles Times Home Magazine*, October 22, 1978. Day of the Dead celebrations.

49 Henle, Zack, *Cooking With Flowers*. Los Angeles: Price! Stern/Sloan, 1971. A short book filled with simple recipes utilizing flowers.

50 Hishijo, Kathy, *Kathy Cooks . . . Naturally*. Honolulu: The Self-Sufficiency Association, 1981. A remarkable guide to using natural foods and exotic fruits. A thousand recipes are included.

51 Hooke, S. H., *Babylonian and Assyrian Religion*. Norman (Oklahoma): University of Oklahoma Press, 1963. Foods used as offerings in ancient times.

52 Jaine, Tom and Nicholas Campion, *Cosmic Cuisine*, San Francisco: Harper & Row, 1988. This astrological cookbook contains numerous tidbits of food magic. It also relates foods to the signs of the zodiac and the planets. Stunning full-color photographs of well-styled dishes.

53 Jensen, Bernard, *Foods That Heal*. Garden City Park (New York): Avery Publishing Company, 1988. Nutritional and historic information about basic foods.

54 Joya, Mock, *Quaint Customs and Manners of Japan*. Tokyo: Superstitions, festivals, and customs, many of which involve food.

55 Kamm, Minnie Watson, *Old Time Herbs for Northern Gardens*. Boston: Little, Brown and Company, 1938. Much food and herb lore from bygone days.

56 Keller, Mitzie Stuart, *Mysterious Herbs and Roots: Ancient Secrets for Beautie, Health, Magick, Prevention and Youth*. Culver City (California): Peace Press, 1978. A fascinating compilation filled with age-old food magic.

57 Kenyon, Theda, *Witches Still Live*. New York: Ives Washburn, 1929. This "modern" book of folklore and magic contains some references to food.

58 Kepler, Kay, *Hawaiian Heritage Plants*. Honolulu: Oriental Publishing Co., 1983. Lore and uses of Polynesian diets.

59 Krutch, Joseph Wood, *Herbal*. Boston: David R. Godine, 1965. The magical associations of plants are included in this work.

60 Leach, Maria, *The Soup Stone: The Magic of Familiar Things*. London: Mayflower, 1954. Salt and turmeric lore; a look at the mysteries of pots and utensils.

61 Leach, Maria (editor), *Standard Dictionary of Folklore, Mythology and Legend*. New York: Funk and Wagnall's, 1972. A treasury of food lore and magic.

62 Leland, Charles Godfrey, *Gypsy Sorcery and Fortune Telling*. New Hyde Park (New York): University Books, 1963. European apple and egg lore.

63 Leyel, C. F., *The Magic of Herbs*. New York: Harcourt, Brace and Company, 1926. Reprint. Toronto: Coles, 1981. Many unusual recipes are found in this book.

64 Leyel, C. F. (editor), *A Modern Herbal*. Two volumes. New York: Harcourt, Brace and Company, 1931. Reprint. New York: Dover, 1971. Some food lore is included in this classic work.

65 Lu, Henry C., *Chinese System of Food Cures, Prevention and Remedies*. New York: Sterling, 1986. An introduction to the use of food as medicine. Fascinating.

66 Malbrough, Ray, *Charms, Spells and Formulas*. St. Paul: Llewellyn Publications, 1985. Some Cajun food magic is included.

67 Malbrough, Ray, *Wildflowers of Louisiana and Their Ritual Uses*. Unpublished paper, 1988. Magical uses of diets.

68 Maple, Eric, *Superstition and the Superstitious*. Hollywood: Wilshire Book Company, 1973. British and American food customs.

69 Manniche, Lise, *An Ancient Egyptian Herbal*. Austin: University of Texas Press, 1989. Egyptian uses of diets.

70 Marquis, Vivienne, and Patricia Haskell, *The Cheese Book*. New York: Fireside, 1965. Cheese lore in antiquity.

71 McGee, Harold, *On Food and Cooking: The Science and Lore of the Kitchen*. New York: Collier, 1988. An extraordinary glimpse of the processes at work while we cook. This massive book contains much ancient culinary lore as well.

72 McNiell, F. Marian, *Halloween: Its Origins, Rites and Ceremonies in the Scottish Tradition*. Edinburgh: The Albyn Press, n.d. Foods of Halloween.

73 Mead, Margaret, and Nicolas Calas (editors), *Primitive Heritage: An Anthropological Anthology*. New York: Random House, 1953. A fascinating collection. Many of the articles mention food or implements used in food preparation.

74 Meyer, Carolyn, *Coconut: The Tree of Life*. New York: William Morrow, 1976. Coconut lore and legend.

75 Moldenke, Harold N. and Alma L., *Plants of the Bible*. Waltham (Massachusetts): Chronica Botanica Co., 1952. Food lore in antiquity.

76 Morgan, Harry T., *Chinese Symbols and Superstitions*. South Pasadena: P. D. and Ione Perkins, 1942. A fascinating look at Chinese symbolism, religion, and folk magic. Food and fruit lore.

77 Neal, Marie C., *In Honolulu Gardens*. Honolulu: Bishop Museum, 1928. This fascinating work includes magic and myth concerning sugar, banana, coconut, and other Polynesian foods.

78 Newmann, Erich, *The Great Mother*. Princeton: Princeton University Press, 1974. Food as related to the Goddess.

79 Newall, Venetia, *An Egg at Easter*. London: Routledge & Kegan Paul, 1971. An exhaustive study of eggs in myth, religion, folklore, and magic. Heavily footnoted.

80 Newall, Venetia, *The Encyclopedia of Witchcraft and Magic*. A & W Visual Press, 1974. Pudding, salt, and pepper lore.

81 Norris, P. E. *About Honey*. London: Thorson's, 1956. Honey folklore and mythology. Sugar is given a cursory examination.

82 Opie, Iona, and Moira Tatem, editors, *A Dictionary of Superstitions.* New York: Oxford University Press, 1989. An impressive, heavily documented collection of superstitions, some of which refer to food.

83 Ortiz, Elizabeth Lambert, *The Complete Book of Mexican Cooking.* New York: Ballantine, 1985. A delightful guide by a woman well versed in this art. Some Mexican food lore is included with many recipes.

84 Perlman, Dorothy, *The Magic of Honey.* New York: Avon, 1974. This useful work contains information on the history and mythological associations of honey.

85 Pitkanen, A. L., and Renan Prevost, *Tropical Fruits, Herbs and Spices, Etc.* Lemon Grove (California): R. Prevost, 1967. Compilation of food lore, legend, and nutritional values.

86 Pliny the Elder, *Natural History.* Cambridge: Harvard University Press, 1956. Pliny, surprisingly skeptical for his time (the first century C.E.), recorded various aspects of food magic in this classic work.

87 Randolph, Vance, *Ozark Superstitions.* New York: Columbia University, 1947. Onion magic.

88 Radbill, Samuel X., "The Role of Animals in Infant Feeding" in *American Folk Medicine.* Editor Wayland D. Hand. Los Angeles and Berkeley: University of California Press, 1976. Fascinating milk information.

89 Rogers, Brant, and Bev Powers-Rogers, Culinary Botany: *The Essential Handbook.* Kent (Washington): PRP; 1988. An invaluable guide to the nomenclature of exotic fruits and vegetables. Some lore is included.

90 Rose, Jeanne, *Jeanne Rose's Herbal Guide to Food.* Berkeley: North Atlantic Books, 1989. A delightful compendium of exotic and homey recipes. The "Organic Culinary Materia Medica" is a treasury of food lore, magic, and legend.

91 Ross, Patricia Fent, *Made in Mexico.* New York: Alfred A. Knopf, 1955. Mexican vanilla lore.

92 Scammell, R. E., *Thistle Eaters Guide.* Lafayette (California): Floreat Press, 1970. A delightful guide to artichoke eating. History and lore is included.

93 Schmidt, Phillip, *Superstition and Magic.* Westminster (Maryland): The Newman Press, 1963. A section titled "Cakes as Offerings" is of great interest.

94 Schnitzer, Rita, *The Secrets of Herbs.* London: Orbis, 1985. Food magic. Beautifully illustrated.

95 Scott, George Ryler, *Curious Customs of Sex and Marriage.* New York: Ace Books, N.D. Wedding cake customs.

96 Shah, Sayed Idries, *Oriental Magic.* New York: Philosophical Library, 1957. Barley.

97 Sharon, Douglas, *Wizard of the Four Winds.* New York: The Free Press, 1978. The ritual uses of lime and sugar.

98 Shurtleff, William, and Akiko Aoyagi, *The Book of Tofu: Food for Mankind.* New York: Ballantine, 1979. An involving, engrossing look at the role of tofu in the past and its potential as a major food in the Western world. Lore and recipes.

99 Simmons, Adelma Grenier, *A Witch's Brew.* Coventry (Connecticut): Caprilands Herb Farm. N.D. Beans.

100 Simmons, Marc, *Witchcraft in the Southwest.* Lincoln: University of Nebraska Press, 1974. Chili lore.

101 Stark, Raymond, *The Book of Aphrodisiacs.* New York: Stein & Day, 1980. Foods as aphrodisiacs and folk magic.

102 Stone, Margaret, *Supernatural Hawaii.* Honolulu: Aloha Graphics and Sales, 1979. Mango.

103 "T", Reverend, *The Voodoo Cookbook.* Santa Barbara: Malcolm Mills Publications, 1984. Food symbolism and magical uses.

104 Tannahill, Reay, *Food in History.* New York: Stein & Day, 1973. Food from prehistory to the present day. A monumental work.

105 Taylor, Demetria, *The Apple Kitchen Cookbook.* New York: Popular Library, 1971. Apple and pie lore.

106 Thompson, C. J. S., *Magic and Healing.* London: Rider & Company, 1947. Eastern food magic.

107 Tillona, Francesca, and Cynthia Strowbridge, *A Feast of Flowers.* New York: Grammercy Publishing Co., 1969. A charming collection of flower cookery.

108 Tonsley, Cecil, *Honey for Health.* New York: Award, n.d. Honey in history and mythology.

109 Toor, Frances, *A Treasury of Mexican Folkways.* New York: Crown, 1973. The lore and magic of pulque and other Mexican beverages and foods. A fascinating book.

110 Villiers, Elizabeth, *The Book of Charms.* New York: Fire side, 1973. Crab and fish lore.

111 Vogel, Virgil J. "American Indian Foods Used as Medicine" in *American Folk Medicine.* Editor Wayland D. Hand. Los Angeles and Berkeley: University of California Press, 1976. Corn.

112 Walker, Barbara, *The Woman's Encyclopedia of Myths and Mysteries.* New York: Harper & Row, 1983. General food lore in past times.

113 Warburton, Diana, *Magiculture: A Book of Garden Charms.* Dorchester (England): Prism Press, 1980. Some food lore is included in this short work.

114 Waring, Phillippa, *A Dictionary of Omens and Superstitions.* New York: Ballantine, 1978. Food magic and customs.

115 Winter, Evelyne, *Mexico's Ancient and Native Remedies.* Mexico City: Editorial Fournier, 1972. A fascinating account of Mexican folk medicine, with cooking magic and ritual uses of herbs.

116 Young, Gordon, "Chocolate: Food of the Gods" in *National Geographic,* November, 1984. An intriguing, short history with glorious color photographs.

117 Younger, William, *Gods, Men and Wine.* Cleveland: The Wine and Food Society/World Publishing, 1966. The full story of wine. The first four chapters are filled with ritual wine use in antiquity.

118 Corrigan, Patricia, "Ice Cream Boasts a Cool History" in *The San Diego Tribune,* Dec. 16, 1987. Ice cream lore.

119 Latimer, Norma, and Gordon Latimer, *English Desserts, Puddings, Cakes and Scones.* Culver City (California): Norma and Gordon Latimer, 1981. Hot-cross buns.

120 Lenher, Ernst and Johanna, *Folklore and Odysseys of Food and Medicinal Plants.* New York: Farrar, Straus and Giroux, 1962. Though this is an interesting source of grain, vegetable, and fruit lore, this work is marred by the lack of a general index and a bibliography.

121 Madsen, William, and Claudia Madsen, *A Guide to Mexican Witchcraft.* Mexico City: Editorial Minutiae Mexicaxna, 1972. This short, comprehensive look at Mexican folk magic describes egg divination.

122 Rhoads, Scot, "How To Eat Meat" in *Rose & Quill,* Vol. 1, No. 1. A satirical, useful, and ultimately spiritual guide for carnivores.

123 Shultes, Richard Evans, *Hallucinogenic Plants.* New York: Golden Press, 1976. Mushrooms and mind-altering plants.

124 Tuleja, Tad, *Curious Customs: The Stories Behind 296 Popular American Rituals.* New York: Harmony, 1987. Fascinating food lore.